KEY TO
A GRAMMAR OF AKKADIAN

Second Edition

HARVARD SEMITIC MUSEUM PUBLICATIONS

Lawrence E. Stager, General Editor
Michael D. Coogan, Director of Publications

HARVARD SEMITIC STUDIES

Jo Ann Hackett and John Huehnergard, editors

Syriac Manuscripts: A Catalogue	Moshe H. Goshen-Gottstein
Introduction to Classical Ethiopic	Thomas O. Lambdin
The Songs of the Sabbath Sacrifice	Carol Newsom
Non-Canonical Psalms from Qumran: A Pseudepigraphic Collection	Eileen M. Schuller
An Exodus Scroll from Qumran	Judith E. Sanderson
You Shall Have No Other Gods	Jeffrey H. Tigay
Ugaritic Vocabulary in Syllabic Transcription	John Huehnergard
The Scholarship of William Foxwell Albright	Gus Van Beek
Features of the Eschatology of IV Ezra	Michael E. Stone
Studies in Neo-Aramaic	Wolfhart Heinrichs, Editor
Lingering over Words: Studies in Ancient Near Eastern Literature in Honor of William L. Moran	Tzvi Abusch, John Huehnergard, Piotr Steinkeller, Editors
A Grammar of the Palestinian Targum Fragments from the Cairo Genizah	Steven E. Fassberg
The Origins and Development of the Waw-Consecutive: Northwest Semitic Evidence from Ugaritic to Qumran	Mark S. Smith
Amurru Akkadian: A Linguistic Study, Volume I	Shlomo Izre'el
Amurru Akkadian: A Linguistic Study, Volume II	Shlomo Izre'el
The Installation of Baal's High Priestess at Emar	Daniel E. Fleming
The Development of the Arabic Scripts	Beatrice Gruendler
The Archaeology of Israelite Samaria: Early Iron Age through the Ninth Century BCE	Ron Tappy
A Grammar of Akkadian (2nd ed.)	John Huehnergard
Key to A Grammar of Akkadian *(2nd ed.)*	John Huehnergard
Akkadian Loanwords in Biblical Hebrew	Paul V. Mankowski
Adam in Myth and History: Ancient Israelite Perspectives on the Primal Human	Dexter E. Callender Jr.
West Semitic Vocabulary in the Akkadian Texts from Emar	Eugen J. Pentiuc
The Archaeology of Israelite Samaria, vol. II: The Eighth Century BCE	Ron E. Tappy
Leaves from an Epigrapher's Notebook: Collected Papers in Hebrew and West Semitic Palaeography and Epigraphy	Frank Moore Cross
Semitic Noun Patterns	Joshua Fox
Eighth-Century Iraqi Grammar: A Critical Exploration of pre-Ḫalīlian Arabic Linguistics	Rafael Talmon
Amarna Studies: Collected Essays	William L. Moran
Narrative Structure and Discourse Constellations: An Analysis of Clause Function in Biblical Hebrew Prose	Roy L. Heller
The Modal System of Old Babylonian	Eran Cohen
Studies in Semitic Grammaticalization	Aaron D. Rubin

KEY TO
A GRAMMAR OF AKKADIAN

Second Edition

by

John Huehnergard

EISENBRAUNS
Winona Lake, Indiana
2005

KEY TO
A GRAMMAR OF AKKADIAN

by
John Huehnergard

2nd edition, 2005

Printed in the United States of America

Library of Congress Cataloging-in-Publication Data

Huehnergard, John
Key to a grammar of Akkadian / by John Huehnergard. — 2nd ed.
p. cm. — (Harvard Semitic studies ; no. 46)
ISBN 1-57506-924-5 (hardback : alk. paper)
1. Akkadian language—Grammar—Problems, exercises, etc.
I. Title II. Series.
PJ3251.H85 2005
492′.182421—dc22

2005020389

The paper used in this publication meets the minimum requirements of the American National Standard for Information Sciences—Permanence of Paper for Printed Library Materials, ANSI Z39.48-1984.⊗™

PREFACE

The present volume is a key to the exercises in my *A Grammar of Akkadian* (HSS 45). Answers to nearly all of the exercises in the thirty-eight lessons are included. It must be emphasized that most sentences, and even phrases, admit of several possible translation variants, and it has not been possible to list them all; the student should be aware of, and allow for, such variation.

Once again it is my pleasant duty to thank a number of individuals who have reviewed parts of the key in its formative stages, and who have saved me from many errors: Patrick Durusau, Esther Flueckiger-Hawker, Daniel A. Foxvog, Matthias Henze, Eugene C. McAfee, Kathryn Slanski, Matthew W. Stolper, Neal H. Walls, Chris Woods, and Norman Yoffee.

I have taken advantage of the publication of this *Key* to provide as well a list of errata in the Grammar that have come to my attention. The errata appear immediately following this preface. (Most of these errata have been corrected in later printings of the Grammar, but it has seemed best to reprint the list here for those with copies of the first printing.)

* * * * *

In the second, revised printing of the *Key*, I have corrected a number of errors brought to my attention by Christopher Frechette, Michael Patrick O'Connor, and especially Avi Winitzer, to whom I express my sincere thanks.

Cambridge, Mass., June 2000

* * * * *

The second edition of the *Key* provides the opportunity to correct additional errors and ambiguities, many of them brought to my attention by Benjamin Thomas and Avi Winitzer, and especially by Michael Patrick O'Connor; I am very grateful to them for taking the time to send these corrections and suggestions for improvement.

Carlisle, Mass., July 2005

Errata

The following errata appear in the first printing of *A Grammar of Akkadian*.

xxxi	lines 11f., read: Izre'el, Sh. *Amurru Akkadian: A Linguistic Study*.(2 volumes; 1991).				
70	line 1, end: read				
125	7th line from end:	for	that silver	read	the silver
165	E. 12, beginning:	for	ERIN$_{2}$MEŠ	read	ERIN$_{2}$.MEŠ
173	12th line from end:	for	pronunced	read	pronounced
251	add note to line 12: read 1 GÍN KUG.BABBAR!(1)				
	note to lines 15–16, end, add:		See Appendix A.		
270	§25.1(a), end 2nd para.:	for	::	read	:
272	5th line from end:	for	lord'.	read	lord';
272	14th line from end:	for	(cf. §24.4) The	read	(cf. §24.4). The
282	§26.1, paradigm, 3mp:	for	*īsû*	read	*īšû*
309	§28.1(a), parad., ptcpl.:	for	*mušēlû*	read	*mušēlûm*
313	§28.4(b), *-iš*, first line, end, add :				
313	§28.4(c):	for	*ayyânum, ayyûm*	read	*ayyānum, ayyum*
314	line 4:	for	(*mal-mal-iš*)	read	(*mal+mal+ -iš*)
326	5th line from end:	for	Texts	read	texts
361	§31.1, Verbal Adj. + 3fs:	for	*nešmât / nešmât*	read	*nešmât / našmât*
403	G. 2, line 26, end:	for	*i-ša-qá-al*	read	*i-ša-qá-al*]
404	H. 1, line 9:	for	*-ki-na-ti-ma*	read	*-ki-na-ši-im*
406	H. 4, add note to line 23: For *ašar* see §30.1(d), end.				
412	§34.1, end:	for	;	read	.
417	G. 1, lines 3, 9, 11:	for	*-na-ṣi-ir*	read	*-na-ṣir*
432	third note to line 55:	for	(see lines 39, 55)	read	(see lines 39, 54)
435	line 10, end:	for	;	read	.
468	E. 6 note:	for	*ḫasûm*	read	*ḫašûm*
469	E. 8 note to line 1:	for	*ḫasûm*	read	*ḫašûm*
533	left column, 12th and 13th lines from end: invert the order of GAN and GÁL				
602	between (5) and (6), insert (5a): The Gt Infinitive and Verbal Adjective have the form *pitarsum*, vs. Bab. *pitrusum*.				
611	Gtn (*i*) Infinitive:	for	*šitarriqum*	read	*šitarruqum*
620	Note 2	for	initial root sibilant and infix *-t-*	read	infix *-t-* to medial root sibilant

628	paradigm of Verbs III–*e*, Durative (see p. 98):		
		for *taleqqe*	read *teleqqe*
		for *taleqqî*	read *teleqqî*
		for *aleqqe*	read *eleqqe*
		for *taleqqeā*	read *teleqqeā*
630	N, Verbs III–*u*, Imp'v, ms:	for *namnu*	read *namni*
	N, Verbs III–*u*, Imp'v, fs:	for *namnu*	read *namnî*
631	line 4:	for *gen.*	read gen.
633	lines 4, 14:	for *gen.*	read gen.

635 line 7: *wûr* should appear at the end of the preceding line (D Vbl. Adj., after slash).

KEY TO THE EXERCISES

LESSON ONE

D. *a/bum*
ā/lum
am/tum
bē/lum
ḫu/rā/ṣum
il/tum
i/lum
kas/pum
mār/tum
mā/rum
qaq/qa/dum
ṣā/bum
šar/ra/tum
šar/rum
war/dum.

E.
1. *mu/šal/li/mum*
2. *i/šāl*
3. *i/din*
4. *id/di/nū/niš/šum*
5. *tab/ni/an/ni*
6. *ni/qī/aš*
7. *e/pē/šum*
8. *kul/lu/mum*
9. *tab/nû*
10. *iš/ši/ak/kum*
11. *rē/dûm*
12. *iq/bi*
13. *pa/ris*
14. *iš/me/ā/nim*
15. *pe/te*
16. *šū/ṣû*

LESSON TWO

B. *aš/ša/tum*
bī/tum
e/mū/qum
ī/num
iš/dum
lib/bum
mu/tum
nā/rum
šī/pā/tum
tup/pum
um/mum
uz/num
a/na
i/na
iš/tu
it/ti

C.
1. *amātum*
2. *wardū*
3. *ummātum*
4. *mārātum*
5. *bēlū*
6. *aššātum*
7. *mutū*
8. *išdātum*
9. *mārū*
10. *ilū*
11. *ilātum*
12. *šarrātum*
13. *emūqū/ emūqātum*
14. *nārātum*
15. *ṭuppū/ ṭuppātum*
16. *ṣābū*
17. *bītātum*
18. *šarrū*

E.
1. *ištu ālim*
2. *ina libbim ša bītim*
3. *itti wardī ša šarratim*
4. *īnān ša bēlim*
5. *ša emūqim/emūqīn/ emūqī/emūqātim*
6. *ina aššātim ša mutī*
7. *qaqqadum ša bēlim*
8. *kaspum u ḫurāṣum ša mārim ša šarrim*
9. *ša ālim*
10. *ina īnīn u uznīn*
11. *ina emūqim ša ilī*
12. *ištu bītim*
13. *itti amtim/wardim*
14. *ina šīpātim ša šarrim*
15. *išdum ša ālim*
16. *ina ṭuppī/ṭuppātim ša mārātim*

F.
1. Ninḫursag is queen of the goddesses; she is queen of the goddesses.
2. You and I are (female) servants of the lord.
3. I am the lord of the city.
4. The womenservants are in the river; they are in the river.
5. The tablet belongs to the lord's son; it belongs to the lord's son.
6. The gods are in the center of town; they are in the center of town.
7. We are the queen's slaves.
8. The king's strength/armed forces are in the city.
9. The husband and wife are in the house with the(ir) sons and daughters; they are in the house.
10. The wool belongs to the (male) slave.
11. The king's strength is the foundation of the city.

G.
1. *ummum ša ilī atti.*
2. *ḫurāṣum ina bītim; ina bītim šū.*
3. *mārū ša amātim attunu; mārātum ša wardī attina.*
4. *ṣābum ša šarrim ina nārim.*
5. *abum ša amtim atta.*
6. *qaqqadum ša kaspim ša ummim.*
7. *iltum ina libbim ša ṣābim.*
8. *šīpātim ša aššatim ina bītim.*

LESSON THREE

B.

da/mā/qum	*ma/rā/ṣum*	*mā/tum*
da/nā/num	*ra/pā/šum*	*qā/tum*
ḫa/lā/qum	*ṣa/bā/tum*	*šar/rā/qum*
ka/šā/dum	*ša/kā/num*	*e/li*
ma/ḫā/ṣum	*ša/rā/qum*	
ma/qā/tum	*a/wī/lum*	

C.1. *dmq; dnn; ḫlq; kšd; mḫṣ; mqt; mrṣ; rpš; ṣbt; škn; šrq.*

C.2.

miqtum: *maqātum, pirs*
naṣbutum: *ṣabātum, naprus*
murappišum: *rapāšum, muparris*
ḫulqum; *ḫalāqum, purs*
kāšidum: *kašādum, pāris*
dummuqum: *damāqum, purrus*
šaḫluqtum: *ḫalāqum, šaprust*
šuṣbutum: *ṣabātum, šuprus*
šarrāqum: *šarāqum, parrās*
damqiš: *damāqum, parsiš*
maškanum: *šakānum, mapras*
murṣum: *marāṣum, purs*
šaknum: *šakānum, pars*
tadnintum: *danānum, taprist*
ritpāšum: *rapāšum, pitrās*
šikānum: *šakānum, pirās*

D.

iḫliq	*ikšud*	*imḫaṣ*
taḫliq	*takšud*	*tamḫaṣ*
taḫliqī	*takšudī*	*tamḫaṣī*
aḫliq	*akšud*	*amḫaṣ*
iḫliqū	*ikšudū*	*imḫaṣū*
iḫliqā	*ikšudā*	*imḫaṣā*
taḫliqā	*takšudā*	*tamḫaṣā*
niḫliq	*nikšud*	*nimḫaṣ*

E.

1. *iḫliq*
2. *akšud*
3. *tašriq*
4. *irpiš*
5. *idmiqū*
6. *nimraṣ*
7. *iṣbat*
8. *taškunā*
9. *imḫaṣā*
10. *tadninī*
11. *anāku u attunu nimqut*

F.

1. The gold and silver of the (male) slaves got lost.
2. You (ms) seized the queen's womanservant.
3. You (fs) struck the thief's son's head with force.
4. The army is in the heart of the land.
5. A god struck the husband's eyes.
6. They (m) stole the wool from the mother's house.
7. The gods placed a king over the land.
8. You (ms) are with the man's daughters.
9. The king's army became strong; they reached the center of the country from the river.

10. The man's household improved.
11. The father and mother hit the(ir) son's ears and hands.
12. The rivers of the lands grew wide.
13. The lord's wife and children fell ill; the lord's household perished.
14. The goddess placed the foundation(s) of the city under the king's authority.
15. The foundation of the city is in the care of the gods.
16. The thief became sick while escaping from the land.
17. I seized the tablets from the thief.
18. She/he began hitting the manservant.
19. The queen became annoyed with the man.
20. I began work on the temple (god's house).

G.
1. *bēlū ša bītim idninū; idmiqū.*
2. *qātīn eli uznīn ša mārtim iškun.*
3. *šarrāqam ina šarāqim nisbat.*
4. *ina ālim anāku.*
5. *ṣābum ša bēlim eli mātim ana kašādim ša mātim imqut/imqutū.*
6. *qātam ša amtim taṣbatā.*

LESSON FOUR

B. 1. *šakānum*
2. *ḫalāqum*
3. *ṣabātum*
4. *maqātum*
5. *kanākum*
6. *šalāmum*
7. *maḫārum*
8. *gamārum*
9. *rapāšum*
10. *maḫāṣum*
11. *balāṭum*
12. *kašādum*

C. 1. *napšātum*; 2. *rapšātum*; 3. *zaprātum*; 4. *šarqātum*

D.

ibluṭ	*iṣbat*	*išlim*
tabluṭ	*taṣbat*	*tašlim*
tabluṭī	*taṣbatī*	*tašlimī*
abluṭ	*aṣbat*	*ašlim*
ibluṭū	*iṣbatū*	*išlimū*
ibluṭā	*iṣbatā*	*išlimā*
tabluṭā	*taṣbatā*	*tašlimā*
nibluṭ	*niṣbat*	*nišlim*

E.

sg.	*wardum ḫalqum*	*amtum ḫaliqtum*
	wardim ḫalqim	*amtim ḫaliqtim*
	wardam ḫalqam	*amtam ḫaliqtam*
pl.	*wardū ḫalqūtum*	*amātum ḫalqātum*
	wardī ḫalqūtim	*amātim ḫalqātim*

F. 1. *kakkū dannūtum*
2. *šikarum ṭābum*
3. *īnān marṣātum*
4. *bēlum ša uznim rapaštim*
5. *ina mārātim damqātim*
6. *alpū ḫalqūtum*
7. *eli eṭlim dannim*
8. *ina šamnim ṭābim*
9. *itti aḫim marṣim*
10. *bītātum maqtātum*
11. *šarrū nakrūtum / nakarūtum / nakirūtum*
12. *šīpātum šarqātum*
13. *ṭuppū kankūtum / ṭuppātum kankātum*
14. *eli mātim nakirtim / nakartim*
15. *ana mutī ṣabtūtim*
16. *išdātum maqtātum*
17. *itti mārim balṭim*
18. *emūqum dannum*
19. *ina nārim rapaštim*
20. *ina libbim gamrim*
21. *kaspum maḫrum*
22. *tībū kašdūtum*

G. 1. I became ill; now I have achieved good health, recovered, grown strong.
2. The gods struck the life of the mighty youth.
3. The wool disappeared from the man's house; the brother of the man caught the thief arriving at the fortress.
4. We annihilated the enemy army with strong weapons.
5. I did not receive fine oil and healthy oxen from the thief.
6. The queen's father is/was not in the temple (house) of the goddess.
7. The women slaves escaped from the master's care.

8. We received tablets from the man's wife; we sealed the tablets.
9. The king's army reached the enemies' fortresses.
10. The slaves arrived at the city to complete the foundation of the house.
11. The mighty king did not strike the captives with the weapons.
12. The favor of the gods befell the young man's brother.
13. You (pl) seized the fine beer from/in the hand of the thief.
14. The man's oxen pleased the lord.
15. The sick slaves escaped from the fortress to the wide river.
16. We did not finish sealing the tablets.
17. I began work on the collapsed house.

H.
1. *alpū ša ummim ša eṭlim šunu.*
2. *šarrum kaspam u ḫurāṣam eli ālim kašdim iškun.*
3. *marṣum šamnam ṭābam eli qaqqadim iškun.*
4. *ummātum ša eṭlūtim libbam ša ālim dannim ikšudā.*
5. *kaspam gamram taknukī.*
6. *bēlū ša ālim šarram ša mātim imḫurū.*
7. *eṭlūtum nak(a/i)rūtum šikaram ša šaknim išriqū, igmurū.*
8. *dannatum eli mātim imqut; nimraṣ.*

LESSON FIVE

B. *issuḫ, tassuḫ, tassuḫī, assuḫ; issuḫū, issuḫā, tassuḫā, nissuḫ.*
iṣṣur, taṣṣur, taṣṣurī, aṣṣur; iṣṣurū, iṣṣurā, taṣṣurā, niṣṣur.

C.
1. *ištu dannatim kašittim*
2. *itti amtim balittim*
3. *šēpān u uznān ša mārtim maḫištim*
4. *eli īnīn ša aššatim maruštim*
5. *ṣabittum*
6. *ḫarrānum qatattum*
7. *ṭuppū kankūtum gamrūtum / ṭuppātum kankātum gamrātum*
8. *kīma iltim dannatim*
9. *iltum pašištum*
10. *ḫarrānātum mādātum u kakkū mādūtum*
11. *napšātum ša eṭlūtim nakrūtim*
12. *ina narkabātim šarqātim*
13. *kīma bītātim naqrātim*
14. *maruštum māttum*
15. *bēlū nasḫūtum*
16. *narkabātum damqātum mādātum*
17. *šikarum mādum*

D.
1. The king anointed the head and neck of the god with fine oil.
2. Hardship came upon the king and the army during the campaign.
3. The brother of the queen rode the excellent chariot to the town.
4. The foundation of the house became narrow; the house collapsed.
5. You (pl) did not give healthy oxen to the man's mother.
6. I placed a hand on the dog's thin neck.
7. We seized the sealed tablets from the thief by force.
8. Trouble confronted the lord.
9. The king supplied the lord with much gold and beer.
10. The lords of the land removed the king; they installed the queen's father.
11. I handed the captive slave over to the man's son to guard; he did not guard the slave; the slave escaped.
12. You (fs) supplied the slave's husband with fine wool; the husband sold the wool.
13. We did not tear down the city and fortresses of the enemy.
14. I myself removed the enemy from the land, in accordance with the gods' will.
15. The god protected the man's life.
16. The dog's foot became diseased/painful.
17. The gods placed the king's foot on the neck(s) of the enemies.
18. The king mustered an expert army; they undertook a campaign.

LESSON SIX

B.

ms	*parsum*	fs	*parištum*	ms	*ṭardum*	fs	*ṭarittum*
	parsim		*parištim*		*ṭardim*		*ṭarittim*
	parsam		*parištam*		*ṭardam*		*ṭarittam*
mp	*parsūtum*	fp	*parsātum*	mp	*ṭardūtum*	fp	*ṭardātum*
	parsūtim		*parsātim*		*ṭardūtim*		*ṭardātim*

C.

1. *rubātum annītum*
   rubātim annītim
   rubātam annītam

   rubâtum anniātum
   rubâtim anniātim

2. *purussûm maḫrûm*
   purussêm maḫrîm
   purussâm maḫriam

   purussû maḫrûtum
   purussê maḫrûtim

3. *šadûm šaplûm*
   šadîm šaplîm
   šadâm šapliam

   šadû šaplûtum
   šadî šaplûtim

4. *rubûm annûm*
   rubêm annîm
   rubâm anniam

   rubû annûtum
   rubê annûtim

5. *kussûm maḫrītum*
   kussîm maḫrītim
   kussiam maḫrītam

   kussiātum maḫriātum
   kussiātim maḫriātim

D.

1. *ekallātum šina*
2. *ana šēpīn ša dayyānim šuāti / šuātu / šâti / šâtu*
3. *eli ḫarrānim šuāti / šâti / šiāti*
4. *kīma šaknim ša mātim šuāti / šâti / šiāti*
5. *kišādum ša kalbim šuāti / šuātu / šâti / šâtu*
6. *ana nakrim ṣabtim šuāti / šuātu / šâti / šâtu*
7. *kakkum šū*
8. *nārum šaplītum šī*
9. *ana napištim šuāti / šâti / šiāti*
10. *ištu bītātim šināti*
11. *ina ṭuppī šaṭrūtim šunūti / ina ṭuppātim šaṭrātim šināti*

E.

1. The judge's eyes did not see.
2. The gods tore out the foundations of that king's throne; an enemy lord took the throne.
3. I handed over an ox to the prince's brother; said ox got sick and died; the prince threw said ox to the dogs.
4. The prince anointed the head of the goddess with fine oil.
5. We did not finish assigning/registering the troops.
6. The lords of the land decided the husband's case; they put (his) wife in a separate house.

7. We did not reach that wide road.
8. The enemy army destroyed the king's palaces; we did not see said ruined palaces.
9. The princesses of the aforementioned city threw much beer down into the river.
10. The prince registered that house to the charge of the judge, and sealed (the tablet).
11. You are not children of the former wife of the prince.
12. The judges rode the chariot from the bank of this river to the mountain.
13. You (ms) drove the thieves and the enemies from the land with a mighty hand.
14. I selected an expert army from among the youths of this city.
15. The aforementioned slaves are under the authority of the king's mother.
16. The masters dispatched said slaves to the house of the sick man.
17. It was not I who wrote the previous tablet of this decision; it was you (fs) who wrote (it).
18. The sick daughter recovered.

LESSON SEVEN

B.

irbi	*izku*	*išme*
tarbi	*tazku*	*tešme* / *tašme*
tarbî	*tazkî*	*tešmî* / *tašmî*
arbi	*azku*	*ešme* / *ašme*
irbû	*izkû*	*išmû*
irbiā	*izkâ*	*išmeā*
tarbiā	*tazkâ*	*tešmeā* / *tašmeā*
nirbi	*nizku*	*nišme*

C.

1. *eqlum zakûm*
   eqlim zakîm
   eqlam zakâm

   eqlētum zakâtum
   eqlētim zakâtim

2. *bēltum rabītum*
   bēltim rabītim
   bēltam rabītam

   bēlētum rabiātum
   bēlētim rabiātim

3. *narûm banûm*
   narîm / *narêm banîm*
   narâm baniam

   narû banûtum
   narî / *narê banûtim*

4. *ṭēmum maḫrûm*
   ṭēmim maḫrîm
   ṭēmam maḫriam

   ṭēmū maḫrûtum / *ṭēmētum maḫriātum*
   ṭēmī maḫrûtim / *ṭēmētim maḫriātim*

5. *kussûm ṣeḫertum*
   kussîm ṣeḫertim
   kussiam ṣeḫertam

   kussiātum ṣeḫ(e)rētum
   kussiātim ṣeḫ(e)rētim

6. *qīštum annītum*
   qīštim annītim
   qīštam annītam

   qīšātum anniātum
   qīšātim anniātim

7. *rubûm ḫadûm*
   rubêm ḫadîm
   rubâm ḫadiam

   rubû ḫadûtum
   rubê ḫadûtim

8. *narkabtum malītum*
   narkabtim malītim
   narkabtam malītam

   narkabātum maliātum
   narkabātim maliātim

D.

1. The ladies' fields filled with much water.
2. The princess gave a report to the youths and (then) rode to the mountains.
3. With the strength of (my) hands I built the foundation of this palace, mustered an excellent army, and installed (it) in the palace.
4. The brother of the prince received a gift from the lady, (and) gave (it) to the prince's son.
5. When we heard that report, we rejoiced.
6. The enemy threw down and destroyed the king's inscribed stela.
7. The water reached from the lower river to the town.

8. Having heard the lady's tablet, I took action concerning that tablet.
9. The hands of those gods built the lands.
10. These female slaves rejoiced on reaching the town.
11. The courage of the mighty king grew, and he took a weapon in (his) hand and struck the enemy.
12. The sick oxen recovered.
13. The child's eyes grew large and became diseased.
14. The lords of the city decided the man's case, and in said case the man's field became free (of claims).
15. The king put the enemies in prison, and so the prison became full.
16. Since you (ms) did not see these tablets, you did not send that male slave.
17. I did not receive the total (amount of) gold from the daughter.

LESSON EIGHT

B. *īḫuz, tāḫuz, tāḫuzī, āḫuz; īḫuzū, īḫuzā, tāḫuzā, nīḫuz.*
illik, tallik, tallikī, allik; illikū, illikā, tallikā, nillik.
īrub, tērub, tērubī, ērub; īrubū, īrubā, tērubā, nīrub.
īšir / īšer, tēšir / tēšer, tēširī / tēšerī, ēšir / ēšer; īširū / īšerū, īširā / īšerā, tēširā / tēšerā, nīšir / nīšer.

C.
1. *dīn(i) qarrādim*
2. *napšātum arkāt ūmim*
3. *ina epišti puḫrim*
4. *qīšti awīlim*
5. *šum(i) narîm / narêm šaṭrim*
6. *akal ālim*
7. *ṣibitti ekallim*
8. *ekal šar(ri) mātim*
9. *eqel bēlet bītim*
10. *kussi rubê / rubi / rubā ālim*
11. *ištu šad(a / i) nakrim*
12. *eli naker dayyānī annîm*
13. *ana amār nārim*
14. *kīma awât ṭēmim šuāti*
15. *kišād kalab rubātim*
16. *ina libbi dannatim rabītim*
17. *qātān u šēpān ša mutim*
18. *itti šakin mātim*
19. *kasap abi šarratim*
20. *ilat bītim ṣeḫrim annîm*
21. *uznā alap mutim*
22. *ina kak(ki) eṭlim*
23. *šikar ṣābim*
24. *mārat šarrāqim damiqtum*
25. *aḫi amtim / wardim*
26. *amat / warad aḫim*
27. *šaman ekallim ṭābum*
28. *šīpāt ekallim šina*
29. *narkabti mārim*
30. *narkabāt mārī mādātum*
31. *marṣūt šadîm šaplîm*
32. *marušti amat bēlim*
33. *ṭuppi ummi aššatim*
34. *eli ḫarrānāt mātim*
35. *epšēt qātim ša ilī* or *epšēt qāt(i) ilī*
36. *ina mê nārim*
37. *emūq šarrim dannum / emūqā(t) šarrim dannātum / emūqū šarrim dannūtum*
38. *eṭlūt ṣābim*
39. *purussû puḫrim maḫrûtum*
40. *ina šemê / šemi awâtim anniātim*

D.
1. *almatti*
2. *ašal*
3. *bāb(i)*
4. *abul*
5. *bašīt*
6. *ḫuluq*
7. *imēr*
8. *kiṣir*
9. *qabê / qabi / qabā*
10. *mānaḫti*

E.
1. We rejoiced at the father's arrival.
2. The great god's hands created humanity.
3. The town's river did not fill with water.
4. The lord's sons married wives and constructed large houses.
5. The food of the lords and ladies improved, but the food of the male and female slaves did not improve.
6. The slaves obeyed the good words of the warrior and entered that fortress.
7. We received fine palace beer from the prince, and gave (it) to the sick woman.

8. I became clear (of claims) in that judgment, and received a sealed tablet.
9. The aforementioned judge traveled to the mountain region and investigated the affairs of the queen's brother.
10. You (fs) did not act according to the king's command, and did not send the escaped womanservant to the city.
11. I gave oil for anointing the head of the god as a gift to the temple, and entrusted (it) to the servant of the temple.
12. The enemy king removed the judges of the city, and also threw the inscribed stela of the previous king into the river.
13. I left much silver of the lord's in a foreign land, and so I have not gone to the lord's city.
14. The royal army undertook a campaign; they charged the enemy army in the enemy fortress, did battle, and conquered that army.
15. I did not receive food or fresh water, and so became ill and did not fare well.
16. Since the land prospered by the strength of the great king, we did not leave the land.
17. When the sick man's days grew long and he recovered, he entered the temple and rejoiced.
18. The king of the land is a just man.

LESSON NINE

C. 1. *an-na* 2. *maḫ-la-aš* 3. *mu-tim* 4. *na-ḫal* 5. *na-la* 6. *nu-bat-tim* 7. *aš-la-tim* 8. *be-rum*

D. 1. *īgur, tāgur, tāgurī, āgur; īgurū, īgurā, tāgurā, nīgur.*
2. *īniš, tēniš, tēnišī, ēniš; īnišū, īnišā, tēnišā, nīniš.*
3. *ibēl, tebēl, tebēlī, ebēl; ibēlū, ibēlā, tebēlā, nibēl.*
4. *imīd, tamīd, tamīdī, amīd; imīdū, imīdā, tamīdā, nimīd.*
5. *išāl, tašāl, tašālī, ašāl; išālū, išālā, tašālā, nišāl.*
6. *išti, tašti, taštî, ašti; ištû, ištiā, taštiā, ništi.*
7. *itūr, tatūr, tatūrī, atūr; itūrū, itūrā, tatūrā, nitūr.*

E. 1. *kītti awātim*
2. *kunuk qarrādim*
3. *ager rubêm*
4. *eqlēt puḫur ālim*
5. *enšūt mātim*
6. *šum(i) ṣabtim*
7. *ūm(i) dīnim*
8. *qīšāt bēlet kussîm*
9. *ṣāb(i) / ummān šarrim*
10. *ṣibittum malītum*
11. *kunukkū ṣeḫ(e)rūtum / kunukkātum ṣeḫ(e)rētum*
12. *narûm šarqum*
13. *mû zakûtum*

F. 1. *agram šuāti ana gamār banê bītim āgur-ma banê bītim ul igmur.* I hired that hireling to finish building the house, but he did not finish building the house.
2. *ina ūmim šâti enšūt mātim idninū u anāku ēniš-ma ul ēšer.* On that day the weak of the land became strong while I became weak and did not prosper.
3. *alpam nišām-ma imraṣ-ma alpam marṣam šuāti ana bēl alpim maḫrîm niddin.* We bought an ox, but the ox got sick, and so we gave said sick ox (back) to the former owner of the ox.
4. *eqlam epšam ana aššat wardim taqīšī.* You (fs) gave a cultivated field to the slave's wife.
5. *šarrum kakkī itti nakirim īpuš-ma nakiram inēr.* The king did battle with the enemy and defeated/slew the enemy.
6. *amtum šāmtum iḫliq-ma ana bīt bēlim ul itūr.* The slave that was purchased escaped and did not return to (her) master's house.
7. *išid kussi šarrim ikūm-ma ūmāt šarrim īrikā.* The foundation of the king's throne endured, and the king's days were prolonged.
8. *awīlum šū bītam u eqlam išām-ma īniš.* When that man purchased a house and field, he became impoverished.
9. *dayyānū ana puḫur ālim illikū-ma ḫurāṣam mādam u šīpātim qatnātim ana rubātim/rubâtim iqīšū.* The judges went to the assembly of the city and gave much gold and fine wool to the princess/princesses.
10. *ummānum nakartum šarram rabiam u māri/mārī šarrim ina ekallim inār.* The enemy army slew the great king and the king's son/sons in the palace.

11. *emūqā ummān nakrim īnišā-ma ummānum šī imqut.* The strength of the enemy's army having become weak, that army fell.
12. *nīnu ina māt nakrim ul nikūn ana mātim annītim nitūr-ma ana dannatim nīrub.* We did not become secure in the land of the enemy; we returned to this land and entered the fortress.
13. *qarrādum kunuk dayyānim īḫuz-ma issuk.*The warrior seized and threw down the judge's seal.
14. *ina kīttim šikar ekallim ul ništi u akal ālim ul nīḫuz.* In truth, we did not drink the palace beer and we did not take the town food.
15. *dayyānum ṭuppam īzim-ma anāku u atta awât ṭuppim kīnātim nīmur.* After the judge made out a tablet, you (ms) and I read the true words of the tablet.
16. *mû nārim šaplītim imīdū-ma nārum irpiš-ma mû eli kišād nārim illikū.* When the water of the lower river increased the river widened and the water flowed over the bank of the river.
17. *šarrum ṭēmam itti eṭlūtim iškum-ma narkabātim ana šadîm annîm irkabū.* After the king gave a report to the youths, they rode the chariots to this mountain.
18. *ina epšētim išarātim ša rubêm šuāti napišti mātim iṭīm-ma mātum iḫdu.* In the just actions of that prince the life of the land became pleasant, so that the land rejoiced.

G. 1. *an-nu-tim; annûtim* 'these (m, g-a)'
2. *maḫ-rum; maḫrum* 'received (ms nom)' or *maḫrûm* 'previous (ms nom)'

LESSON TEN

C. 1. *an-nam*
2. *ge-re*
3. *sé-be*
4. *ti / til-la-tim*
5. *be-en-nu / be-nu*
6. *ḫal-la-ti*
7. *ṣé-nam*
8. *zi-mu*
9. *eg-rum*
10. *mu-ḫu-tim*
11. *ṭì-dim*

D. 1. *imūt, tamūt, tamūtī, amūt; imūtū, imūtā, tamūtā, nimūt.*
2. *išīb, tašīb, tašībī, ašīb; išībū, išībā, tašībā, nišīb.*
3. *īkul, tākul, tākulī, ākul; īkulū, īkulā, tākulā, nīkul.*
4. *urid, turid, turdī, urid, urdū, urdā, turdā, nurid.*
5. *īriq, tēriq, tēriqī, ēriq; īriqū, īriqā, tēriqā, nīriq.*

E. 1. *ittīni*
2. *elīka*
3. *kīma šunūti*
4. *elīšu*
5. *ittīkina*
6. *kīma šuāti / šuātu / šâti / šâtu*
7. *ittīya u ittīša*
8. *elīšunu*
9. *kīma šināti*
10. *elīkunu*
11. *ana šuāšim / šâšim / šiāšim*
12. *elīšina*
13. *kaspam ittīki amḫur*

F. 1. *ṭēmam itti amtim aškum-ma ana mārat šarratim aṭrud.* Having given a report to the female slave, I sent (her) to the queen's daughter.
2. *qarrādum šū ina bītim ušib ḫarrānam ittīni ul illik.* That warrior remained in (his) house; he did not undertake the campaign with us.
3. *ina dīnim eqlam zakâm anniam amḫur-ma ākul bēl eqlim maḫrûm imraṣ-ma ul išlim-ma imūt.* I received this field free of claims in a judgment and used (it); the previous owner of the field fell ill, did not recover, and died.
4. *šībum marṣum ana wardī ḫalqūtim mê ṭābūtim ana šatêm u aklam ana akālim iqīš.* The sick old man gave the escaped slaves fresh water to drink and food to eat.
5. *eṭlam šuāti ilqû-ma ana bīt ilim ublū.* They took and carried that youth to the temple.
6. *šarram mārū šarrim ina ekallim inērū.* The king's sons slew the king in the palace.
7. *ṭēmam ana watarti bītim šuāti taṣbatā-ma karān bītim ana bēl bītim taddinā.* You (pl) took action concerning the excess (land) of that estate and gave the vineyard of the estate to the owner of the estate.
8. *ina šattim šâti nišū mātim bīt ilim laberam iqqurā-ma bītam eššam ibniā.* In that year the people of the land tore down the old temple and build a new temple.
9. *mār dayyānim ṣeḫrum bēltam īḫuz-ma nišū iḫdâ.* When the judge's young son married the lady, the people rejoiced.

10. *ana mātim itti ummānim nitūr-ma ina ālim nušib.* After we returned to (our) land with the army, we remained in the city.
11. *iltum rabītum lemuttam ina mātim iprus.* The great goddess kept evil from the land.
12. *awât šībūtim kīnātim ešmē-ma enšam šuāti ul amḫaṣ.* I heeded the elders' just words and did not strike that weak man.
13. *akalum ina eqlētim īter-ma nišū mādam īkulā.* Food became exceeding(ly abundant) in the fields, and so the people had much to eat (lit.: ate much).
14. *dannatum šī ana šanātim mādātim ilbir-ma ina šattim annītim imqut.* The aforementioned fortress endured for many years, but in this year it collapsed.
15. *agram ana naṣār kunuk awīlim tāgurī-ma šū kunukkam išriq.* You (fs) hired a hireling to guard the boss's seal, but he himself stole the seal.
16. *alpū mādūtum ša rubêm imūtū alpī mītūtim ittīni ul išām.* Many of the prince's oxen died; he did not buy the dead oxen from us.
17. *ḫurāṣum watrum ana ekallim īrum-ma ḫurāṣum imīd-ma libbi šarrim iṭīb.* Excess gold entered the palace; because the gold increased, the king's heart was satisfied.

G. 1. *ag-rum; agrum* 'hireling (nom)'
2. *maḫ-ri-tim; maḫrītim* 'foremost (fs, gen)'
3. *na-ak-rum; nakrum* 'enemy (ms, nom)'
4. *iq-ti-nu; iqtinū* 'they (m) became thin'

LESSON ELEVEN

C.

1. *mu-gur*
2. *sa-ap-ḫu-um*
3. *ze / zé-rum / ru-um*
4. *sa-ad-rum / ru-um*
5. *ṣe / ṣé-re-tim*
6. *šu-gi-tim*
7. *tal-la-šu*
8. *ḫu-ub-tim*
9. *se / sé-ek-rum / ru-um*
10. *ab-nam*
11. *šu-ḫu-rum / ru-um*
12. *šu-ub-tim*

D.

iṯhe, teṯhe, teṯhî, eṯhe / aṯhe; iṯhû, iṯheā, teṯheā, niṯhe.
ulid, tulid, tuldī, ulid; uldū, uldā, tuldā, nulid.

E.

1. *lemuttaša*
2. *šībū(tū)ya*
3. *karākkunu*
4. *kunukkūšina banûtum / kunukkātūšina baniātum*
5. *ṣāb(ū)šu / ummāššu ša ẹmūqim*
6. *edēssu*
7. *watarti eqlīšunu epšim*
8. *ana mītūtīšina kalîšunu*
9. *sinnišāt mātīšunu*
10. *kišāssu qatnum*
11. *maruštaka u maruštī*
12. *šarrani u šarrassu*
13. *ṣuḫārtaša annītum*
14. *nakāssunu*
15. *ūmū arkūtum / ūmātum arkātum ša šanātīšu*
16. *dayyānī kīnum / išarum*
17. *puḫuršunu rabûm*
18. *awātī kīttum*
19. *awâtūya kīnātum*
20. *purussâšunu amḫur.*
21. *abī u aḫūšu*
22. *epištaki damiqtum*
23. *epšētūki damqātum*
24. *qāssa / qātūša maruštum*
25. *uzuššu rapaštum*
26. *uznāšu rapšātum*
27. *agerkina u agrī*
28. *mussa / mutūša*
29. *ina ṭuppīya kankim šuāti / šuātu / šâtu / šâti*
30. *itti narkabātīkunu eššētim kalîšina*
31. *ṭēm(ū)ki gamrum*
32. *eli kussīka*
33. *alpūni šalmūtum*
34. *ina šamnīya u šikarīya ṭābūtim*
35. *napištaša ša maruštim*
36. *kasapkunu šarqum*
37. *išissu maqtum / išdāšu maqtātum*
38. *amassu ḫaliqtum*
39. *nēmettašina watartum*
40. *mārī u mārātūya*
41. *narî šaṭrum*
42. *nišūki ḫadiātum*
43. *kīma ṣabtīka naṣrim*
44. *āl(ū)šu kalûšu*
45. *ina bītīša parsim*
46. *ištu mêšu zakûtim*
47. *rašê*
48. *nakeršu / nakaršu ṭardum*
49. *rubûni u aššassu*
50. *ḫarrāššina šaplītum*

F.

1. *ṣāb šarrim iṣam mādam ikkisū-ma iṣam naksam ana ekallīšu ublū.* The king's troops cut down a lot of wood and carried the cut wood to his palace.
2. *nišū ina puḫrim ipḫurā-ma kasapšina u ḫurāssina ana qarrādim dannim ipqidā.* When the people gathered in assembly, they entrusted their silver and gold to the mighty warrior.

3. *ina dīnim šâtu wardī u amātim aršī-ma adīni ana bītīya ul īrubū.* In that judgment I acquired male and female slaves, but they have not yet entered my house.
4. *sinništum šī mārī mādūtim ana mutīša ulid-ma kalûšunu īširū.* That woman bore her husband many children, and all of them prospered.
5. *šarrum ummānam rabītam ikṣur-ma ana mātim nakartim iṭḫē-ma kakkī īpuš-ma bēlša nakeršu issuḫ.* The king organized a great army, approached the enemy land, did battle, and removed its lord, his enemy.
6. *abūšunu u ummašunu ana ālīšunu maḫrîm itūrū-ma ina ālim šuātu ušbū-ma išībū-ma imūtū.* Their father and mother returned to their earlier town, and remained, grew old, and died in that town.
7. *dayyānū kaspī kalâšu kīma nēmettīya ilqû-ma adīni šīpātim ul ašām.* The judges took all my silver as my tax, and so I have not yet bought (any) wool.
8. *abī amassu ana ilīšu ana balāṭīšu iqīš.* My father dedicated his female slave to his god for his life('s sake).
9. *ina ṭeḫê aḫīša ṣeḫrim īnāša mê imlâ-ma aḫāša ul iṭṭul.* At her young brother's approach her eyes filled with water, so that she did (i.e., could) not see her brother.
10. *ilum lemnum ana ṣuḫārim šuātu ina ḫarrānim īšir-ma ṣuḫārum ilam ul īmur.* An evil god charged that young man on the road, but the young man did not see the god.
11. *iṣam kalâšu ša bēlīkunu takṣurā ina kīttim epištum annītum īn bēlīkunu imḫur.* You collected all your (mp) lord's wood; in truth this deed pleased your lord.
12. *sinništam šâti mussa īzim-ma ana bīt abīša itūr.* Her husband left that woman and she returned to her father's house.
13. *kalbum annûm ša bēlīki ul kalabki šū.* This dog belongs to your (fs) lord; it is not yours.
14. *ina šattim šuāti šarrāqum šū eqelni watram īkul-ma kaspam nēmettani ittīšu ul nimḫur.* In that year said thief used our extra field, but we did not receive (any) silver (as) our tribute from him.
15. *ina paḫār nišī ilū iḫdû.* The gods rejoiced at the gathering of the people.

G.

1. *šu-um-šu la-be-ru-um; šumšu laberum* 'his/its (m) ancient name (nom)'
2. *en-šu-um an-nu-um; enšum annûm* 'this weak man (nom)'
3. *na-sa-ak-šu-nu; nasākšunu* 'their (m) throwing (nom-acc)'
4. *ag-ru-tim; agrūtim* 'hirelings (gen-acc)'
5. *be-la-šu; bēlāšu* 'his lord (acc)'

LESSON TWELVE

C. 1. *du-uk-šu*
2. *úr-ḫu-um*
3. *šu-um-gur*
4. *gi-mil*
5. *si / sí-(ik-)kum*
6. *na-ad-rum / ru-um*
7. *ru-up-šu-um*
8. *pé-ṣi / ṣí-tum*
9. *mu-uš-ḫu-(uš-)šu-um*
10. *sa-(as-)sa-tum*

D. *iḫeppe / iḫappe, teḫeppe / taḫappe, teḫeppî / taḫappî, eḫeppe / aḫappe; iḫeppû / iḫappû, iḫeppeā / iḫappeā, teḫeppeā / taḫappeā, niḫeppe / niḫappe.*

ikannuš, takannuš, takannušī, akannuš; ikannušū, ikannušā, takannušā, nikannuš.

imalla, tamalla, tamallî, amalla; imallû, imallâ, tamallâ, nimalla.

inakkis, tanakkis, tanakkisī, anakkis; inakkisū, inakkisā, tanakkisā, ninakkis.

isaḫḫap, tasaḫḫap, tasaḫḫapī, asaḫḫap; isaḫḫapū, isaḫḫapā, tasaḫḫapā, nisaḫḫap.

E. 1. *piam tašakkanī*
2. *ina libbīšunu*
3. *inassukū*
4. *pān(ā)ša / pānīša ana banêm / epēšim išakkan*
5. *ana / ša pī šīb(ūt)īšina*
6. *tarabbiā*
7. *pān(ā)šunu / pānīšunu aṣabbat*
8. *ikaṣṣarū*
9. *elīkunu / ina muḫḫīkunu*
10. *tarakkabā*
11. *nimaqqut*
12. *irappiš*
13. *ina maḫar / pān(i) sinništim šuāti / šiāti / šâti*
14. *inaṭṭalā*
15. *tamaḫḫaṣā*
16. *ana maḫar / ṣēr šaknim*
17. *imalla*
18. *ana maḫar / ṣēr ṣābim / ummānim*
19. *libbaki imarraṣ*
20. *pānī / pānīya ašakkan*
21. *ina pān(i) awātim annītim*
22. *inaqqarū*
23. *taballuṭ / tašallim*
24. *ina / ša qāt(i) dayyānī*
25. *ileqqeā*
26. *nikaššad*
27. *ina bīrīšunu*
28. *nigammar*
29. *tašaṭṭar*
30. *ašallim*
31. *mārū / mār(i) šiprīkina*
32. *nišemme / nišamme*
33. *niḫaddu*
34. *takannakā*
35. *adannin*
36. *iṭarrad*
37. *izakku*
38. *imaḫḫarā*
39. *inassaḫ*
40. *idammiq*
41. *anaṣṣar*
42. *ana pān(i) ṣuḫārim šuāti / u / šâti / u*
43. *tapaqqidī*
44. *ina birīt karānī annûtim*
45. *išattû*
46. *nipaššaš*
47. *bēlū / bēl(i) ḫubullīni*
48. *anakkis*
49. *iḫalliqā*
50. *iqattin*
51. *ipaḫḫurū*
52. *taraššî*
53. *ipaššaḫū / ipaššiḫū*

F. 1. *ilum rabûm pīšu īpuš-ma awâtīšu kalâšina nišme.* When the great god opened his mouth, we heard all his words.

2. *ṭuppātim labirātim teḫeppē-ma eššētim tašaṭṭar.* You (ms) will/should break the old tablets and write new ones.
3. *ina epēšim annîm bēlī pānīya ula ubil-ma libbī imraṣ.* In this action my lord did not favor me, and so I became annoyed.
4. *ṣuḫārātūni eqlam šuāti šipram adīni ul īpušā u ana bīt abīšina itūrā.* Our employees (f) have not yet worked that field; moreover, they have returned to their father's house.
5. *mû ina nārim imīdū-ma eqlētīya rapšātim isḫupū.* When the water increased in the river, it covered my vast fields.
6. *narê ḫepûtim ša nakrīya ina ālīšu āmur.* I saw my enemy's smashed stelae in his city.
7. *kaspam mādam ana bēl ḫubullīka tanaddim-ma ṭuppi/ṭuppī ḫubullīka iḫeppû.* If you (ms) give a lot of silver to your creditors, they will break/ invalidate your debt tablet/tablets.
8. *ina epištim annītim libbi iltim ipaššaḫ.* At this deed the goddess's mind will become calm.
9. *awāt/awât dīnim šuāti maḫar dayyānim igammarū mār šiprīšunu ana ṣēr bēlīšunu iṭarradū.* They (m) will settle the affair(s) of this case before the judge (and) send their messenger(s) to their lord.
10. *ilum lemnum nišī bītim šâti isḫup-ma imūtā.* An evil god overwhelmed the people of that house, and they died.
11. *ina šattim annītim iṣam naksam watartani kīma nēmettīni ana ekallim niddin.* This year we gave our extra cut timber to the palace as our tax.
12. *nakrī kanšum ana maḫrīya illik-ma ana šēpīya imqut.* My subjected enemy came toward me and fell at my feet.
13. *sinnišātum šina itti mutīšina ina ālīni ušbā-ma mārī u mārātim mādūtim uldā-ma napšātūšina iṭībā.* After those women settled in our town with their husbands, they had many sons and daughters, and their lives improved.
14. *nišū mātātim kalîšina ina pānīya ikannušā.* The people of all lands (will) bow down before me.
15. *aḫī awātam annītam maḫrīya iškun qāssu ana epēš bītīšu išakkan.* My brother informed me of this matter: he will begin to build his house.

G.

1. *aṣ-bat; aṣbat* 'I seized'
2. *il-bi/bé-ru; ilbirū/ilberū* 'they (m) endured'
3. *iš-ri-iq; išriq* 'she/he stole'
4. *pí-šu; pīšu* 'his mouth'
5. *ik-nu-uš; iknuš* 'he/she bowed down'
6. *ap-ru-ús; aprus* 'I decided'
7. *maḫ-ri-šu-nu; maḫrīšunu* 'before them (m)' or 'their (m) previous one (m)'
8. *aṣ-ṣe-ri-šu; aṣ-ṣērīšu* 'toward him'

LESSON THIRTEEN

C.
1. GEME$_2$-*sa*
2. MU DUMU
3. KUG.BABBAR SAG.DU-*šu*
4. KUG.SIG$_{17}$-*ṣi* / *ṣí*
5. *iš-ru-uk*
6. *qé-ru-ub*
7. *az-bi-il*
8. *šu-mu-ut*
9. *še-be* / *bé-rum* / *ru-um*
10. *mil-kum*
11. *šu-uk-nu-uš*
12. *du-(úr-)ru-si* / *sí*

D. *iḫḫaz, taḫḫaz, taḫḫazī, aḫḫaz; iḫḫazū, iḫḫazā, taḫḫazā, niḫḫaz.*
irrub, terrub, terrubī, errub; irrubū, irrubā, terrubā, nirrub.
inniš, tenniš, tennišī, enniš; innišū, innišā, tennišā, ninniš.
itamma, tatamma, tatammî, atamma; itammû, itammâ, tatammâ, nitamma.

E.
1. *tappût eṭlūtim šunūti ul nillak.*
2. *enniš.*
3. *ṣuḫārtaša taḫḫaz.*
4. *nēmettakunu ina maḫar* / *pān(i) ebūrim ikaṣṣarū.*
5. *âm nikkal.*
6. *kalab šarrāqim ul tammarī.*
7. *ilū kalûšunu ina šamê ipaḫḫurū.*
8. *nīš(i) rubêm itammâ.*
9. *pīka ul teppeš* / *teppuš.*
10. *rēš(i) tappê iššir* / *idammiq.*
11. *ana pānīkina*
12. *ina birīt narkabātim eššētim anniātim*
13. *ina maḫrīka* / *pānīka ikannušū.*
14. *elīšunu* / *ina muḫḫīšunu*

F.
1. *ûm ina eqlētim īter* / *itter-ma nišū bābtim annītim âm watram ana kaspim inaddinā.* There was/will be an excess of grain (i.e., the grain became/will become excessive) in the fields, and so the people of this district will sell the excess grain.
2. *mār šiprīya ina qāt bēl ḫubullīya ēzim* / *ezzim-ma šū šiprī ippeš.* I left/will leave my messenger in the charge of my creditor(s), and he will do my work / the tasks.
3. *ina ūmim šuāti īnāni šamšam ul iṭṭulā.* On that day our eyes did not see the sun.
4. *anāku u aššatī ina pāni rugummêm šâti ul nipaššaḫ.* My wife and I are not content with the aforementioned penalty.
5. *ana maḫar bēltīya eṭḫē-ma īšša ul amḫur-ma pānīya ul ubil.* I approached my lady, but I did not please her, and so she did not forgive me.
6. *alpī šalmūtim aggar-ma eqlī šipram eppeš.* I will hire healthy oxen and work my field.
7. *ūmū marṣim ul irrikū-ma ul iballuṭ.* The sick man's days will not be long, and he will not recover.
8. *agrū iṣam mādam ikkisū-ma ana pī ṭēm bēlīšunu iṣam šuāti ana dannatim* / *dannātim ublū.* The hirelings cut down much timber and

brought said timber to the fortress/fortresses according to their lord's/ lords' instruction.

9. *tappê ḫurāṣam mādam iršī-ma ṭuppi tappûtīni kankam iḫpē-ma ḫurāṣam adīni ul nizūz.* My partner acquired a lot of gold, but since he broke our sealed partnership tablet, we have not yet shared the gold.

10. *dannatum mātam šâti isḫup-ma nišū mādātum imūtā-ma sinnišātum mārī ul uldā.* Famine having overwhelmed that land, many people died, and women did not have children.

G. 2. *Eqlam itti Ālikum mār Arwûm Takūm-mātum mārat Amurrûm u Rabbatum ummaša išāmā. Ālikum mār Arwûm Sumu-ramê u mārūšu kalûšunu ana Takūm-mātim irgumū-ma, dayyānū ina bīt Šamaš rugummêšunu issuḫū. ... Dīn bīt Šamaš. ...*

Takūm-mātum daughter of Amurrûm and Rabbatum her mother bought a field from Ālikum son of Arwûm. Ālikum son of Arwûm, Sumu-ramê and all his children brought suit against Takūm-mātum, but the judges, in the temple of Šamaš, rejected their suit. (Oath. Names of judges.) Judgment of the temple of Šamaš. (Witnesses.)

3. x *kaspam ešrētum*! *itti Šamaš Kišūšû ilqe. Ana Anum-abī ana ipṭerīšu iddin. Ina ūm ebūrim âm ana Šamaš inaddin. ...*

Kišūšû received x silver, a tithe, from Šamaš. He gave (it) to Anum-abī for his ransom. On the day of the harvest, he will give grain (equivalent to the value of the silver) to Šamaš. (Witnesses.)

H. 1. MU *maḫ-ri-tum; šattum maḫrītum* 'previous year'

2. ŠE-*ki* KI DUMU.MUNUS-*šu tam-ḫu-ri; âki itti mārtīšu tamḫurī* 'you (fs) received your grain from his daughter'

3. ÌR KUG.BABBAR KI *il-tim il-qé; wardum kaspam itti iltim ilqe* 'the slave received silver from the goddess'

4. *še-pí* DINGIR *ap-šu-uš; šēpī ilim apšuš* 'I anointed the god's feet'

5. KUG.SIG$_{17}$ MUNUS *nu-bi-il; ḫurāṣ sinništim nubil* 'we carried the woman's gold'

6. SAG É ^{d}UTU; *rēš(i) bīt(i) Šamaš* 'the top of the Šamaš temple'

7. GEME$_{2}$-*ki; amatki* 'your (fs) servant'

LESSON FOURTEEN

C. 1. *qí-bi / bí-šum / šu-um*
    2. *pil / píl / pí-il-šum / šu-um*
    3. *ta-ap-ta-ṭar*
    4. *ṭe / tè-mu-um*
    5. *nu-tar*
    6. *ne-šum / šu-um*
    7. *ta-du-uk*
    8. *mu-še-pí-šum / šu-um*
    9. *qá-dum / du-um*
    10. DI.KUD.MEŠ KÁ.DINGIR.RA^{ki}
    11. ÌR.MEŠ *ša* ^{d}UTU
    12. KUG.BABBAR GEME$_2$ LUGAL

D. 1. *tadukkā*
    2. *libbašu itīab*
    3. *imuttū*
    4. *tašīab*
    5. *nizâz / niparras*
    6. *ikunnū*
    7. *aqīaš*
    8. *tašammī*
    9. *tašāmī*
    10. *itâr*
    11. *itūr*
    12. *iturrā*
    13. *itūrā*
    14. *imīad*
    15. *tenerrā*
    16. *tenērā*
    17. *adīan*
    18. *idinnū*
    19. *itibbū*
    20. *imiddā*
    21. *nimât*
    22. *ikân*
    23. *appal*
    24. *tezzibī*
    25. *temmidā*
    26. *iddiš*
    27. *enniš*
    28. *teššerī*

E. 1. *mannum dīnī u dīkki idīan?* Who will judge my case and your (fs) case?
    2. *ana ṣēr awīlim allik-ma ina pānīšu aqbī-ma šū qabê īpul.* I went to the boss and spoke in his presence, and he himself answered my speech.
    3. *qarrādum šū kaspam mādam kīma nēmettim elīni īmid-ma nēmettam šuāti ul nippal.* That warrior imposed much silver upon us as a tax, but we will not pay said tax.
    4. *nišū ālim akalam itti šarrim imḫurā-ma ina warkiāt ūmī isaddarā-ma ina ebūrim âm šamnam u ḫurāṣam ana šarrim inaddinā.* The people of the town received food from the king, and so in the future they will regularly give grain, oil, and gold to the king at harvest-time.
    5. *bēl ummānim ana dâk nakrim qabâšu iškun.* The lord of the army promised to defeat the enemy.
    6. *am-mīnim ṭuppātum sadrātum ana maḫar abīya lā illakā.* Why are the regular documents not going to my father?
    7. *eqlam kiriam u karānam itā bāb bīt Šamaš nišâm-ma alpam niggar-ma eqlam šipram nippeš.* We will buy a field, orchard, and vineyard next to the gate of the Šamaš temple, hire an ox, and work the field.
    8. *mamman ṣeḫram anniam ana mārūtim ul ileqqē-ma imarraṣ-ma imât.* If no one adopts this child, he will become sick and die.
    9. *ayyītam mātam šarrum ana mārīšu ana epēš bēlūtim iqīaš?* Which land will the king bestow upon his son to rule?
    10. *ina rēš šattim annītim ayyumma ina nišī ekallim šarram idūk-ma ina muḫḫi kussīšu ušib.* At the beginning of this year someone among the palace staff killed the king, and sat upon his throne.
    11. *kaspam ḫalqam ul āmur; minâm eppeš u mannum tappûtī illak?* I have not found the missing silver; what shall I do, and who will help me?

12. *mimma šumšu ša bītīšunu ina bābtīni ul nīmur.* We have not seen anything at all from (lit. of) their house in our district.
13. *mātum ana šarrim šuāti iknuš-ma ina bēlūtīšu ipšaḫ-ma lemuttum mimma elīša ul imqut.* When the land bowed down to that king and became content in his lordship, no evil befell it.
14. *ina warkiāt ūmim mamman mimma ina qātīka ul ileqqe.* In future no one will take anything from you (ms).

F. 1. *Aššum bīt kīdim Nīši-īnīšu mārat Abunānum ana Erišti-Ayya mārat Sîn-ēriš irgum-ma, dayyānī šarrim ikšudā-ma, dayyānū awâtīšina īmurū-ma, šērtam Nīši-īnīšu īmidū. Ul itâr-ma Nīši-īnīšu mārat Abunānum ana Erišti-Ayya mārat Sîn-ēriš ul iraggum. Nīš Šamaš Ayya ... u Samsu-iluna šarrim itmâ.*

Concerning a house in the open country Nīši-īnīšu daughter of Abunānum sued Erišti-Ayya daughter of Sîn-ēriš, so they approached the king's judges, and when the judges investigated their affairs, they imposed a penalty on Nīši-īnīšu. Nīši-īnīšu daughter of Abunānum will not sue Erišti-Ayya daughter of Sîn-ēriš again. They swore by the life of Šamaš, Ayya, ..., and king Samsu-iluna. (Witnesses. Date.)

2. *Ana eqlim bītim amtim wardim u kirîm ... itā Bizīzāna u iškarim ša Šamaš Bēlessunu u Napsānum u Mātātum mārat Iṣi-darê ana Mayyatum u Sumu-rāḫ mārī Azalīya irgumū-ma, dayyānū ina bīt Šamaš rugummêšunu issuḫū. Ul iturrū-ma ana warkiāt ūmī ana eqlim bītim amtim wardim u kirîm ša Mayyatum u Sumu-rāḫ Bēlessunu Napsānum u Mātātum mārat Iṣi-darê ištu zikarim adi sinništim mārū Amurrûm ana Mayyatum u Sumu-rāḫ ul eraggamū. Dīn bīt Šamaš ina Ebabbar. Nīš Šamaš Ayya ... u Ṣabium itma.* PN_1 – PN_5, *dayyānū.* (Witnesses. Date.)

For a field, a house, a female slave, a male slave, and the orchard ... next to Bizīzāna, and the *iškarum*-field of Šamaš, Bēlessunu and Napsānum and Mātātum daughter of Iṣi-darê sued Mayyatum and Sumu-rāḫ, the children of Azalīya, but the judges rejected their claims in the temple of Šamaš. In future Bēlessunu, Napsānum, and Mātātum daughter of Iṣi-darê, (or any) children of Amurrûm from male to female will not again sue Mayyatum and Sumu-rāḫ for the field, house, female slave, male slave, and orchard of Mayyatum and Sumu-rāḫ. A judgment of the temple of Šamaš in Ebabbar. They (! text: sg.) swore by the life of Šamaš, Ayya, ..., and Ṣabium. PN_1 – PN_5, judges.

3. *x kaspam ... itti Qīšū'a ... Ikkā-kīnā ... u Warad-Kūbi ... ana tappûtim ... ilqû. Išammū, inaddinū; ummiāššu*[*nu*] *ippalū*-[*ma*], *nēmela izuz*[*zū*] ...

Ikkā-kīnā and Warad-Kūbi received x silver from Qīšū'a for a partnership. They will buy (and) sell; they will pay their lender, and divide the profit ...

4. *Maḫar Libūram maḫar Šeš-batuk maḫar Warassa maḫar Paluḫ-rigimšu — maḫrīšunu ina bāb gagîm Lamassī mārat Aḫūšina amtam ana Šamaš-ṣulūlī ipqid. Amtum imât, iḫalliq-ma ša Lamassī ul awāssa.*

Before Libūram, before Šeš-batuk, before Warassa, before Paluḫ-rigimšu — before them, in the cloister gate, Lamassī daughter of Aḫūšina entrusted a female slave to Šamaš-ṣulūlī. If the slave dies (or) escapes, it is not Lamassī's affair. (Date.)

G. 1. *qá-tam ša* DUMU.MUNUS-*šu ta-aṣ-bat; qātam ša mārtīšu taṣbat.* You (ms) helped his daughter.

2. KÁ É-*ša ta-mu-ri; bāb(i) bītīša tāmurī.* You (fs) saw the door of her house.

3. KI DI.KUD.MEŠ *di-nam am-ḫu-úr; itti dayyānī dīnam amḫur.* I received a judgment from the judges.

4. *ig-mu-ru; igmurū.* They (m) finished.

5. ÌR *an-nu-um ik-nu-uš; wardum annûm iknuš.* This male slave bowed down.

LESSON FIFTEEN

C.

1. MÁŠ ^{d}UTU
2. LUGAL KALAM
3. $^{(giš)}$MÁ DI.KUD
4. ABUL KÁ.DINGIR.RA^{ki}
5. É ^{d}EN.LÍL
6. *ú-bil / bíl / bi-il*
7. *ú-gal / ga-(al-)la-ab*
8. *pa-du-ú*
9. *tam / ta-(am-)mar*
10. *ú-kal / ka-al*
11. *ne-(e-)rum / ru-um*
12. *e-de-šum / šu-um*
13. *iš-ḫu-un*
14. *pa-qá-dum / du-um*
15. *ša-al-mu-tum*
16. *ša-ṭar na-ri-šu*

D.

1. *ubbal*
2. *uṣṣab*
3. *ulid*
4. *tulladī*
5. *iṭibbam*
6. *tubbalānim*
7. *itterū*
8. *nurdam*
9. *tadinnī*
10. *taddinī / taqīšī*
11. *ušib*
12. *idukkū*
13. *ikūnā*
14. *ikunnā*
15. *tuššabā*

E.

1. *tašpuram*
2. *taqiššam*
3. *nikaššadam*
4. *tulladīm*
5. *ippalūnim*
6. *tēmidānim*
7. *ubilam / ublam*
8. *iḫalliqūnim*
9. *iḫdâm*
10. *tanaddinīm*
11. *ileqqeam*
12. *taṣṣurānim*
13. *tazūzam*
14. *idukkam*
15. *nušbam*
16. *tašammam*
17. *imallânim*
18. *išmeam*
19. *taturrīm*
20. *tapḫurānim*
21. *iteḫḫeam*
22. *turdam*
23. *tērubam*
24. *iṭarradūnim*
25. *ibnûnim*
26. *idmiqānim*
27. *tamqutīm*

F.

1. *ilū kalûšunu ištu šamê ana erṣetim urradūnim-ma ina puḫrim ipaḫḫurū-ma purussê mātim iparrasū.* When all the gods come down from the sky to the earth, they will gather in assembly and decide the judgments of the land.
2. *aḫūni maḫrīni kiam iškun umma šū-ma: mutum šū šīpātim qatnātim ana aššatīšu isaddar-ma ipaqqid.* Our brother informed us as follows: "That husband will regularly supply his wife with fine wool."
3. *ina ṭuppīka pānîm kiam tašpuram umma attā-ma: ina eleppīya arkam-ma ištu nārim šaplītim adi nārim elītim allik.* In your (ms) previous tablet you wrote to me as follows: "I boarded my ship and went from the lower river to the upper river."
4. *šikarum ana šatêm u ûm ana akālim ana ṣērīya adīni ul illikūnim; am-mīnim atti mamman lā tašapparīm? ina kīttim amarraṣ-ma amât.* Beer to drink and grain to eat have not yet come to me; why do you (fs) not send someone here? In truth, I will get sick and die.
5. *sinništum šī ana šaknim aššum kirîm itā karān rubātim irgum-ma dayyānū ana pī awât šībūtīšu rugummâša issuḫū-ma šērtam sinništam īmidū; u nīš Šamaš itma.* That woman sued the governor concerning the orchard next to the princess's vineyard, but the judges

rejected her suit in accordance with the words of his witnesses, and they imposed a fine on the woman; moreover, she swore by the life of Šamaš.

6. *ana mīnim mār(ū) šiprīni ištu erṣetim elītim adīni lā urdūnim?* Why have our messengers not yet come down from the upper country?

7. *ina uznīya šarratam ešme umma šī-ma: šarrum išarum mutī kakkī itti nakrim ippeš-ma qaqqad nakrim imaḫḫaṣ; ina epšētim anniātim išid bēlūtīšu u šumšu rabiam išakkan; kiam iqbiam.* I heard the queen with my (own) ears: "The just king, my husband, will do battle with the enemy, and smite the enemy's head; by these deeds he will establish the foundation of his rule and his great reputation"; thus she said to me.

8. *ṭuppī ina kunukkīya akannakam-ma ana bēlīya ina qāt tappêya ašapparam.* I will seal my tablet with my seal and send it to my lord in the care of my partner(s).

9. *ayyum ilum lemuttam u maruštam anniātim elīya iškun?* Which god has imposed this evil and hardship upon me?

10. *watarti šamnim kīma ṣibtim ana awīlim amaddad-ma anaddin.* I will weigh out and pay the boss the excess of the oil as interest.

11. *ina ūmim šâti mannum idannim-ma mannum inniš?* On that day, who will become strong and who will weaken?

12. *minâm ana maḫrīya tašapparānim u minâm ana maḫrīkunu ašapparam?* What will you (mp) send to me, and what will I send to you?

G. 1. *x ê ḫubullim — ṣibat êm y âm uṣṣab — itti Anum-pīša Šū-ilīšu mār Ibbi-Sîn ilqe. Ana ebūrim ina maškanim âm ṣibassu imaddad. Maḫar Iturrum Ilšu-abūšu mārī Ilī-ublam, maḫar Sîn-emūqī mār Pīṣāya.*

An interest-bearing (loan of) x barley — (as) the interest of the barley he will add y barley — Šū-ilīšu son of Ibbi-Sîn received from Anum-pīša. At harvest-time, at the threshing floor he will pay the barley (and) its interest. Before Iturrum (and) Ilšu-abūšu sons of Ilī-ublam; before Sîn-emūqī son of Pīṣāya.

2. *Šamaš-āpilī itti Šaḫamatim Mārat-Ištar mā[rtīša] u Tarībum mārī[ša] Bunene-abī u Ḫuššūtum ... aššassu ... ana mārūtim ilqû. U ina mārī Bunene-abī u Ḫuššūtum Šamaš-āpilī aḫūšunu rabûm. Šumma ana warkiāt ūmī Šamaš-āpilī ana Bunene-abī u Ḫuššūtum "ul abī atta; ul ummī atti" iqabbi, ... ana ka[spim] inaddinūšu. U šumma Bunene-abī u Ḫuššū[tum ana] Šamaš-āpilī mārīšunu "ul mārūni atta" iqabbû, ina bītim ītellû ...*

Bunene-abī and Ḫuššūtum ... his wife ... adopted Šamaš-āpilī from Šaḫamatum, Mārat-Ištar her daughter, and Tarībum her son. And among the children of Bunene-abī and Ḫuššūtum Šamaš-āpilī is their eldest brother. If in future Šamaš-āpilī says to Bunene-abī and Ḫuššūtum, "You are not my father; you are not my mother," ... they may sell him. And if Bunene-abī and Ḫuššūtum say to Šamaš-āpilī their son, "You are not our son," they will forfeit the estate ... (Witnesses. Date.)

3. *x kaspam ana šâm ê(m) itti Sîn-bēl-aplim ana qabê Zababa-ilum mār Ibni-Adad Nabû-malik mār Marduk-muballiṭ u Sîn-aḫam-iddinam mār Bēlīya ilqû. [I]na maḫīr êšunu âm imaddadū.*

   Nabû-malik son of Marduk-muballiṭ and Sîn-aḫam-iddinam son of Bēlīya received from Sîn-bēl-aplim, on the authorization of Zababa-ilum, x silver for buying barley. They will (re)pay the barley at the going rate of their barley. (Witnesses. Date.)

H. 1. GEME$_2$.MEŠ É.GAL GIŠ *na-ak-sa-am ša* É.GAL *ub-la; amāt ekallim iṣam naksam ša ekallim ublā.* The palace slaves (f) carried the cut wood of the palace.

2. LUGAL *dan-nu-um* KALAM-*tam ša na-ak-ri-šu is-ḫu-up; šarrum dannum mātam ša nakrīšu isḫup.* The mighty king overwhelmed the land of his enemy.

3. DUMU.MUNUS.MEŠ KUG.SIG$_{17}$ DI.KUD GAL *iš-ri-qá; mārātum ḫurāṣ dayyānim rabîm išriqā.* The daughters stole the chief judge's gold.

4. *qí-iš-ta-am ša-ri-iq-ta-am ú-la iṣ-bat; qīštam šariqtam ula iṣbat.* She did not seize the stolen gift.

LESSON SIXTEEN

C. 1. *i-ma-(ag-)gar*
    2. *i-gi / gi₄-gi / gi₄*
    3. *na-ra-tum*
    4. *iṣ-ba-ta*
    5. *ra-pa-aš / áš-tam*
    6. *qá / qar-ra-dum /*
       du-um
    7. *e-ti-qá-am*
    8. *i-zu-(úz-)zu-um*
    9. *ma / mar-ra-tim*
  10. *pa-ra-su / sú-um*
  11. *al-qú-ú*
  12. KALAM-*su / sú*
  13. MÁŠ ᵈAMAR.UTU
  14. ⁽ᵍⁱˢ⁾MÁ.MEŠ-*ia*
  15. EN *ú-ṣur / sú-úr*

D. 1. *bābam petē-ma lūrub*
    2. *nēmettakunu kalâša aplā / šuqlā / muddā*
    3. *dīkkina lidīnū-ma etqā*
    4. *lūtiq*
    5. *ṭuppaki lā takannakī*
    6. *ridānim*
    7. *šamakkunu watram ayy-imḫurā*
    8. *napišti mārātīya ṭardātim uṣrā*
    9. *ṣāb(ā)ni / ummānni i nipqid*
  10. *lā ipaššašū*
  11. *lā tamaqqut-ma lā tamât*
  12. *tūrīm-ma pānīki i nīmur*
  13. *nīš(i) šarrim lā tatammî*
  14. *šibānim*
  15. *šikaram ṭābam šiti*
  16. *aššatam aḫuz*
  17. *eleppam malītam lirkab*
  18. *pīki petî / pitî / epšī-ma qabâki lušme*
  19. *alpī šalmūtim lirdû*
  20. *alkīm*
  21. *ṣeḫrūtim lā tenerrā / tadukkā*
  22. *ak(a)lam mādam aklā-ma šilmā / bulṭā*
  23. *iṣam anniam ikis-ma eli / ina muḫḫi bītīni lā imaqqut*
  24. *lā teṭeḫḫeā(nim)*
  25. *erbīm*
  26. *ana iltim damiqtim tiklī*
  27. *tebeā*
  28. *mamma(n) ayy-ikšudam*
  29. *ḫarrānam ṣabat*
  30. *kakkī epšā*
  31. *qīštam rabītam qīšīm-ma luḫdu*
  32. *ē-nimūt*
  33. *pānīya uṭlā-ma ḫudâ*
  34. *lemuttam annītam ayy-āmur-ma ilī pānīya libil*
  35. *bābam qatnam bini*
  36. *awâtīya kīnātim lušpur*
  37. *kunukkam ḫepeam*
  38. *qaqqad nakrīya kanšim maḫṣī*
  39. *mê idnam*
  40. *mimma šumšu lā išammā*
  41. *i niḫliq*
  42. *ilī pilaḫ*
  43. *ūmūšu līrikū-ma līširū / lidmiqū* or *ūmātūšu līrikā-ma līširā / lidmiqā*
  44. *lā ilabbir*
  45. *âm eli erṣetim kuṣrā*
  46. *nārum elītum ayy-irpiš*
  47. *rubātum eništum lišlim / libluṭ-ma māram lilid.*
  48. *eqlam sudur-ma ṣib / sudur-ma eqlam ṣib*
  49. *pišaḫ / pišiḫ*
  50. *ṣibittašina uqrā*

E. 1. *am-mīnim dīn ṣuḫārtīya lā idīnū? warkassa purus-ma dīšša dīn.* Why was my servant's case not judged? Investigate (ms) the circumstances of her case and judge her case (or, so that you may judge her case).

    2. *aḫī ṣeḫrum ina ḫarrān šarrim awīlum šanûm ilikšu lā illak.* My

young brother is on a royal campaign. Another man may not work his *ilkum*-land.

3. *abullam peteānim-ma ana ālim lūrum-ma nakrī napištī lā inakkis.* Open (pl) the city gate that I may enter the city, lest my enemy cut off my life.
4. *ilī warassu palḫam lirdē-ma maruštum mimma ayy-imqutam.* May my god lead his reverential servant (i.e., me), so that no hardship befall me.
5. *eṭlam ayyam ana mārūtim eleqqē-ma šū ilkī illakam?* Which youth shall I adopt, so that (lit., and) he will do my *ilkum*-service for me?
6. *nišū rapšātum kalûšina bēlūt Marduk ilim rabîm liplaḫā.* Let the all wide people revere the lordship of Marduk, the great god.
7. *mīnam ina pāni šībūtim taqabbî? mimma lemnam ē-taqbî.* What will you (fs) say before the witnesses? You should not say anything bad.
8. *warkat sinništim šuāti ša mārātīšā; ul ša mutīša šī.* That woman's estate belongs to her daughters; it does not belong to her husband.
9. *awīlum šū amtam ḫaliqtam ina ṣērim iṣbat-ma ana bēlīša irde; bēl amtim šâti kaspam ana awīlim liddin.* That man caught the escaped slave in the steppeland and conducted (her) to her master; the master of said slave must give silver to the man.
10. *ū lū eqlī litūram ū lū eqlam šaniam kīma eqlīya liddinūnim.* Either let my field return to me or let another field like my field be given me.
11. *anāku u aḫī tappûtam i nīpuš.* May my brother and I do business together.
12. *ana qabê mannim ṭēm têrtim šuāti ana maḫrīya lā tašpuram?* By whose command have you (ms) not sent me a report of that oracle?
13. *warkat bītīya laberim limqut-ma bītam eššam eppeš.* Should the rear of my old house collapse, I will build a new house.
14. *mārū eqlētim zakâtim ša abīšunu mītim limdudū-ma lizūzū.* The sons should measure and divide the free fields of their deceased father.
15. *âm šaqlam ina qāt wardīki taklim kuṣrīm-ma šuprīm.* Collect (fs) and send the weighed grain in the care of a trusted servant of yours.
16. *šarram imḫurū-ma umma šunū-ma mimma šarqam ša bēlim ina qātīni liṣbatū-ma šērtam dannatam līmidūniāti.* They approached the king, saying: "Should they seize anything stolen of the lord's in our possession, let them impose a severe penalty on us."
17. *aḫi abīki ina amār ṭuppīki annîm litbeam-ma ana ālīni lillikam.* On seeing this tablet of yours (fs), your father's brother should set out to come here to our city.

F. 1. *Aḫu-waqar mār Šāt-Adad itti Šāt-Adad ummīšu Ṣillī-Adad mār Erīb-Sîn ana mārūtīšu ilqe. U mārī šanûtim Ṣillī-Adad liršī-ma Aḫu-waqar aḫum rabûm. Aḫu-waqar ana Ṣillī-Adad abīšu "ul abī atta" iqabbī-ma Aḫu-waqar ana kaspim inaddin. U Ṣillī-Adad abūšu ana Aḫu-waqar mārīšu "ul mārī atta" iqabbī-ma ina bītim ... ittaṣṣi.*

Ṣillī-Adad son of Erīb-Sîn adopted Aḫu-waqar son of Šāt-Adad from Šāt-Adad his mother. And should Ṣillī-Adad acquire other children, Aḫu-waqar is the old(est) brother. If Aḫu-waqar says to Ṣillī-Adad his father, "You are not my father," he may sell Aḫu-waqar. And if Ṣillī-Adad his father says to Aḫu-waqar his son, "You are not my son," he will forfeit his house ...

2. *[1 r]ugbam itti Nunu-rīšat Nannatum ana šattīšu īgur. Kiṣrī x kaspam [išaq]qal.*

   Nannatum leased one roof from Nunu-rīšat for one year. He will weigh out x silver (as) payment. (Witnesses. Date.)

3. ^{1} 4 MA.NA KUG.BABBAR ^{2} MÁŠ ^{d}UTU *ú-ṣa-ab* ^{3} 1 SAG.ÌR *ì-lí-ma-ṭá-ar* ^{4} 1 SAG.ÌR ^{d}UTU-*na-ap-še-ra-am* ^{5} 8 GÍN KUG.BABBAR *i-na* 1 *šattim*(MU.1.KAM) ^{6} *ki-iṣ-ru-šu-nu* ^{7} KI *e-ri-iš-ti-*^{d}UTU LUKUR ^{d}UTU ^{8} DUMU.MUNUS ^{d}EN.ZU-*ri-im*-URI^{ki} ^{9} ^{Id}EN.ZU-*ri-im*-URI^{ki} ^{10} DUMU É.BABBAR$_{2}$-*lu-mur* ^{11} ITI DUMU.ZI ŠU.BA.AN.TI ^{12} ITI DUMU.ZI ^{13} KUG.BABBAR *ù* MÁŠ.BI *išaqqal* (Ì.LAL.E)

   4 manā kaspam — ṣibat Šamaš uṣṣab — 1 wardam Ilī-maṭar 1 wardam Šamaš-napšeram — 8 šiqil kaspum ina 1 šattim kiṣrūšunu — itti Erišti-Šamaš nadīt Šamaš mārat Sîn-rīm-Ur Sîn-rīm-Ur mār Ebabbar-lūmur waraḫ Dumuzi ilqe. Waraḫ Dumuzi kaspam u ṣibassu išaqqal.

   Sîn-rīm-Ur, son of Ebabbar-lūmur, received from Erišti-Šamaš the *nadītum* of Šamaš, the daughter of Sîn-rīm-Ur, 4 minas of silver — he will pay the interest of Šamaš — 1 slave Ilī-maṭar, 1 slave Šamaš-napšeram — 8 shekels of silver per year is their payment — (in) the month of Dumuzi. In the month of Dumuzi he will pay the silver and its interest.

G. 1. *na-ak-ru-ti-šu i-na* ^{giš}TUKUL-*šu i-du-uk; nakrūtīšu ina kakkīšu idūk* 'He killed his enemies with his weapon.'

2. *ma-ri ku-nu-uk-ki-ia i-na* É-*ia iṣ-ṣur; mārī kunukkīya ina bītīya iṣṣur* 'My son guarded my seal in my house.'

3. DINGIR.MEŠ GAL.MEŠ LUGAL-*ru-ut* KALAM-*tim i-na qá-ti-ia iš-ku-nu; ilū rabûtum šarrūt mātim ina qātīya iškunū* 'The great gods placed the kingship of the land in my hand(s).'

LESSON SEVENTEEN

C.
1. *ú-nam / na-(am-) maš / ma-aš / áš*
2. *ni-mar*
3. *e / et̩-t̩e / t̩è-(et-) tum*
4. *ka-ba-tum*
5. *ge-(er-)rum / ru-um*
6. *maš / ma-aš / áš-kum / ku-um*
7. *i / ir-ru*
8. *ka-su / sú-(ú-)um*
9. *ú-la-(ab-)bar*
10. *ni-ša-(ap-)pár*
11. *i-ku-un*
12. *mar-ṣú-um*
13. *ni-ma-(ag-)gàr*
14. IGI GUD-*šu* / GUD.NI
15. *ši-pa-at* EN-*ia*

D.
1. *amatka ḫaliqtam aptat̩ar.*
2. *bābam labiram tattaqrī.*
3. *ṣuḫārtani ana mārūtim nilteqe.*
4. *ana iltim šuāti / šâti / šiāti ittaklū.*
5. *ana mātim šaplītim tettebeā.*
6. *rubâm marṣam iptašaš.*
7. *šikaram t̩ābam ištatiā.*
8. *et̩lūtim (ana maḫrīya / ṣērīya) tat̩t̩ardam.*
9. *ḫurāṣam mādam tartaši.*
10. *ilū ina šamê iptaḫrū.*
11. *dayyānam aššum šarratim iptat̩rū.*
12. *aḫ / kišād nārim elītim et̩t̩eḫeam.*
13. *bēl pī / āḫatīki iṣṣabtā-ma lēssu / lētāšu imtaḫṣā.*
14. *rēš ṣabtūtim ana šēpī šaknim imtaqut.*
15. *narkabtī ana pānīka aštaknam.*
16. *sinništam šanītam ina ṣibittim kīma* (or *ana pī*) *ṣimdat šarrim iktalû.*
17. *kalbī ul nišme.*
18. *eqlētum rapšātum mê imtalâ.*
19. *šumma awīlum t̩uppam īzim-ma iktanak, mamma(n) lā ipette.*
20. *nišū šum(ā)ka iptalḫā.*
21. *īnāya šamšam ittat̩lā.*
22. *dīššunu ina bābtīšunu igdamrū.*

E.
1. *awīlum šū alpīya īgur-ma inanna alpūya šunu iḫtalqū awīlum šū šīm(i) alpīya liddinam ū lū alpī šanûtim kīma alpīya lišāmam.* That man hired my oxen, and now said oxen of mine have disappeared. That man must either give me the price of my oxen or buy me other oxen like my oxen.
2. *šumma mutum aššassu izzib ana maḫar šarrim illak-ma warkassu iparrasū.* If a husband wants to divorce his wife, he will go before the king and the circumstances of his case will be investigated.
3. *warki ummīni mišil kaspīša ana aḫīni ṣeḫrim ana pī têrtīša niqīš.* After our mother's death, we gave half of her silver to our young(est) brother in accordance with her instruction.
4. *ummānātīka kalâšina ana ṣērīya redeam-ma ḫarrānam i niṣbat-ma nakram u ummāššu i ninēr.* Conduct all your (ms) forces to me, that we may take to the road and slay the enemy and his force.
5. *Enlil ina puḫur ilī bēlūt mātātim ana Marduk iddin u bēlūt šamê ana Šamaš iddin.* Enlil in the assembly of the gods gave dominion of the lands to Marduk and he gave dominion of the sky to Šamaš.

6. *awīlum aḫûm itebbē-ma ina kussi šarrūtim uššab.* A foreign man will arise/appear and sit on the throne of kingship.
7. *itti ṣuḫārīya ridānim-ma tappûtam ittīya epšā.* Come down (pl) with my servant and do business with me.
8. *eqlētim ana mê nizzim-ma ayyumma eqlētim šipram ul ippeš.* If we abandon the fields to the water, no one will work the fields.
9. *anumma ṭēm ilkim šuāti ana bēlīya aštapram bēlī âm mimma ana wardīšu lā ikallâm âm šupram-ma lā amât.* I have now sent the report of that *ilkum* to my lord; may my lord not withhold any grain from his servant; send me grain, lest I die.
10. *šarrum dannum nēmettam rabītam eli nišī šināti iškun am-mīnim nēmettašina ana ekallim lā ublānim?* The mighty king imposed a great tribute on those people; why have they not brought their tribute to the palace?
11. *am-mīnim rittaki eli aḫ mārtīki taškunī?* Why did you (fs) place your hand on your daughter's arm?
12. *ṣābīya/ummānātīya lupqid-ma ana maḫāṣ nakrīya lillikū.* I must muster my troops that they may go to strike my enemy/enemies.
13. *aḫûtum ištu mātim lemuttim ikšudūnim-ma ana erṣetīka ītiqūnim inanna aḫûtum šunu mār šiprīya ina erṣetīka iṣṣabtū mār šiprīya ina qātīšunu puṭram-ma litūram.* Hostile people arrived from an evil country and crossed into your (ms) land; now those hostile people have seized my messenger in your land; ransom my messenger from their possession, that he may return to me.
14. *ina šattim šuāti aššatī maḫrītum māram uldam.* In that year my previous wife bore me a son.
15. *bēltī pānītum kiam iqbiam umma šī-ma inanna iṣam damqam ina libbi šadî ana eleppētīya amrā-ma iksā eleppētīya šināti biniānim-ma ana maḫrīya redeānim.* My former lady said to me as follows: "Now find (pl) and cut down fine wood for my boats in the mountains; build said boats of mine and conduct (them) to me."
16. *ša pī ṭuppim annîm kiriam itā/itê kišād nārim mudud-ma ana ṭuppīka ṣib.* In accordance with this tablet, measure (ms) and add the orchard next to the river-bank to your tablet.

F. 195 *šumma mārum abāšu imtaḫaṣ rittašu inakkisū.* If a son has struck his father, his hand will be cut off.

205 *šumma warad awīlim lēt mār awīlim imtaḫaṣ uzuššu inakkisū.* If a man's slave has struck the cheek/side of a member of the *awīlum* class, his ear will be cut off.

247 *šumma awīlum alpam īgur-ma īššu uḫtappid kaspam mišil šīmīšu ana bēl alpim inaddin.* If a man hired an ox and has blinded its eye, he will give the owner of the ox silver (equal to) half its value.

14 *šum-ma a-wi-lum* DUMU *a-wi-lim ṣe-eḫ-ra-am iš-ta-ri-iq id-da-ak.*

šumma awīlum mār awīlim ṣeḫram ištariq iddâk. If a man has kidnapped (lit., stolen) the young son of a man (or, a young member of the *awīlum* class), he will be executed.

G. 1. *Bāštum ... mārat Uṣi-bītum Rīmum mār Šamḫatum ana aššūtim u mutūtim īḫuz. ... [Šum]ma Bāštum [ana] Rīmum [mut]īša "ul mutī [att]a" iqtabi, [Bāš]tum ana nārim inaddû. [Šu]mma Rīmum [an]a Bāštum aššatīšu "ul aššatī atti" iqtabi, x kaspam išaqqal. Nīš Šamaš u Samsu-iluna itmû.*

Rīmum son of Šamḫatum married (lit., took in "wife-and-husband-hood') Bāštum ... daughter of Uṣi-bītum. If Bāštum says to Rīmum her husband, "You are not my husband," Bāštum will be thrown into the river. If Rīmum says to Bāštum his wife, "you are not my wife," he will pay out x silver. They swore by the life of Šamaš and Samsu-iluna. (Witnesses.)

2. *1 šiqil kaspam ana ēṣidim itti Ilī-iqīšam muʾir ṣāb(i) bāb(i) ekallim Sîn-šar-ilī mār Šēlebum ilqe. Ana ūm ebūrim ina eqlim pīḫat Uṣriya iššiakkim ēṣidum illak. Ul illak-ma kīma ṣimdat šarrī.*

Sîn-šar-ilī son of Šēlebum received 1 shekel of silver as a harvester from Ilī-iqīšam director of the palace work force. On the day of the harvest he will work as a harvester in a field (that is) the responsibility of Uṣriya the farmer. If he does not work, (the penalty will be) according to the royal regulation. (Witnesses. Date.)

H. 1. MAŠ ŠÁM Ì *ta-ad-di-na-am-ma i-na* DUB-*pí-ia áš-ta-ṭar; mišil šīm(i) šamnim taddinam-ma ina ṭuppīya aštaṭar.* You gave me half the value of the oil, and I have recorded (it) in my tablet.

2. ^{giš}TUKUL.MEŠ *ša* ERIN_2 ^{d}AMAR.UTU *ì-lí-šu iṣ-ṣur; kakkī ša ṣāb(i)/ummān Marduk ilīšu iṣṣur.* He guarded the weapons of the army of Marduk, his god.

LESSON EIGHTEEN

C.

1. *ú-na-(ak)-kar*
2. *iš-tap / ta-(ap)-pár*
3. Ì(.GIŠ)-*šu*
4. TAB.BA.MEŠ-*a / ia*
5. É A.ZU
6. ḪA.LA A.BA-*ka*
7. NÍG.GA DINGIR
8. MAŠ ŠÁM
9. GUD.MEŠ URU-*ka*
10. A.MEŠ A.ŠÀ
11. IGI MAŠ.EN.GAG / MAŠ.GAG.EN
12. MÁŠ KUG.BABBAR
13. *i-na* ŠÀ DUB
14. $^{(giš)}$TUKUL.MEŠ ERIN$_2$
15. *iṭ-ru-da-(ak)-ku-(uš)-ši*
16. *a-pa-lum*
17. *ir-te-de*
18. *ṭe / ṭè / ṭe$_4$-ḫa-am*
19. *eṭ-lam / la-am*
20. *da-(an)-núm / nu-um*

D.

1. *apallassu*
2. *tabtaqrāšunūti*
3. *lā takallâniššī*
4. *ayy-iqīšakkim*
5. *usuqšunūti*
6. *tarīabši*
7. *ītaḫassi / ilteqēši*
8. *nītezibšināti*
9. *pilaḫšunūti*
10. *annītum imtaqtam*
11. *īterbā(nik)kum*
12. *šīpātim šuqulšim*
13. *lissuḫūši*
14. *atakkal(ak)kim*
15. *tattalkīnniāšim*
16. *abullam eptēkunūšim / epteakkunūšim*
17. *ātamarkināti*
18. *lā tereddeāniššunūti*
19. *ayy-idūkūninni / inērūninni*
20. *ītarik*
21. *tētetqāninni*
22. *irtagmākum*
23. *tētešrā / taddamqā*
24. *idīnūšunūti*
25. *ētepussināšim / ētepessināšim*
26. *šērtam ītemissi*
27. *iddamqam*
28. *nītagarka*
29. *tētenšā*
30. *ul(a) īkul*
31. *ītediš*
32. *ātapalkuššu / ātaplakkuššu*
33. *idukkanni*
34. *iktabissum*
35. *izzaqap*

E.

1. *dayyānū warkat muškēnim šuāti iprusū-ma muškēnum baqrī irtaši inanna šū u mārūšu baqrī kīma ṣimdat šarrim līpulū.* The judges investigated the circumstances of that commoner's case, and that commoner has incurred legal claims; now he and his sons must pay the claims according to the royal decree.
2. *rubûm ina ḫarrānim imarraṣ-ma imât.* The prince will sicken and die on a campaign.
3. *inanna ṭupp(āt)īka ša alpīka ša qātīya assadar-ma aštaprakkum.* I have now arranged and sent you (ms) your tablets of your oxen (that are) in my charge. (Or, I have now regularly sent you ...)
4. *adīni ṣuḫārtaka ul aṭrudakkum anumma aṭṭardakkušši libbaka mimma lā imarraṣ.* I have/had not yet sent your servant to you; I have herewith sent her to you; do not be angry at all.
5. *bēlum pānûm ša eqlim annîm ina pānī ilkim eqelšu īzim-ma šaniam ana epēš šipir eqlim annîm aštaṭar.* The previous owner of this field abandoned his field because of the *ilkum*-work; I have now assigned another to work this field.

6. *ūmam šâtu šarrum piam iškunam-ma pānī ṣābim ṣeḫrim aṣbat-ma šarrāqī ina birīt Bābilim u ālīni aḫ nārim niṣbassunūtī-ma terḫatam šariqtam ina qātīšunu ul nīmur.* That day, when the king gave me an order, I led a small force, and we seized the thieves between Babylon and our town at the river bank; but we did not find the stolen bride-price in their possession.
7. *aḫī epištam lemuttam annītam ayy-īpušanni.* May my brother not do this evil thing to me.
8. *mārū abim kīma emūq zīttīšu âm šamnam u šīpātim ana aḫīšunu ṣeḫrim inaddinū mišil karānim ul inaddinūšum.* The father's children will give their young brother grain, oil, and wool according to the value of his inheritance; they will not give him half the vineyard.
9. *šattam šuāti šarrum itti ṣābīšu / ummānīšu ana ālim aḫîm ittiq-ma pilšam ina abul ālim ipallaš.* That year the king will cross with his army to a foreign city, and breach that city's gate.
10. *tappê išpuram umma šū-ma ana êm šuāti bēl pīḫatim šukum-ma maruštī lā imīad u ummānam aplannī-ma išdam maqtam lūpuš ummānam ul tappalannī-ma pīḫatam šuāti ina muḫḫīka išakkanū.* My partner wrote me, "Assign (ms) a delegate to that barley, lest my difficulty increase; and pay me for the work-force, that I may rebuild the collapsed foundation. If you do not pay me for the work-force, that responsibility will be assigned to you.
11. *asûm ša lētim šaplītim kaspam u ṣibassu ana bēl ḫubullīšu liddin kaspam u ṣibassu ul imaḫḫarūšū–ma iddâk.* The physician of the lower district must pay the silver and its interest to his creditors; should they not receive the silver and its interest from him, he will be executed.
12. *ina têrētim šalmātim u ina qabê Enlil bēlīšu šarrani išarum ana epēš kakkī itti nakrīni pānīšu iškum-ma mātātum nakarātum kalûšina iknušāšum-ma narâm ša šarrūtīšu rabītim ibni.* When, with favorable omens and by the command of his lord Enlil, our just king decided to wage war on our enemies, and all hostile lands bowed down to him, he built a stela of his great kingship.

F. 21 *šumma awīlum bītam ipluš, ina pāni pilšim šuāti idukkūšū-ma iḫallalūšu.* If a man broke into a house, he will be executed and hung in front of that breach.

60 *šumma awīlum eqlam ana kirîm zaqāpim ana nukaribbim iddin, nukaribbum kiriam izqup 4 šanātim kiriam urabba, ina ḫamuštim šattim bēl kirîm u nukaribbum mitḫāriš izuzzū bēl kirîm zīttašu inassaq-ma ileqqe.* If a man gave a field to a gardener to plant an orchard, (and) the gardener planted the orchard, he will tend the orchard for four years; in the fifth year the owner of the orchard and the gardener will share equally; the owner of the field will have first choice of his share (lit., will choose and take his share).

167 *šumma awīlum aššatam īḫuz-ma mārī ulissum, sinništum šī ana šīmtim ittalak, warkīša sinništam šanītam ītaḫaz-ma mārī ittalad, warka abum ana šīmtim ittalku, mārū ana ummātim ul izuzzū; šerikti ummātīšunu ileqqû-ma makkūr bīt abim mitḫāriš izuzzū.* If a man married a wife and she bore him children, (and) that woman has

passed on, and after her (death) he has married another woman and she has born children, after the father has passed on the children will not share according to the mothers; they will receive their mothers' dowry, but they will share the property of the father's estate equally.

183 *šumma abum ana mārtīšu šugītim šeriktam išrukšim ana mutim iddiššī kunukkam išṭuršim, warka abum ana šīmtim ittalku ina makkūr bīt abim ul izâz.* If a father presented a dowry to his daughter, a junior wife, gave her to a husband, (and) inscribed a sealed document for her, after the father has passed on, she will not share in the property of the father's estate.

218–220 218 *šumma asûm simmam kabtam ina karzil siparrim īpuš-ma awīlam uštamīt ū lū nakkapti awīlim ina karzil siparrim iptē-ma īn awīlim uḫtappid rittašu inakkisū.* 219 *šumma asûm simmam kabtam wardam muškēnam ina karzil siparrim īpuš-ma uštamīt, wardam kīma wardim irīab.* 220 *šumma nakkaptašu ina karzil siparrim iptē-ma īššu uḫtappid, kaspam mišil šīmīšu išaqqal.* 218 If a physician treated a serious wound with a bronze lancet and has killed the man, or has opened a man's temple with a bronze lancet and blinded the man, his hand will be cut off. 219 If a physician treated a slave or a commoner for a serious wound with a bronze lancet and has killed (him), he will repay slave for slave. 220 If he opened his temple with a bronze lancet and has blinded him, he will pay out half his value.

246 *šum-ma a-wi-lum* GUD *i-gur-ma šēp*(GÌR)*-šu iš-te-bé-er ù lu la-bi-a-an-šu it-ta-ki-is* GUD *ki-ma* GUD *a-na be-el* GUD *i-ri-a-ab.*

šumma awīlum alpam īgur-ma šēpšu išteber ū lū labiāššu ittakis, alpam kīma alpim ana bēl alpim irīab. If a man rented an ox and has broken its foot or has cut its neck tendon, he will repay ox for ox to the owner of the ox.

G. 1. *1 amtam Mād-dumuq-bēl[tim] itti Erišti-Šamaš mār‹at› Šū-pīša Lipit-Eštar ... ana amtim īguršī. Idī amātim x âm ... imaddad.*

Lipit-Eštar hired a slave, Mād-dumuq-bēltim, from Erišti-Šamaš daughter of Šū-pīša, as a slave. He will weigh out x barley, the wage of slaves ... (Witnesses. Date.)

2. *Kiriam ša Sîn-magir Mār-Amurrim ana kaspim išām. Anum-bānî ana ṣimdat šarrim aššum kirîm šâti ibqur-ma ana dayyānī illikū-ma dayyānū ana bāb Ninmar iṭrudūšunūtī-ma ana dayyānī ša bāb Ninmar Anum-bānî ina bāb Ninmar kiam iqbi, umma šū-ma: "mār Sîn-magir anāku; ana mārūtim ilqeanni; kunukkī ul iḫpû." Kiam iqbīšunūšim-ma kiriam u bītam ana Anum-bānî ubirrū. Itūr Sîn-muballiṭ kiriam Anum-bānî ibqur-ma ana dayyānī illikū-ma dayyānū ana ālim u šībūtim iṭrudūšunūtī-ma ... šībūtum pānûtum ša Mār-Amurrim "ina bāb Ninmar Anum-bānî 'mārum anāku' itma" iqbû-ma kiriam u bītam ana Anum-bānî ubirrū. Sîn-muballiṭ lā itâr-ma lā ibaqqar. Nīš Šamaš Marduk u Ḫammu-rapi šarrim itma.*

Mār-Amurrim purchased the orchard of Sîn-magir for silver. Anum-bānî brought suit for that orchard according to the royal decree. When they went to the judges, the judges sent them to the gate of Ninmar, and Anum-bānî said to the judges of the gate of Ninmar, in the gate of

Ninmar, as follows: "I am the son of Sîn-magir; he adopted me; my sealed document was not broken (i.e., annulled)." Thus he said to them, and so they confirmed the orchard and estate to Anum-bānî. Sîn-muballiṭ again laid claim against Anum-bānî for the orchard; they went to the judges, and when the judges sent them to the city and the witnesses, the previous witnesses of Mār-Amurrim said, "In the gate of Ninmar Anum-bānî swore, 'I am the son,'" and so they confirmed the field and estate to Anum-bānî. Sîn-muballiṭ may not bring suit again. He swore by the life of Šamaš, Marduk, and King Ḫammurapi. (Witnesses.)

3. [1] ^{I}*eš$_4$-tár-um-mi* MU.NI [2] DUMU.MUNUS *bu-za-zu-um* [3] *ù la-ma-sà-tum* [4] KI *bu-za-zu-um* AD.TA.NI [5] *ù la-ma-sà-tum* AMA.A.NI [6] ÌR-^{d}EN.ZU DUMU *ib-ni-*^{d}EN.ZU [7] *a-na a-šu-ti-im ù mu-tu-ti-im* [8] *i-ḫu-sí* [9] $^{2}/_{3}$ MA.NA KUG.BABBAR [10] *ù* 1 SAG.ÌR ^{d}KI.ŠUB-LUGAL MU.NI [11] *te-er-ḫa-sà* [12] *a-na la-ma-sà-tum* [13] *ù bu-za-zu-um* [14] ÌR-^{d}EN.ZU *iš-qú-ul* [15] *a-na wa-ar-ki-it* UD-*mi-im* [16] *zu*(!)*-za-bu*(!)*-um la-ma-sà-tum* [17] *ù ma-ru bu-za-zu-um* [18] *ú-la i-ra-ga-mu* [19] ÌR-^{d}EN.ZU *eš$_4$-tár-um-mi* [20] *i-zi-ma* [21] 1 MA.NA KUG. BABBAR Ì.LAL.E [22] *eš$_4$-tár-um-mi* ÌR-^{d}EN.ZU [23] *i-zi-ma* [24] *iš-tu di-im-ti-im* [25] *i-na-pa-ṣú-ni-ši.*

Eštar-ummī šumša mārat Buzāzum u Lamassatum itti Buzāzum abīša u Lamassatum ummīša Warad-Sîn mār Ibni-Sîn ana aššūtim u mutūtim īḫussi. $^{2}/_{3}$ *manā kaspam u 1 wardam Kišub-lugal šumšu terḫassa ana Lamassatum u Buzāzum Warad-Sîn išqul. Ana warkīt ūmim Buzāzum Lamassatum u mārū Buzāzum ula iraggamū. Warad-Sîn Eštar-ummī izzim-ma, 1 manā kaspam išaqqal. Eštar-ummī Warad-Sîn izzim-ma, ištu dimtim inappaṣūnišši.*

Warad-Sîn son of Ibni-Sîn received in marriage a certain Eštar-ummī daughter of Buzāzum and Lamassatum from Buzāzum her father and Lamassatum her mother. Warad-Sîn paid out two-thirds mina of silver and 1 male slave, Kišub-lugal by name, (as) her bride-price to Buzāzum and Lamassatum. In future Buzāzum, Lamassatum and Buzāzum's children will not contest. Should Warad-Sîn leave Eštar-ummī, he will pay out 1 mina of silver. Should Eštar-ummī leave Warad-Sîn, she will be hurled from the tower (or: she will be thrown out of the district).

LESSON NINETEEN

1. A.ŠÀ A.BA/AD A.ZU
2. ŠÀ ITI
3. NÍG.GA TAB.BA*ia*
4. ^{giš}KIRI$_6$ DAM.GÀR
5. ḪA.LA DAM
6. UDU.MEŠ/UDU.ḪI.A-*ki*
7. SÍG URU
8. Á(.BI)(.MEŠ) GUD (.MEŠ/ḪI.A)-*ša*
9. *lu-uš-ṭú-úr*
10. *bu-dam/da-am*
11. *ú-ta-(aš/áš)-šar*
12. *qú-lam/la-am*
13. *a-na-(ad)-di-in*
14. *li-ḫu-uz-ma li-te-er*
15. *kar-tap/ta-(ap)-pu-um*
16. *ḫa-lum/lu-um*

D. 1. *nirtāmšunūti*
2. *taddīnāšu*
3. *muškēnū imtūtū*
4. *artībšunūti*
5. *iddūkniāti* / *ittērniāti*
6. *tattaldīšum*
7. *nittablaššināti* / *nitbalaššināti*
8. *šamallû ittūrūnim*
9. *itetrā/itatrā*
10. *ništāmšu*
11. *aqtīssināti/aštarakšināti*
12. *taddūkīši*
13. *ittardakkim*
14. *ikūnū*
15. *mitḫāriš nizzūssu*
16. *tattašbī*
17. *libbašu ina maḫīr illaku iṭṭīb*
18. *anumma attaṣab*
19. *imtīdā* / *ītetrā/ītatrā*
20. *ištībū* / *iltabrū*
21. *baqrū ša taršû*
22. *ina warḫim ša tazkurī*
23. *qīštum ša tanassaqūšim*
24. *adi pilšim ša (ina) idi* (or *ša itê/itā) abullim*
25. *bēl pīḫatim ša lēssu/lētāšu tamḫaṣu*
26. *watartum ša anassaḫu*
27. *ana rubêm ša irabbû-ma idanninu*
28. *ṣimdat šarrim ša aššumīša niḫdû* (or *ša niḫdûšim*)
29. *mātum elītum ša ana pîm uššabu* / *ušbu*
30. *tamkārum ša šamnam takaṣṣarāšum*
31. *kīma šarrāqim ša iṣbatū(šū)-ma iklû(šu)*
32. *dannatum ša ilbirū-ma nakrum isḫupu* (or *isḫupūši*)
33. *qarrādum ša lā iblutū-ma/ išlimū-ma ana šīmtīšu illiku*
34. *dayyānum ša purussâšu lā amḫuru*
35. *adi nārim rabītim ša ana kišādīša/aḫīša nirkabu*
36. *eṭlum ša terḫassa īrišūšu* (or *ša ittīšu terḫassa īrišu*)
37. *muškēnum ša tappûssu alliku* or *muškēnum ša qāssu aṣbatu*
38. *aklum mala nišammu*
39. *awāt kīttim ša iqbû*
40. *ilum ša šum(ā)šu nizkuru*

E. 1. *tappê šīm(i) eleppīya ša īgurū-ma iḫliqu lišqulam.* My partner must weigh out to me the price of my boat, which he rented and which disappeared.

2. *ana eṭlim ša immer(āt)īya u šīpātīya tublūšum luqbi.* I must speak to the youth to whom you transported my sheep and my wool.

3. *aššum ṭēm tappêya ašpurakkunūšim mala ša ippalūkunūti ṭēmam šuprānim.* I wrote to you (mp) about my partners' report; however much they pay you, send me a report.

4. *šarrāq makkūr bīt Šamaš išriqu bāb bītīšu iṣbatū-ma rittašu ikkisū aḫi mār šiprīya šū.* The thief who stole the property of the Šamaš temple was seized at the entry of his house and his hand was cut off; he is my messenger's brother.
5. *ūmam šuāti awīlum ša kirīni ikkalu imraṣ-ma imūt.* That day the man who was using our orchard got sick and died.
6. *šattam šuāti nakrū ša elīšunu ina ṣērim nimqutū-ma ittīšunu kakkī nīpušu ina pāni kakkīni dannūtim ipṭurū.* That year the enemies upon whom we fell in the back country and with whom we did battle dispersed before/because of our mighty weapons.
7. *sinništum ša mār(ū)ša ina ṣibittim imtaḫranni inanna ū lū dīn mārīša purus ū lū mār(ā)ša puṭur.* The woman whose son is in prison approached me; now, either render her son's verdict or release her son.
8. *tappûya attunu am-mīnim eqlam mala pī kanīkīya lā tanaddinānim.* You are my partners; why will you not give me a field in accordance with my sealed document?
9. *šumma awīlum pānīšu ana ezēb aššatīšu ištakan sinništum šī ana bīt abīša itâr u mārūša kalûšunu ša ana mutīša uldu ittīša uššabū.* If a man has decided to divorce his wife, that woman will/may return to her father's house; moreover, all of her children that she bore her husband will/may live with her.
10. *eqlum šū ša idi kirīya ul ana pašārim.* That field that is beside my orchard is not for sale.
11. *tamkārum šū mišil bītīšu u bīšīšu ana ṣeḫrim ša ana mārūtim ilqû išruk ina pāni šībūtim ṭuppam išṭur-ma īzibšum inanna mamman ṣeḫram šuāti lā ibaqqar.* The aforementioned merchant bestowed half of his estate and his property on the young man whom he had adopted; he wrote out and deposited for him a tablet in the presence of witnesses; now no one may lay claim against that young man.
12. *mār(ū)ka anāku am-mīnim kīma mārīka šanûtim lā tarammanni?* I am your son; why do you (ms) not love me like your other children?

F. 104 *šumma tamkārum ana šamallêm âm šīpātim šamnam ū mimma bīšam ana pašārim iddin, šamallûm kaspam isaddar-ma ana tamkārim utār; šamallûm kanīk kaspim ša ana tamkārim inaddinu ileqqe.* If a merchant gave a trading agent barley, wool, oil, or any property to sell, the trading agent will regularly return silver (or: will record and return silver) to the merchant; the trading agent will receive a sealed document of the silver that he gives the merchant.

119 *šumma awīlam eʾiltum iṣbassū-ma amassu ša mārī uldūšum ana kaspim ittadin, kasap tamkārum išqulu bēl amtim išaqqal-ma amass[u] ipaṭṭar.* If a financial liability "seized" a man and he has sold his slave who bore him children, the owner of the slave may pay the silver the merchant paid and so redeem (or, to redeem) hi[s] slave.

150 *šumma awīlum ana aššatīšu eqlam kiriam bītam ū bīšam išrukšim, kunukkam īzibšim, warki mutīša mārūša ul ibaqqarūši; ummum warkassa ana mārīša ša irammu inaddin; ana aḫîm ul inaddin.* If a man bestowed a field, orchard, house, or property on his wife, (and) made out a sealed document for her, after (the death of) her husband

her sons will not bring suit against her; the mother may give her inheritance to her child whom she loves; she will not give (it) to an outsider.

249 *šumma awīlum alpam īgur-ma ilum imḫassū-ma imtūt, awīlum ša alpam īguru nīš ilim izakkar-ma ūtaššar.* If a man rented an ox, and a god struck it and it has died, the man who rented the ox will swear by a god and be released.

6 *šum-ma a-wi-lum* NÍG.GA DINGIR *ù* É.GAL *iš-ri-iq a-wi-lum šu-ú id-da-ak ù ša šu-úr-qá-am i-na qá-ti-šu im-ḫu-ru id-da-ak.*

šumma awīlum makkūr ilim ū ekallim išriq awīlum šū iddâk; u ša šurqam ina qātīšu imḫuru iddâk. If a man stole property of a god or the palace, that man will be executed; moreover, whoever received stolen property from him will be executed.

G. 1. *1 alap 3 šanātim ša itti Sîn-nādin-šumi mār Etel-pī-Marduk šangêm ana niqi nabrî Iddin-Marduk rēdîm mār Zababa-nāṣir ilqû. Ana warḫim ešrim 1 alap 3 šanātim ana Sîn-nādin-šumi mār Etel-pī-Marduk šangîm inaddin.*

1 3-year-old ox that the *rēdûm*-soldier Iddin-Marduk son of Zababa-nāṣir received from Sîn-nādin-šumi son of Etel-pī-Marduk the temple administrator for an offering at (lit., of) the Nabrû-festival. In the tenth month he will give 1 3-year-old ox to Sîn-nādin-šumi son of Etel-pī-Marduk the temple administrator.

2. *x šīpātim ša ekallim šīm(i) y kaspim ša Ilšu-ibni ... ina ekallim imḫuru ... itti Ilšu-ibni ... Tarībum mār Ibbi-Šamaš Ipqu-Mama Bēlīyātum mārū Ilšu-ibni u Kubburum ilqû. Ūm ekallum kaspam irri[šu] ekallam kaspam ippalū.*

x palace wool worth y silver, which Ilšu-ibni ... got from the palace, Tarībum son of Ibbi-Šamaš, Ipqu-Mama (and) Bēlīyātum children of Ilšu-ibni, and Kubburum received from Ilšu-ibni. When the palace demands the silver, they will pay the palace the silver. (Witnesses. Date.)

3. [1] 1 KUG.[BABBAR] [2] MÁŠ ^{d}UTU *ú-ṣa-ab* [3] KI *Anum*(AN)*-pi*$_{4}$*-ša* [4] ^{I}*šar-*⌜*ma*⌝*-*^{d}*Adad*(IŠKUR) [5] DUMU ^{d}[*Adad*(IŠKUR)*-r*]*a-bi* [6] ŠU.BA.AN.TI [7] *ana ūm ebūrim* (UD.BURU$_{14}$.ŠÈ) [8] *ma-ḫi-ir i-la-ku* [9] ŠE-*am imaddad*(Ì.ÁG.E).

x kaspam — ṣibat Šamaš uṣṣab — itti Anum-pīša Šarma-Adad mār [Adad-r]abi ilqe. Ana ūm ebūrim maḫīr illaku âm imaddad.

Šarma-Addad son of Adad-rabi received x silver — he will add the interest of Šamaš — from Anum-pīša. On the day of the harvest he will measure out barley at the going rate (lit., the rate that goes). (Witnesses.)

LESSON TWENTY

C. 1. ITI *iḫ-li-qú*
    2. ŠÀ DÙG
    3. AGA.ÚS.MEŠ KALAM/KUR
    4. AGA DINGIR
    5. NIN DAM.GÀR
    6. Á(.BI) ANŠE.MEŠ/ḪI.A *a-gu-ru*
    7. *i-na ma-ḫi-ri-im*
    8. *i-šar / ša-ra-kam / ka-am*
    9. *el-te-qé*
    10. *iq-ti-in*
    11. *li-pu-(us/ús)-su/sú*
    12. *ṭú-úr-di-im*
    13. *lu-mur / mu-úr*
    14. *i-ma-(aḫ)-ḫar*
    15. *ma-ḫa-ṣum / ṣu-um / ṣú-um*

D. 1. *itti āgerīšu*
    2. *(sinništum) ēpišet annītim*
    3. *ṣābitānum*
    4. *māḫirat šikarim*
    5. *kakkum māḫiṣum*
    6. *rākibum*
    7. *aḫḫū nāṣir(ūt) aḫḫātim*
    8. *nākisūt iṣṣī*
    9. *šēmiat awât Ellil*
    10. *ilum bānî*
    11. *ilum ālik pānīya*
    12. *wardū wāšib(ūt) ālim šuāti*
    13. *pēt(i) bābim*
    14. *ilum rāʾimki / iltum rāʾimtaki*
    15. *šattum ēribtum*
    16. *pāqid kanīkātim*
    17. *šāpir rēdî*
    18. *bāqirānum*

E. 1. *anumma imēram nasqam ana qīštīki attadnakkim inanna qīšātim mādātim ana maḫrīya šuprī*. I have herewith given you (fs) a select donkey as your gift; now send to me many gifts.
    2. *ina lā šādidim eleppum ša nadīt Šamaš īguru ana ṣērīša ul illik*. For want of a tower, the boat that the *nadītum* of Šamaš rented did not go to her.
    3. *il(ān)ū rabûtum agê bēlūtim iqīšūnim*. The great gods bestowed on me the crown of lordship.
    4. *asûm eqlam labiram ša šamallûm īrišūšu išdud-ma kīma zītti šamallêm išrukšum*. The physician surveyed the old field that the trading agent demanded of him and gave (it) to him as the agent's share.
    5. *šāpirī išpuram umma šū-ma "ša pilšam ina bītim eššim iplušū-ma makkūram išriqū ṣabat"; inanna awīlê šunūti aṣṣabat-ma šērtam kabittam ētemissunūti*. My overseer wrote me, "Arrest those who made a breach in the new house and stole the property"; I have now arrested those men and imposed a serious penalty on them.
    6. *aḫum ša napištašu kīma napištīya arammu atta*. You are a brother whose life I love as my (own) life.
    7. *amraṣ-ma pî ēpuš-ma ilat šamê bēltī azkur-ma umma anākū-ma ayy-amūt luslim īnāya šamšam liṭṭulā-ma uznāya qabâki lišmeā*. When I became sick I opened my mouth and invoked the goddess of heaven, my mistress: "May I not die; let me recover; may my eyes see the sun and my ears hear your speech."
    8. *šamnam ana qaqqad marṣim šupuk-ma libluṭ*. Pour oil on the head of the sick man that he may recover.

9. *ālānû nakrūtum ṣabtūtīšunu ana ḫurāṣim mādim ipaššarū.* The enemy cities will release their prisoners for a lot of gold.
10. *apil šarrim ana pāni kašād abīšu ana šīmtīšu ittalak.* The king's heir has gone to his fate before his father's arrival.
11. *ṣuḫārû šunu mê zakûtim lištû-ma lā imuttū.* Let those servants drink pure water, lest they die.
12. *âm ša ina bīt aḫātīya/aḫḫātīya ašpuku mitḫāriš nizâz.* We will divide equally the grain that I stored in my sister's/sisters' house.
13. *ayyumma bīšam ša rubâtim lā nāṭilātim mala iḫliqu irībšināšim.* Someone replaced for them however much of the blind princesses' property had disappeared.

F. 278 *šumma awīlum wardam amtam išām-ma waraḫšu lā imlā-ma bennī elīšu imtaqut ana nādinānīšu utār-ma šayyāmānum kasap išqulu ileqqe.* If a man bought a male (or) female slave and while he has not (yet) completed one (lit., his) month (of service) epilepsy has befallen him, he may return him to his seller; the buyer in question will receive the silver he paid out.

279 *šumma awīlum wardam amtam išām-ma baqrī irtaši nādinaššu baqrī ippal.* If a man bought a male (or) female slave and (s)he has incurred legal claims, his seller will pay the claims.

175 *šum-ma lu* ÌR É.GAL *ù lu* ÌR MAŠ.EN.GAG DUMU.MUNUS *a-wi-lim i-ḫu-uz-ma* DUMU.MEŠ *it-ta-la-ad be-el* ÌR *a-na* DUMU.MEŠ DUMU. MUNUS *a-wi-lim a-na wa-ar-du-tim ú-ul i-ra-ag-gu-um.*

šumma lū warad ekallim ū lū warad muškēnim mārat awīlim īḫuz-ma mārī ittalad bēl wardim ana mārī mārat awīlim ana wardūtim ul iraggum. If a palace slave or a *muškēnum*'s slave married an *awīlum*' s daughter and she has borne children, the slave's owner will not lay claim to the children of the *awīlum*'s daughter for slavery.

G. 1. [*Aplūt*] *Šât-Ayya nadīt Šamaš mārat Šamaš-ilum. Amat-Mamu nadīt Šamaš mārat Ša-ilīšu rēdīt warkatīša. Eqlam ina Gamīnānum itā eqel Ibānum-qāssu u itā eqel Aḫūni mār Abba, x bītam epšam ina gagîm idi bīt Muḫaddītum mārat Abdim, mimma annîm Šât-Ayya nadīt Šamaš ummaša ana Amat-Mamu mārat Ša-ilīšu iddin. Eqlam ina Gamīnānum itā eqel Sîn-rēmēnī u itā eqel Nabi-Šamaš, eqlam ina Qablum itā eqel Bēlšunu, 1 amtam, mimma annîm Ša-ilīšu abūša u Šamuḫtum ummaša ana Amat-Mamu mārtīšunu iddinū. Ina aḫḫīša ana ša irammu aplussa inaddin.*

The estate of Šât-Ayya the *nadītum* of Šamaš, daughter of Šamaš-ilum. Amat-Mamu the *nadītum* of Šamaš, daughter of Ša-ilīšu, is the heir of her estate. A field in Gamīnānum next to the field of Ibānum-qāssu and next to the field of Aḫūni son of Abba, x built house in the *gagûm* next to the house of Muḫaddītum daughter of Abdum, all of this Šât-Ayya the *nadītum* of Šamaš, her mother, gave to Amat-Mamu daughter of Ša-ilīšu. A field in Gamīnānum next to the field of Sîn-rēmēnī and next to the field of Nabi-Šamaš, a field in Qablum next to the field of Bēlšunu, a female slave, all of this Ša-ilīšu her father and Šamuḫtum her mother gave to Amat-Mamu their daughter. Among her brothers, she may give her inheritance to the one she loves.

2. [1] ^{I}*ša-ḫi-ra* [...] [2] ^{I}*be-le-sú-nu ù* [3] ^{I}*a-sà-tam i-ḫu-*[*uz*] [4] *5 ma-ri ú-li-súm* [5] *i-na 5 ma-ri ša a-sà-tum* [6] *a-na!*(UD) *ša-ḫi-ra ul-du* [7] ^{I}*ia-ku-na-am* [8] *ma-ra-šu ra-bi-a-am* [9] ^{I}*ša-ḫi-*[*ra a-n*]*a ma-ru-ti-šu il-qé* [10] *a-na wa-ar-ki-a-at* UD-*mi* [11] ^{I}*a-sà-tum* [12] *a-aḫ-ḫu-ša* [13] *a-na ša-ḫi-ra* [14] *ú-ul i-ra-ga-mu* [15] MU ^{d}UTU ^{d}*a-a* ^{d}AMAR.UTU [16] *ù ḫa-am-mu-ra-pí* [17] *itmû*(IN. PÀD.DÈ.MEŠ).

Šaḫira [...] *Bēlessunu u Asatum īḫu*[*z*]. *5 mārī ulissum. Ina 5 mārī ša Asatum ana Šaḫira uldu Iakūnam mārāšu rabiam Šaḫi*[*ra an*]*a mārūtīšu ilqe. Ana warkiāt ūmī Asatum aḫḫūša ana Šaḫira ul iraggamū. nīš Šamaš Ayya Marduk u Ḫammurapi itmû.*

Šaḫira [son of ...] married Bēlessunu and Asatum. She bore him 5 children. Among the 5 children whom Asatum bore to Šaḫira, Šaḫira adopted Iakūnum (as) his oldest son. In future Asatum (and) her brothers will not contest against Šaḫira. They swore by the life of Šamaš, Ayya, Marduk, and Ḫammurapi. (Witnesses. Date.)

LESSON TWENTY-ONE

C. 1. UDU LÚ
2. ANŠE ŠEŠ-*ia*
3. Á BÀD
4. AGA-*šu*
5. NIN AGA.ÚS
6. *i-na-(ad)-din/di-in*
7. *i-na-(aʾ)-ʾì-du-nim/ni-im* or *i-na-i-du-nim/ni-im*
8. *ú-ul im-ḫur/ḫu-úr*
9. *i-diṅ/di-in*
10. *na-ʾa$_4$/a-dum/du-um*
11. *pu-uḫ/úḫ-rum/ru-um*
12. *te-eš-mi-i*
13. *el-te-i* (*el-te-ʾì*)
14. *wa-ṣum/ṣu-(ú)-um/ṣú-(ú)-um*
15. *la-(aʾ/a)-bu-um*
16. *šar-kam/ka-am*
17. *wa-ra-dam/da-am*
18. *li-gu-ra-nim/ni-im*

D. 1. *ēteliam.*
2. *ištu bīt šāpirim ṣî.*
3. *ana bābtīšunu/kiṣrīšunu niqerreb/niṭeḫḫe.*
4. *īnīn ana bašīt* (etc.) *mannim iššû?*
5. *ina rēš dūrim idīšunūti.*
6. *elê šadîm eleʾʾi/elê/elî.*
7. *aplum ana abīšu liʾʾid.*
8. *mātam kalâša taltawiā.*
9. *iqterbānim/iṭṭeḫeānim.*
10. *eqlētim nadiātim šuddā.*
11. *mīnam/minâm rubûm naʾdum/nādum išpuk?*
12. *šiprum/ṭēmum/qabûm/awātum ittaṣi.*
13. *teqribīm/teṭḫîm.*
14. *meḫer ṭuppīya adīni ul uṣiam.*
15. *šatê šikarim ul eleʾʾi/elê/elî.*
16. *kunukkam eššam idi.*
17. *ilawwûniāti.*
18. *itti qīštīša eliā.*
19. *rubātum iqerribam/iṭeḫḫeam.*
20. *alwīšu.*
21. *ina wardūtīkunu tēteliānim.*
22. *lemnum ilteʾīšu/iltêšu.*
23. *aḫka aššum ummīya taddi.*
24. *ina bābim ṣi.*
25. *ištu bītim nittaṣiam.*

E. 1. *šumma ṭuppum šanûm ša purussêm annîm īliam ṭuppam šuāti iḫeppû.* If another tablet of this decision should appear, that tablet will be destroyed.

2. *wāšib bītim kiṣram gamram ana maḫīr illaku ana bēl bītim u nēmettašu watartam ana ekallim lisdur-ma liddin.* The resident of the house must regularly give the entire payment at the going rate to the owner of the house and his additional tax to the palace.

3. *šaknum meḫer kanīkīya kankim īrišanni/irrišanni.* The governor asked/will ask me for a copy of my sealed document.

4. *nadītum lā balittum ištu gagîm adi ūm rugummêm lā uṣṣi.* The unwell *nadītum* must not leave the *gagûm* until the day of the lawsuit.

5. *wardum lā taklum ša šum bēlīšu lā izkuru lēssu amḫaṣ-ma šinnāšu uṣiānim.* When I struck the cheek of the untrustworthy slave who would not mention the name of his owner, his teeth came out.

6. *nišū ḫadiātum ša ina pānī šarrim ipḫurā-ma awâtīšu nasqātim išmeā libbašina ipšaḫ.* The heart of the joyful people who gathered in the king's presence and heard his choice words was appeased.

7. *inanna ṣuḫārû ša ana pānīya taškunu ana alpī ša ēzibūšunūti liʾʾidū-*

šunūšim-ma baqrī ayy-iršû. Now the servants whom you put at my disposal must pay attention to the oxen that I left behind, and not incur any debts.

8. *inanna mātum annītum iddanim-ma ittīni ittakir kiṣrīka kuṣur-ma ittīša kakkī epuš.* Now this land has become strong and become hostile against us; organize (ms) your contingents and do battle with it.
9. *aššatum maḫrītum terḫatam u šeriktam ana mārīša ša irammu išarrak ana aḫîm lā ipaššaršināti.* The first wife may bestow the bride-price and the dowry upon her child(ren) whom she loves; she may not sell them to an outsider.
10. *našê maruštim annītim ša ilī elīya īmidu ul eleʾʾi.* I am not able to bear this burden that my god has imposed upon me.

F. 3 *šumma awīlum ina dīnim ana šībūt sarrātim uṣiam-ma awāt/awât iqbû lā uktīn, šumma dīnum šū dīn napištim, awīlum šū iddâk.* If a man came forth in a legal case for (presenting) false testimony (lit. testimony of falsehoods), and has not proved the word/words he spoke, if that case is a capital case, that man will be executed.

106 *šumma šamallûm kaspam itti tamkārim ilqē-ma tamkāršu ittakir, tamkārum šū ina maḫar ilim u šībī ina kaspim leqêm šamallâm ukām-ma šamallûm kaspam mala ilqû adi 3-šu ana tamkārim inaddin.* If a trading agent took silver from a merchant, but has disputed (it) with his merchant, said merchant will, before god and witnesses, convict the trading agent of taking the silver, and then the trading agent will give the merchant up to three times however much silver he took.

200 *šum-ma a-wi-lum ši-in-ni a-wi-lim me-eḫ-ri-šu it-ta-di ši-in-na-šu i-na-ad-du-ú.*

šumma awīlum šinni awīlim meḫrīšu ittadi, šinnašu inaddû. If a man has knocked out the tooth of a man of his own rank, his tooth will be knocked out.

G. 1. *Tarām-Sagil u Iltani mārat Sîn-abūšu Warad-Šamaš ana aššūtim u mutūtim īḫussināti. Tarām-Sagil ū Iltani ana Warad-Šamaš mutīšina "ul mutī atta" iqabbī-ma ištu dimtim inaddûniššināti. U Warad-Šamaš ana Tarām-Sagil ū Iltani aššātīšu "ul aššatī atti" iqabbī-ma ina bītim ... ītelli. U Iltani šēpī Tarām-Sagil imessi, kussīša ana bīt ilīša inašši, zēni Tarām-Sagil Iltani izenne, kunukkīša ul ipette.*

Warad-Šamaš married Tarām-Sagil and Iltani daughter of Sîn-abūšu. Should Tarām-Sagil or Iltani say to Warad-Šamaš their husband, "you are not my husband," they will be thrown down from a tower. Should Warad-Šamaš say to Tarām-Sagil or Iltani his wives, "You are not my wife," he will forfeit the estate ... Moreover, Iltani will wash the feet of Tarām-Sagil (and) will carry her chair to her temple, (and) Iltani will hate whoever hates Tarām-Sagil, will not open her sealed documents. (Witnesses.)

2. *x šamnam ... itti Šumšunu ... ana qabê Bāšti-ilʾabi Inbūša mār Baziya ilqe. Ūm ebūrim ana nāši kanīkīšu y âm ... imaddad.*

Inbūša son of Baziya received x oil ... from Šumšunu ... by order of Bāšti-ilʾabi. On the day of the harvest he will measure out y grain ... to the bearer of his (debt-)document. (Witnesses. Date.)

3. [1] É *ni-ši-i-ni-šu* [2] KI *ni-ši-i-ni-šu* [3] ^{Id}UTU-*du-ur-a-li* [4] É *a-na ki-iṣ-ri* [5] *a-na* MU.1.KAM *ú-še-ṣí* [6] $^{1}/_{3}$ GÍN 15 ŠE KUG.BABBAR [7] Ì.LAL.E [8] ITU *ti-ri-im* [9] UD.1.KAM *i-ru-ub* [10] ITU *Isin*(EZEN)-*a-bi* [11] *i-ga-mar-ma ú-ṣí* [12] IGI ^{d}UTU [13] IGI ^{d}*a-a* [14] IGI ^{d}*ma-*[*ma*] [15–16] MU *s*[*a-am-su*]-*i-lu-ni*.

Bīt Nīši-īnīšu itti Nīši-īnīšu Šamaš-dūr-āli bītam ana kiṣrī ana 1 šattim ušēṣi. $^{1}/_{3}$ *šiqil 15 uṭṭet kaspam išaqqal. Waraḫ Tirim ūmam maḫriam irrub, waraḫ Isin-abi igammar-ma uṣṣi. Maḫar Šamaš, maḫar Ayya, maḫar Ma*[*ma*]*; šanat S*[*amsu*]*-iluni.*

Šamaš-dūr-āli rented the house of Nīši-īnīšu from Nīši-īnīšu as a house for rent (payment) for one year. He will weigh out one-third shekel and 15 grains of silver. He will enter on the first day of the month of Tirum; he will leave completely in the month of Isin-abi. Before Šamaš, before Ayya, before Mama; year of Samsu-iluna.

LESSON TWENTY-TWO

C. 1. $^{\text{(giš)}}$GU.ZA ŠEŠ-*ku-nu*
2. SAG ZÉ
3. BÀD URU
4. NIN LÚ *kab / ka-ab-tim / ti-im*
5. ZAG *ù* GÙB
6. *wa-ar-ka-at* $^{\text{(lú)}}$ÚS
7. *ik / i-kir / ki-ir*
8. *am-mi-nim lu-(ud)-din / di-in*
9. *ur / úr-ṣa-am še / še*$_{20}$*-eb-ra-am*
10. *eš-me-ma al / a-lik / li-ik*
11. *lu-uš-pur / pu-ur / úr*
12. *ú-ul ta-aš / áš-ṭur / ṭú-ur / úr*
13. *a-túr / tu-(ur / úr)-ra-am*
14. *ṭú-uḫ / úḫ-dam / da-am*
15. *e-(i / ʾi)-il-tum / tu-um*

D. 1. *eqlētūni (ina) mê imlâ; eqlētūni (ina) mê maliā.*
2. *šum(ū)šu līli; šum(ū)šu lū eli.*
3. *ina ālānī / ālānê annûtim wašbā; ... uššabā.*
4. *nārātum šapliātum irappišā; rapšā.*
5. *ē-tamraṣ; ul marṣāta.*
6. *mītat; imtūt.*
7. *ṣāb(i) / ummān nakrim iqerribanniāšim / iṭeḫḫeanniāšim* (or pl. *iqerribūninniāšim / iṭeḫḫûninniāšim*); (*ṣābum*) *qerbam / ṭeḫiam* (or pl. *qerbūnim / ṭeḫûnim*) / (*ummānum*) *qerbet / ṭeḫiat.*
8. *tabluṭī / tašlimī; balṭāti / šalmāti.*
9. *dūrum ilbir; labir.*
10. *ina nišī abāta; abi nišī atta.*
11. *ina šamê bēlēti; bēlessina atti.*
12. *sinnišātina; sinnišātum ša ana karānim īrubā attina.*
13. *qarrādū lū paḫrū; lipḫurū.*
14. *ālānū / ûni imtaqtū; maqtū.*
15. *awâtim ša ina narîya šaṭrā azzakar.*
16. *ina šadî ezbētunu.*
17. *mārum ša waldūšim atta; mārtum ša waldassim anāku.*
18. *lū dannāta; lā enšēta.*
19. *annītum narkabtum ša ana dayyānim šaddat.*
20. *ina emūqim / emūqī(n) / emūqātim kaliāku.*
21. *rubânu; rubû palḫūtum nīnu.*
22. *ul šamallê šū.*
23. *šinnāya šebrā / ḫepiā.*
24. *eṭlēku.*
25. *qaqqad šarratim šamnam ṭābam* (or, *ina šamnim ṭābim*) *pašiš.*
26. *ina kišādīšu kīma kalbim ṣabit.*
27. *naʾdāku / nādāku; aḫī ul anaddi.*
28. *ana šumēlim saḫer.*
29. *imittašu lawiat / saḫrat.*

E. 1. *āl(ū)ka šū ittīka inakkir-ma ana šarrim ša ittīka nakru isaḫḫur-ma ina kakkī tadâkšū-ma ālam šuāti talawwī-ma dūr(ā)šu tanaqqar u išid kussi šarrūtīšu tanassaḫ.* That city of yours (ms) will become hostile to you and turn to a king who is hostile to you, but you will kill him with weapons, surround that city, and tear down its walls; further, you will uproot the foundation of its/his royal throne.

2. *têrētūya ša epšānim ul išarā têrētum šina lemnā ina šībūtīya bītī ul iššer.* The omens that were done for me are not favorable; said omens are bad. In my old age my house will not prosper.

3. *kīma kīttim ša Šamaš u Marduk rāʾimka išrukūnikkum âm ša*

maḫrīka mudud-ma šupuk. In accordance with the honesty that Šamaš and Marduk, who love you (ms), have bestowed upon you, measure and store up the grain that is before you.

4. *mut aḫātīya ilikšu ul šalim ṣibtam watartam kīma ṣimdat šarrim lā temmissu.* The *ilkum* of my sister's husband is in not good shape; do (ms) not impose on him extra interest according to the royal decree.
5. *awīlam taklam ša naʾdū-ma tatakkalūšum ina mātim šuāti pūḫi šāpirim šukun.* Install in that land as the prefect's replacement a trustworthy man who is careful and whom you trust.
6. *nadītum ša ina gagîm wašbat kiam iqbiam umma šī-ma inanna immerātum imtīdā-ma našâšina ul eleʾʾi mamman šupram-ma tappûtī lillik.* The *nadītum* who lives in the *gagûm* said as follows to me: "Now the sheep have increased and I am unable to support them; send (ms) someone to help me."
7. *šumma martum waṣiat agûm ištu mātim uṣṣi.* If the gall bladder protrudes, the crown will leave the land.
8. *kaspum ša nitbalu ana šīm kirîm šanîm ul imaṣṣi.* The silver we brought is not sufficient for the price of another orchard.
9. *suḫur-ma šīpātim qatnātim šāmam-ma leqeam.* Seek (ms) out, buy, and bring me (some) fine wool.
10. *lēt bāʾerim amḫaṣ-ma rittašu ešber-ma ana maṣṣarī apqissu.* I struck the cheek of the fisherman, I broke his hand, and I entrusted him to the watchmen.
11. *balum bēl pīḫatim meḫer kunukkīya īpušū epištašunu annītum ul damqat.* Without the knowledge of the commissioner they made a copy of my seal; this deed of theirs was not proper.

F. 26 *šumma lū rēdûm ū lū bāʾerum ša ana ḫarrān šarrim alākšu qabû lā illik ū lū agram īgur-ma pūḫšu iṭṭarad lū rēdûm ū lū bāʾerum šū iddâk munaggeršu bīssu itabbal.* If either a footsoldier or a "fisherman" whose going on a royal campaign was commanded did not go, or hired a hireling and has sent (him as) his substitute, said footsoldier or "fisherman" will be executed; his denouncer will take his estate for himself.

33 *šumma lū ša ḫaṭṭātim ū lū laputtûm ṣāb(i) nisḫātim irtaši ū lū ana ḫarrān šarrim agram pūḫam imḫur-ma irtede lū ša ḫaṭṭātim ū lū laputtûm šū iddâk.* If either a "captain" or a "lieutenant" has had deserters/has acquired conscripts(?) or accepted and has led a hireling as substitute on a royal campaign, said "captain" or "lieutenant" will be executed.

7 *[š]um-ma a-wi-lum lu* KUG.BABBAR *lu* KUG.SIG$_{17}$ *lu* ÌR *lu* GEME$_2$ *lu* GUD *lu* UDU *lu* ANŠE *ù lu mi-im-ma šum-šu i-na qá-at* DUMU *a-wi-lim!*(LUM) *ù lu* ÌR *a-wi-lim ba-lum ši-bi ù ri-ik-sa-tim iš-ta-am ù lu a-na ma-ṣa-ru-tim im-ḫu-ur a-wi-lum šu-ú šar-ra-aq id-da-ak.*

šumma awīlum lū kaspam lū ḫurāṣam lū wardam lū amtam lū alpam lū immeram lū imēram ū lū mimma šumšu ina qāt mār awīlim ū lū warad awīlim balum šībī u riksātim ištām ū lū ana maṣṣarūtim imḫur awīlum šū šarrāq iddâk. If a man has purchased or accepted for safekeeping either silver or gold or a male slave or a female slave or an ox or a sheep or a donkey or anything at all from a member of the *awīlum* class or an *awīlum*'s slave without witnesses and contracts, said man is a thief; he will be executed.

128 *šum-ma a-wi-lum aš-ša-tam i-ḫu-uz-ma ri-ik-sa-ti-ša la iš-ku-un* MUNUS *ši-i ú-ul aš-ša-at.*

šumma awīlum aššatam īḫuz-ma riksātīša lā iškun sinništum šī ul aššat. If a man married a woman but did not conclude her contracts, that woman is not a wife.

G. 1. *šumma kakki imittim ina rēš martim šakim-ma martam irde, kakki qūlim.* If the right mark is located at the top of the gall bladder and led the gall bladder, the mark of silence.

2. *šumma libbum kīma iškī immerim, amūt Maništīšu ša ekallûšu [i]dūkūšu.* If the heart is like a sheep's testicles, the (liver) omen of Maništīšu, whose palace officials killed him.

3. *šumma imitti libbi qê [ṣubb]ut, kiṣir libbi ilim ana awīlim [ul pa]ṭer.* If the right side of the heart is held by filaments, the anger of the god against the man is not ended.

4. ⸢*šum*⸣*-ma um-mu-um ra-bi-tum i-ta-ri-ik ap-lu-um ra-bu-ú-um* ^{giš}GU.ZA*-am i-ṣa-ba-at šum-ma ṣe-ḫe-er-tum i-ta-ri-ik ap-lu-um ṣe-eḫ-ru-um* ^{giš}GU.ZA*-am i-ṣa-ba-at.*

šumma ummum rabītum ītarik, aplum rabûm kussiam iṣabbat; šumma ṣeḫertum ītarik, aplum ṣeḫrum kussiam iṣabbat. If the large "mother" has become long, the elder heir will take the throne; if the small one has become long, the younger heir will take the throne.

5. *šum-ma mar-tum ḫa-al-qá-at da-am-qá-at.*

šumma martum ḫalqat, damqat. If the gall bladder is missing, it is good.

6. *šum-ma mar-tum ma-li-at-ma mu-ša wa-ar-qú ra-du-um i-la-ak.*

*šumma martum maliat-ma mûša warqū, rādum illak.*If the gall bladder is full and its liquid is yellow, a cloudburst is coming.

7. *šum-ma mar-tum ṣa-bi-it be-el ma-a-tim i-ma-a-at.*

šumma martum ṣabit, bēl mātim imât. If the gall bladder is held (in place?), the lord of the land will die.

H. 1. *Šamaš-nūrī mārat Ibbi-Ša(ḫ)an itti Ibbi-Ša(ḫ)an abīša Bunene-abī u Bēlessunu išāmūši. Ana Bunene-abī aššat; ana Bēlessunu amat. Šamaš-nūrī ana Bēlessunu bēltīša "ul bēltī atti" iqabbī-ma ana kaspim inaddišši. Ana šīmīša gamrim x kaspam išqulū. ... Awāssa gamrat; libbašu ṭāb. Ana warkiāt ūmim awīlum ana awīlim lā ibaqqar. Nīš(i) Šamaš Marduk u Ḫammurapi itmû.*

Bunene-abī and Bēlessunu bought Šamaš-nūrī daughter of Ibbi-Ša(ḫ)an from Ibbi-Ša(ḫ)an her father. To Bunene-abī she is a wife; to Bēlessunu she is a slave. If Šamaš-nūrī says to Bēlessunu her mistress, "You are not my mistress," she may sell her. They weighed out x silver as her full price. ... Her transaction is settled; his heart is satisfied. In future one may not contest against the other. They swore by the life of Šamaš, Marduk, and Ḫammurapi. (Witnesses. Date.)

2. ^{1} [A.ŠÀ]-*um ma-la ma-ṣú-ú* ^{2} [K]I ^{d}*na-bi-um-ma-lik* ^{3} ^{Id}EN.ZU-*ra-bi* ^{4} DUMU *ig-mil-*^{d}EN.ZU ^{5} *a-na e-re-šu-tim* ^{6} *ú-še-ṣí* ^{7} *ki-ma i-mi-ti-šu* ^{8} *ù šu-mé-li-šu* ^{9} *ši-ip-ra-am i-ip-pu-uš* ^{10} *ši-ip-ra-am ú-ul* [*i*]-*pu-uš-ma* ^{11} *mi-iš-la-ni-šu* ŠE-*a-a*[*m*] ^{12} *i-le-qé* ^{13} IGI *na-ra-am-*^{d}IŠKUR ^{14} DUMU ^{d}EN.ZU-*be-el-ì-lí* ^{15} IGI *ri-iš-*^{d}*Girra*(GIBIL) ^{16} DUMU ^{d}EN.ZU-*e-ri-ba-am.*

[*Eql*]*um mala maṣû* [*it*]*ti Nabium-mālik Sîn-rabi mār Igmil-Sîn ana errēšūtim ušēṣi. Kīma imittīšu u šumēlīšu šipram* [*i*]*ppuš. Šipram ul ippuš-ma mišlānīšu â*[*m*] *ileqqe. Maḫar Narām-Adad mār Sîn-bēl-ilī; maḫar Rīš-Girra mār Sîn-erībam.*

Sîn-rabi son of Igmil-Sîn rented in tenancy a field, as far as it extends, from Nabium-mālik. He will work (the field) like his right (neighbor) and his left (neighbor). Should he not work (it), he (the owner) will (nevertheless) receive his half share of grain. Before Narām-Adad son of Sîn-bēl-ilī; before Rīš-Girra son of Sîn-erībam.

LESSON TWENTY-THREE

C.

1. *qabal* / *qablā martim;* MURUB$_4$ ZÉ
2. *sebet(ti) šiqil ḫurāṣum;* 7 GÍN KUG.SIG$_{17}$
3. *ešrā bābū* / *bābātum;* 20 KÁ(.MEŠ)
4. *rebûm kiṣrum;* 4 *ki-iṣ-rum*
5. *sebiat šikarim;* IGI.7.GÁL *ši-ka-ri-im*
6. *tišēšeret bāʾerū;* 19 ŠU.ḪA.MEŠ
7. *sebûm pagrum;* 7 *pa-ag-rum*
8. *samānat qarrādū lēʾûtum;* 8 *qar-ra-du le-ú-tum*
9. *šeduštum iltum;* 6 *il-tum*
10. *šumēl qaqqad ṣabtim;* GÙB SAG.DU *ṣa-ab-tim*
11. *šediš*$^?$ *meāt ṭuppū* / *ṭuppātum;* 6 ME DUB(.MEŠ/ḪI.A) (or, *nēr ṭuppū* / *ṭuppātum;* GÍŠ-U DUB(.MEŠ/ḪI.A))
12. *tiše napšātum;* 9 *na-ap-ša-tum*
13. *ṭuppī kilallīn* / *ṭuppātim kilattīn eḫpe* / *ešber;* DUB(.MEŠ/ḪI.A) *ki-la-al-li-in* / *ki-la-at-ti-in eḫ-pé* / *eš-be* / *bé-er*
14. *samuntum rubātum;* 8 *ru-ba-tum*
15. *šanûm ṭēmum;* 2 *ṭe* / *ṭè* / *ṭe*$_4$*-mu-um*
16. *ṭēmum šanûm; ṭe* / *ṭè* / *ṭe*$_4$*-mu-um ša-nu-(ú)-um*
17. *šalāšat kur âm ašām;* 3 ŠE.GUR *a-ša-am*
18. *par(asr)ab ileqqe.* KINGUSILA *i-le-eq-qé*
19. *ešer qīšātum* / *šerkētum;* 10 *qí-ša-tum* / *še-er-ke-tum*
20. *ḫamušti ak(a)lim išî;* IGI.5.GÁL *ak* / *a-ka-li-im i-ši-i*
21. *mišil puḫrim;* MAŠ *pu-uḫ* / *úḫ-ri-im*
22. *birīt šinā iṣṣī; bi-ri-it* 2 GIŠ(.MEŠ)
23. *šalušti ḫubullim;* IGI.3.GÁL *ḫu-bu-ul-lim*
24. *erbeā* / *erbâ manā kaspum;* 40 MA.NA KUG.BABBAR
25. *šinšeret šūt-rēšim naʾdūtum* / *nādūtum;* 12 *šu-ut*-SAG *na-(aʾ)-du-tum*
26. *(ana) šalāšat warḫī; (a-na)* ITI.3.KAM
27. *sebe ubānātum;* 7 ŠU.SI(.MEŠ)
28. *išātum ištēn bītam eššam īkul;* IZI 1 É *eš-ša-am i-ku-ul*
29. *kilallā* / *ūni nissaḫur; ki-la-al-la* / *lu-ni ni-is-sa-ḫur*
30. *ešret nēmettim;* IGI.10.GÁL *ne* / *né-me-et-tim*
31. *ḫamšat tappû;* 5 TAB.BA.MEŠ
32. *šalāš sât ûm;* 3 BÁN ŠE
33. *itā šalāšat kirî;* ÚS.SA.DU 3 KIRI$_6$.MEŠ
34. *abullum maḫrītum* / *pānītum;* ABUL *maḫ-ri-tum* / *pa-ni-tum*
35. *Adad šinipiāt(im)* / *šittīn imḫur;* ^{d}IŠKUR ŠANABI / *ši-it-ti-in im-ḫur*
36. *ḫamšum pilšum;* 5 *pí-il-šum*
37. *imitti kussîm;* ZAG $^{(\text{giš})}$GU.ZA
38. *šaluštum zīttum;* 3 ḪA.LA
39. *ištēššerûm asûm;* 11 $^{(\text{lú})}$A.ZU
40. *šalāšat meḫrū ibšû* / *šalāš meḫrētum ibšiā;* 3 *me-eḫ-ru* / *re-tum ib-šu-ú* / *ib-ši-a*
41. *arkab; ar-kab* / *ka-ab*
42. *šipram tašpur; ši-ip-ra-am ta-aš* / *áš-pur* / *pu-ur* / *úr*
43. *ṭupšarrum ipṭur;* $^{(\text{lú})}$DUB.SAR *ip-ṭur* / *ṭú-ur* / *úr*
44. *ikkir; ik* / *i-kir* / *ki-ir*

45. *aṣṣabat; aṣ/a-ṣa-bat/ba-at*
46. *rabiat/rebiat/rabât/rebât watartim;* IGI.4.GÁL *wa-tar/ta-ar-tim*
47. *šalāšā šībūtum;* 30 $^{(\text{lú})}$IGI.MEŠ
48. *(ana) šeššet ūmī; (a-na)* UD.6.KAM
49. *(ina) rebūtim šattim; (i-na)* MU.4.KAM
50. *ṭēmum ištēn; ṭe/ṭè/ṭe*$_4$*-mu-um iš-te-en*

D. 1. *šumma rēdûm ša maṣṣarūt kanīkī šarratim paqdassum pūḫšu īgur warkassu lū parsat.* If a foot-soldier to whom safe-keeping of the queen's sealed documents was entrusted has hired a substitute, his case must be investigated.

2. *aššatum māram ša mussa pānûm ana mārūtim ilqû lā ibaqqaršu ina dīnim lā iraggumšum.* The wife may not bring suit against a son whom her previous husband adopted; she may not lay a complaint against him in a legal case.

3. *ana mātātim šināti tellī-ma kakkī nakrīka mala maṣû tešebber.* You (ms) will go up to those lands and break your enemy's/enemies' weapons, however many there are.

4. *ana dūrim laberim ša ālim šuāti ēlī-ma nišū ālim ittīya ikkerā-ma erēbam ul elē.* When I went up to the old wall of that town, the people of the town were hostile to me and I could not enter.

5. *anumma bāʾerum šū imēram anniam balum riksātim ana ḫamšat šiqil kaspim u šittā sât êm ittadnam.* Said "fisherman" has herewith given me this donkey, without contracts, for five shekels of silver and two seahs of barley.

6. *šamallûm eš(e)ret šiqil kaspam ša ina qāti/qātī tamkārim imḫuru ana aḫātīšu/aḫḫātīšu išruk.* The trading agent gave his sister(s) the ten shekels of silver that he had received from the merchant.

7. *ina dīn šarrum idīnu mamman ul iraggum.* No one will contest a verdict the king has rendered.

8. *šeššet warḫī šarrāqam ša pilšam ina bītīya iplušū-ma makkūrī ḫalqam ina qātīšu iṣbatū ina ṣibittim iklûšu.* For six months the thief who broke into my house and in whose possession my missing property was seized was held in prison.

9. *ṣuḫārê šunūti kalâšunu bēlessunu ana ištēn manā kaspim iptaṭar-šunūti.* Their mistress has ransomed all those servants for one mina of silver.

10. *ana Ellil tatakkal/tattakal-ma rubûm ayyum kussi šarrūtīka iṣabbat u mannum lemuttam ippeška.* If you (ms) trust/have trusted Enlil, what prince can seize your royal throne, and who can do you harm? (Or, You have trusted Enlil, and so what prince ...)

11. *warki abim mārū ummašunu aššum purussêm annîm lā ibaqqarū u ummum baqrī šanûtim ul iraššî.* After the death of (their) father the children may not sue their mother because of this decision; and the mother will not incur additional legal claims.

12. *inanna šarrum šūt-rēšīšu ana maḫrīka iṭṭarad ittīšunu ana aḫ nārim elītim rid-ma nīš ilim zukur.* Now the king has sent his court officials to you (ms); go down to the bank of the upper river with them to swear by the life of the god.

E. 133–133b 133 *šumma awīlum iššalil-ma ina bītīšu ša akālim* [*i*]*bašši* [*aš*]*šassu* [*bīssu i*]*ṣa*[*bba*]*t* [*u pagarš*]*a* [*inaṣṣa*]*r* [*ana bīt(im) šanî*]*m* [*ul irr*]*ub.* 133b *š*[*umm*]*a sinništum šī* [*pa*]*garša lā iṣṣur-ma ana bīt(im) šanîm īterub sinništam šuāti ukannūšī-ma ana mê inaddûši.* 133 If a man has been carried off (as booty), but there is something to eat in his house, his wife will take over his house, and protect herself; she will not enter another house/the house of another man. 133b If that woman has not protected herself, but has entered another house/the house of another man, that woman will be convicted and thrown into the water.

200–201 200 *šumma awīlum šinni awīlim meḫrīšu ittadi, šinnašu inaddû* 201 *šumma šinni muškēnim ittadi šalušti manā kaspam išaqqal.* 200 If a man has knocked out the tooth of a man of his own rank, his tooth will be knocked out. 201 If he has knocked out the tooth of a *muškēnum*, he will pay out one-third mina of silver.

273 *šumma awīlum agram īgur ištu rēš šattim adi ḫamšim warḫim šediš*$^{?}$ *uṭṭet kaspam ina ištēn ūmim inaddin ištu šeššim warḫim adi taqtīt šattim ḫamiš uṭṭet kaspam ina ištēn ūmim inaddin.* If a man hired a hireling, from the beginning of the year until the fifth month he will give six grains of silver for one day; from the sixth month until the end of the year he will give five grains of silver for one day.

277 *šumma awīlum elep šūš kurrī īgur ina ištēn ūmim šuduš/šeššat kaspam idīša inaddin.* If a man hired a sixty-kur boat, for one day he will give one-sixth (shekel) of silver (as) its hire.

59 *šum-ma a-wi-lum ba-lum be-el* ^{giš}KIRI$_6$ *i-na* ^{giš}KIRI$_6$ *a-wi-lim i-ṣa-am ik-ki-is* MAŠ MA.NA KUG.BABBAR *i-ša-qal.*

šumma awīlum balum bēl kirîm ina kiri awīlim iṣam ikkis mišil manā kaspam išaqqal. If a man cut down a tree in a man's orchard without the permission of the owner of the orchard, he will pay out one-half mina of silver.

204 *šum-ma* MAŠ.EN.GAG *le-e-et* MAŠ.EN.GAG *im-ta-ḫa-aṣ* 10 GÍN KUG. BABBAR *i-ša-qal.*

šumma muškēnum lēt muškēnim imtaḫaṣ eš(e)ret šiqil kaspam išaqqal. If a *muškēnum* has struck the cheek of a *muškēnum*, he will pay out 10 shekels of silver.

268–269 268 *šum-ma a-wi-lum* GUD *a-na di-a-ši-im i-gur* 2 BÁN ŠE Á-*šu* 269 *šum-ma* ANŠE *a-na di-a-ši-im i-gur* 1 BÁN ŠE Á-*šu.*

268 *šumma awīlum alpam ana diāšim īgur šittā sât ûm idūšu.* 269 *šumma imēram ana diāšim īgur išteat sât ûm idūšu.* 268 If a man hired an ox for threshing, its hire is two seahs of barley. 269 If he hired a donkey for threshing, its hire is one seah of barley.

F. 1. *šumma* [*ina amūtim*] *erbe/erba naplasā*[*tu*]*m šarrū ḫammê kibrāt mātim itebbûnim annûm imaqqutam annûm itebbe.* If in the liver there are four lobes, usurper kings will rise up in the peripheries of the land; one will fall, the other will succeed (remain standing).

2. *šumma naplaštum ana padānim iqterbam Turukkûtum ana šarrim iqerrebūnim awīlšu‹nu› ekallam ibêl.* If the lobe has come near the path, the Turukkians will come near the king; their man (leader) will rule the palace.

3. *šumma ina libbi na[ṣ]raptim padānum šarrum māssu ana pīšu uššab.* If there is a path within the depression, the king's land will dwell according to his command (or, will be obedient to his command).
4. *[šumm]a martum [l]ibbaša lipiam mali kak(ki) Šarru(m)-kīn.* If the center of the gall bladder is full of fat, the mark of Sargon.
5. *šumma martum isḫur-ma ubānam iltawe šarrum mātam nakar[t]am i[ṣa]bba[t].* If the gall bladder rotated and has surrounded the finger, the king will take a foreign country.
6. *šum[m]a martum isḫur-ma muḫḫam ša ubānim iltawi šarrum sukkalmaḫḫašu inassaḫ.* If the gall bladder rotated and has surrounded the top of the finger, the king will remove his chief minister.
7. *šumma martum itbē-ma muḫḫi ubānim iṣṣabat šarrum ālam nakram qāssu ikaššad.* If the gall bladder arose and has seized the top of the finger, the king will personally conquer a foreign city (lit., the king's hand will conquer ...).
8. *šumma izbum errūšu ina muḫḫīšu šaknū bīšam ša mātim šâti [mā]tum [ša]nītum itabbal.* If the intestines of a foetus are at its skull(?), another land will carry off that land's possessions.
9. *šumma izbum uznāšu īnīšu iktatmā awīlum iḫalliq.* If the ears of a foetus have covered its eyes, the man will perish.
10. *šum-ma ma-ra-tum 5-iš šar-ru ḫa-am-me-e i-te-eb-bu-ú-nim.*

    šumma marrātum ḫamiš šarrū ḫammê itebbûnim. If the gall bladders are five, usurper kings will appear on the scene.
11. *šum-ma mar-tum pa-nu-ú-ša a-na šu-me-li-im ša-ak-nu-ú* DINGIR-*šu e-li a-wi-li-im ša-bu-us.*

    šumma martum pānūša ana šumēlim šaknū il(ū)šu eli awīlim šabus. If the front of the gall bladder is located on the left, his god is angry with the man.
12. *šum-ma mar-tum qá-ab-la-šu ṣa-ab-ta-a šar-ra-am šu-ut-re-ši-i-šu i-du-uk-ku-šu.*

    šumma martum qablāšu ṣabtā šarram šūt-rēšīšu idukkūšu. If the middle of the gall bladder is "held", his court officials will kill the king.
13. *šum-ma mar-tum iṭ-bu-ú-ma it-ta-ṣí ru-bu-ú-um i-na da-an-na-tim uṣ-ṣí.*

    šumma martum iṭbū-ma ittaṣi rubûm ina dannatim uṣṣi. If the gall bladder sank and has (re-)emerged, the prince will emerge from difficulty (or, go out of the fortress).
14. *šum-ma mar-tum i-mi-ta-ša da-ma-am bu-ul-la-am pa-ši-iš* É.GAL-*la-am i-ša-tu-um i-ka-al.*

    šumma martum imittaša damam bullâm pašiš ekallam išātum ikkal. If the right side of the gall bladder is smeared with ... blood, fire will consume the palace.
15. *šum-ma mar-tum i-na a-bu-ul-lim na-di-a-at ni-ku-úr-tum da-an-na-tum.*

    šumma martum ina abullim nadiat nikurtum dannatum. If the gall bladder is lying in the "city gate," severe hostility.

16. DIŠ *iz-bu-um qá-qá-as-sú ka-a-a-nu-um ša-ki-in-ma ù iš-tu li-ib-bi pi-šu qá-qá-as-sú ša-nu-um wa-ṣi šar-ru-um šar-ra-am i-na* ^{giš}TUKUL-*ki i-da-ak-ma a-la-ni-šu na-we-šu du-ra-ni-šu er-ṣe-es-sú ù ṭe-eḫ-ḫe-šu qá-as-sú-ú i-ka-aš-ša-ad.*

šumma izbum qaqqassu kayyānum šakim-ma u ištu libbi pīšu qaqqassu šanûm waṣi, šarrum šarram ina kakkī idâk-ma ālānīšu nawêšu dūrānīšu erṣessu u ṭeḫḫêšu qāssu ikaššad. If the normal head of a foetus is in place, but also a second head protrudes from its mouth, king will kill king with weapons, and personally conquer his towns, his surrouding areas, his walls, his land, and his nearby lands.

G. 1. *Eqlam mala qāssu ikaššadu ugāram* [*š*]*a Ṭābātum šūṣūt Awīl-Sîn itti Awīl-Sîn mār Mār-erṣetim Gimillum mār Warad-eššešim eqlam ana errēšūtim ana išteat šattim ušē*[*ṣi*]. *Ana ūm ebūrim šittīn errēšu, šaluš bēl eqlim.*

Gimillum son of Warad-eššešim rented a field, as much as its/his share amounts to, the arable land of Ṭābātum, the leasehold of Awīl-Sîn, from Awīl-Sîn son of Mār-erṣetim, for tenancy, for one year. On the day of the harvest, two-thirds the tenant (will take), one-third the owner of the field (will take). (Witnesses. Date.)

2. ^{1} 1 GÍN KUG.BABBAR ^{2} ŠÁM 3 ^{udu}ŠU.GI.NA ^{3} *ša* É ^{d}UTU ^{4} *e-si-iḫ-ti* ^{I}DUMU-UD.20.KAM ^{5} *ù* ÌR-^{d}30 DUMU.MEŠ *e-ṭi-rum* ^{6} *qá-ti* DUMU-UD.20.[KA]M ^{7} *ù* ÌR-^{d}EN.Z[U] ^{8} *na-ás-ḫa-a-ma* ^{9} ^{I}30-*na-di-in-šu-mi* DUMU ^{d}UTU-*mu-ba-lí-iṭ* ^{10} 3 ^{udu}ŠU.GI.NA *a-na* UD.15.KAM ‹*ub*›-*ba!-lam!* ^{11} *ú-ul ub-ba-lam-ma* ^{12} 1 GÍN KUG.BABBAR!(DIŠ) Ì.LAL.E. ^{13} IGI *ta-ri-ba-tum* DUB.SAR ^{14} ⌜ITU⌝ *Šabāṭim*(ZÍZ.A) UD.27.KAM ^{15} MU *am-mi-di-ta-na* LUGAL.E ^{d}URAŠ UR.SAG GAL.LA$^{?}$

Ištēn šiqil kaspum — šīm šalāšat šuginê ša bīt Šamaš — esiḫti Mār-ešrîm u Warad-Sîn mārī Ēṭirum. Qāti Mār-ešrîm u Warad-Sîn nasḫā-ma, Sîn-nādin-šumī mār Šamaš-muballiṭ šalāšat šuginê ana ūmim ḫamiššerîm ‹ub›balam. Ul ubbalam-ma, ištēn šiqil kaspam išaqqal. Maḫar Tarībatum ṭupšarrim. Waraḫ Šabāṭim, ūmam ešrā sebet, šanat Ammiditana šarrum ana Uraš qarrādim rabîm ...

One shekel of silver — the value of three sheep-offerings of the temple of Shamash — is the assignment of Mār-ešrîm and Warad-Sîn sons of Ēṭirum The claim of Mār-ešrîm and Warad-Sîn is withdrawn, and Sîn-nādin-šumī son of Šamaš-muballiṭ will bring the three sheep-offerings on the fifteenth day. If he does not bring (them), he will pay one shekel of silver. Before Tarībatum the scribe. Month of Šabāṭum, day 27, year Ammiditana the king to Uraš the great warrior ... (i.e., Ammiditana year 27).

LESSON TWENTY-FOUR

C.
1. É ^{d}EN.ZU
2. LÚ.KÚR-*šu*
3. BÀD URU-*ni*
4. *ta-sa-(ad)-dar* / *da-ar*
5. LÚ.MEŠ
6. ^{I}DUMU-*eš*$_{4}$-*tár*
7. GÌR $^{(giš)}$GU.ZA
8. EME KUR/KALAM
9. 2 BÁN ŠE
10. IGI.4.GÁL *te-er-ḫa-tim* / *ti-im*
11. Ì(.GIŠ) $^{(lú)}$ŠU.ḪA
12. ZAG ZÉ
13. MURUB$_{4}$ GÌR.PAD.DU-*ša*
14. GÙB UDU
15. 5 GÍN KUG.SIG$_{17}$

D.
1. *zakât*
2. *izakku*
3. *uzakkāši*
4. *zukkât*
5. *bullissi*
6. *kilallīšunu tumalla*(/*tamla*)
7. *išātum qurrubet* / *ṭuḫḫât*
8. *muḫaddi iltīšu*
9. *uptaḫḫeraššunūti*
10. *lidammiqū(nin)niāti* / *-niāšim*
11. *ittaṣiānim*
12. *aḫam ayy-iddû*
13. *wardum ša tuḫalliqu*
14. *altawīšu* / *assaḫuršu*
15. *dūram kullimāninni*
16. *tabāl terḫatim ul elē* / *elʾe*
17. *ilum mutakkilki* / *ilum ša utakkalūki*
18. *tībam limdī*
19. *nišū kunnušā* / *nišī ukannišū*
20. *munâšunūti*
21. *nārum ruppuštum*
22. *ṭupšarram udannim-ma utammi*
23. *nussaḫḫeršu*
24. *uqerribūniššunūti*
25. *lā unakkaršu*
26. *tēteliam*
27. *bulussu* / *balāssu* / *napištašu ulabbarū*
28. *lupaššiḫšu*
29. *šūt-rēšīšu ukabbit*
30. *ulammassināti*

E.
1. *tabnâni* 'you (pl) built for me' ‹ *tabniānim* or *tabnânni* 'you (ms) built me' ‹ *tabnianni*
2. *ilqâ* 'they (f) took'‹ *ilqeā* or 'he took for me' ‹ *ilqeam*
3. *arda maḫrâ arâb* 'I will give back the previous slave' ‹ *wardam maḫriam arīab*
4. *awâtīya nasqāti šemâ* 'hear (ms Vent. or pl) my choice words' ‹ *awâtīya nasqātim šemeā* / *šemeam*
5. *ṭēmu* / *ṭēmū ša tašpura* / *tašpurā* 'the report/reports that you (ms) sent me/you (pl) sent' ‹ *ṭēmum* / *ṭēmū ša tašpuram* / *tašpurā*
6. *ana šarrati rabīti* 'for the great queen' ‹ *ana šarratim rabītim*
7. *ana šarrāti rabâti* 'for the great queens' ‹ *ana šarrātim rabiātim*
8. *lemuttu imqutam-ma aštaprakku* 'evil befell me and so I have written to you (ms)' ‹ *lemuttum imqutam-ma aštaprakkum*

F.
1. *rēdû u bāʾerū lēʾûtum ištu erṣetim qerubtim urradūnim-ma ṣābī aḫûtim ša ištu šadî ītiqū inerrū.* Able footsoldiers and "fishermen" will come down from a nearby land and slay the foreign troops who have crossed from the mountains.

2. *warki ḫāwirīya rubātum kunukka šīpātim u šeššet kur âm ana šeriktim išruka.* After the death of my husband, the princess gave me a seal, wool, and six kor of grain as a gift.
3. *šumma appi lišān kalbim nakis bīt awīlim imaqqut-ma ul ibannīšu.* If the tip of a dog's tongue is cut off, the man's house will fall and he will not (re-)build it.
4. *mamman lēt aḫātīya imḫaṣ-ma šinnīša iddi inanna šumma tarammanni têrta šukum-ma awīlam šuāti ṣubbit-ma ina ṣibitti idīšu u meḫer ṭuppīya šupra.* Someone struck my sister's cheek and knocked out her teeth; now if you (ms) love me give instructions, and seize that man and throw him in prison; further, send me a copy of my tablet.
5. *muḫḫi qarrādim u qablāšu marṣū u ubānāt rittīšu ša šumēlim šebrā.* The warrior's skull and hips are sore; and the fingers of his left hand are broken.

G. 190 *šumma awīlum ṣeḫram ša ana mārūtīšu ilqûšū-ma urabbûšu itti mārīšu lā imtanūšu, tarbītum šī ana bīt abīšu itâr.* If a man did not include among his children a youngster whom he had adopted and raised, that adopted child may return to his father's house.

192 *šumma mār gerseqqêm ū lū mār sekretim ana abim murabbīšu ū ummim murabbītīšu "ul abī atta; ul ummī atti" iqtabi, lišāššu inakkisū.* If a domestic's son or a *sekretum*'s son has said to the father who raised him or the mother who raised him, "you are not my father; you are not my mother," his tongue will be cut off.

215–217 215 *šumma asûm awīlam simmam kabtam ina karzil siparrim īpuš-ma awīlam ubtallit ū lū nakkapti awīlim ina karzil siparrim iptē-ma īn awīlim ubtallit, eš(e)ret šiqil kaspam ileqqe.* 216 *šumma mār muškēnim, ḫamšat šiqil kaspam ileqqe.* 217 *šumma warad awīlim, bēl wardim ana asîm šinā šiqil kaspam inaddin.* 215 If a physician treated a man for a serious wound with a bronze lancet, and has saved the man, or else opened a man's temple with a bronze lancet, and has saved the man's eye, he will receive ten shekels of silver. 216 If (it is) a member of the *muškēnum* class, he will receive five shekels of silver. 217 If (it is) a man's slave, the slave's owner will give the physician two shekels of silver.

221 *šumma asûm eṣemti awīlim šebertam uštallim ū lū šerʾānam marṣam ubtallit, bēl simmim ana asîm ḫamšat šiqil kaspam inaddin.* If a physician has repaired a man's broken bone or has healed a sore tendon, the patient (lit., "owner of the wound") will give the physician five shekels of silver.

122 *šum-ma a-wi-lum a-na a-wi-lim* KUG.BABBAR KUG.SIG17 *ù mi-im-ma šum-šu a-na ma-ṣa-ru-tim i-na-ad-di-in mi-im-ma ma-la i-na-ad-di-nu ši-bi ú-kál-lam ri-ik-sa-tim i-ša-ak-ka-an-ma a-na ma-ṣa-ru-tim i-na-ad-di-in.*

šumma awīlum ana awīlim kaspam ḫurāṣam ū mimma šumšu ana maṣṣarūtim inaddin, mimma mala inaddinu šībī ukallam riksātim išakkam-ma ana maṣṣarūtim inaddin. If a man wishes to give silver, gold, or anything to a man for safekeeping, he will show whatever he would give to witnesses, make out contracts, and then he may give (it) for safekeeping.

138 *šum-ma a-wi-lum ḫi-ir-ta-šu ša* DUMU.MEŠ *la ul-du-šum i-iz-zi-ib* KUG.BABBAR *ma-la ter-ḫa-ti-ša i-na-ad-di-iš-ši-im ù še-ri-ik-tam ša iš-tu* É *a-bi-ša ub-lam ú-ša-lam-ši-im-ma i-iz-zi-ib-ši.*

šumma awīlum ḫīrtašu ša mārī lā uldūšum izzib, kaspam mala terḫatīša inaddiššim u šeriktam ša ištu bīt abīša ublam ušallamšimma izzibši. If a man wishes to divorce his wife who has not born him children, he will give her as much silver as her bride-price, and also repay to her the dowry that she brought from her father's house, and then he may divorce her.

196–199 196 *šum-ma a-wi-lum i-in* DUMU *a-wi-lim úḫ-tap-pí-id i-in-šu ú-ḫa-ap-pa-du* 197 *šum-ma* GÌR.PAD.DU *a-wi-lim iš-te-bé-er* GÌR.PAD.DU-*šu i-še-eb-bé-ru* 198 *šum-ma i-in* MAŠ.EN.GAG *úḫ-tap-pí-id ù lu* GÌR.PAD.DU MAŠ.EN.GAG *iš-te-bé-er* 1 MA.NA KUG.BABBAR *i-ša-qal* 199 *šum-ma i-in* ÌR *a-wi-lim úḫ-tap-pí-id ù lu* GÌR.PAD.DU ÌR *a-wi-lim iš-te-bé-er mi-ši-il* ŠÁM-*šu i-ša-qal.*

196 *šumma awīlum īn mār awīlim uḫtappid, īššu uḫappadū.* 197 *šumma eṣemti awīlim išteber, eṣemtašu išebberū.* 198 *šumma īn muškēnim uḫtappid ū lū eṣemti muškēnim išteber, ištēn manā kaspam išaqqal.* 199 *šumma īn warad awīlim uḫtappid ū lū eṣemti warad awīlim išteber, mišil šīmīšu išaqqal.* 196 If a man has blinded the eye of a member of the *awīlum* class, his eye will be blinded. 197 If he has broken a man's bone, his bone will be broken. 198 If he has blinded a *muškēnum*'s eye or has broken a *muškēnum*'s bone, he will weigh out one mina of silver. 199 If he has blinded the eye of a man's slave or has broken the bone of a man's slave, he will weigh out half his value.

H. 1. *šumma padānū šinā, ālik ḫarrā[ni]m ḫarrāššu [i]kaššad.* If the paths are two, the expeditionary force will reach its goal.

2. *šumma padānum adi šalāšīšu purrus, ālik ḫarrānim ḫarrānum ana ḫarrānim inaddiššu / inaddīšu, ūmūšu iriqqū.* If the path is separated into three parts, the road will give/throw the expeditionary force to (still another) road, (so that) its days will be empty.

3. *šumma maṣraḫ martim kunnuš, šarrum nakrum ana šarrim ikannuš.* If the cystic duct of the gall bladder is bent, a foreign king will bow down to the king.

4. *šum-ma mar-tum ap-pa-ša a-na* KÁ É.GAL-*im ša-ki-in ṭa-ar!*(RI)-*du-ú-um ša ku-uš-šu-du a-na* URU-*li-šu i-ta-ar.*

šumma martum appaša ana bāb ekallim šakin, ṭardum ša kuššudu ana ālīšu itâr. If the tip of the gall bladder is located at the palace gate, an exile who was chased out will return to his town.

5. DIŠ *iz-bu-um qá-qá-as-su ka-a-a-nu-um ša-ki-in-ma ù ša-nu-um i-na i-mi-tim ša-ki-in ti-bu-um ka-aš-du-um* LÚ.KÚR-*ka ma-at-ka ú-ḫa-al-la-aq.*

šumma izbum qaqqassu kayyānum šakim-ma u šanûm ina imittim šakin, tībum kašdum, nakerka mātka uḫallaq. If the normal head of the foetus is in place, but there is also a second located on the right, a successful attack: your enemy will destroy your land.

I. 1. *Ana aplūt Tabni-Eštar mārat Nabi-Sîn. Bēlessunu mārat Nūr-ilīšu aḫīša. Adi Tabni-Eštar balṭat Bēlessunu Tabni-Eštar ipallaḫ, ukabbassi. Šumma (iplaḫši), bītum ša gagîm u bušêša mala ibaššû (ina gagîm) ša Bēlessunu. Nīš(i) Šamaš Marduk u Sumu-la-il ša pī ṭuppim annîm unakkaru.*

Concerning the estate of Tabni-Eštar daughter of Nabi-Sîn. Bēlessunu is the daughter of Nūr-ilīšu her brother. As long as Tabni-Eštar is alive, Bēlessunu will revere Tabni-Eštar (and) honor her. If (she reveres her), the estate of the *gagûm,* however much there is (in the *gagûm*) belongs to Bēlessunu. The oath of Šamaš, Marduk, and Sumu-la-il (is upon) whoever alters the wording of this tablet. (Witnesses.)

J. 2. *Ana Nabium-atpalam qibī-ma; umma Bēlānum-ma. Šamaš u Marduk liballiṭūka. Lū balṭāta, lū [š]almāta. Ana šu[lm]īya tašpura[m]; ša[l]māku. Šalāmka ana dāriātim Marduk liqbi. Ištu inanna šinā ūmī anāku ana Sippar allakam. Aššum ṣuḫārê ša tašpuram: ana Mār-Šamaš aštapram, inaddinakkum.*

Speak to Nabium-ataplam; thus Bēlānum. May Šamaš and Marduk keep you in good health. Be healthy, be well. You wrote about my well-being; I am well. May Marduk command/proclaim your wellness forever. Two days from now I myself am coming to Sippar. Concerning the servants about whom you wrote me: I have written to Mār-Šamaš to give (or, (and) he will give) (them) to you.

3. *Ana Sîn-erībam qibī-ma; umma Tarībatum. Mišil šiqil kaspam ana Būratum idin.*

Speak to Sîn-erībam; thus Tarībatum. Give half a shekel of silver to Būratum.

4. *Ana Ibbi-Sîn ša Marduk uballaṭu qibī-ma; u[mm]a Attâ-ma. Šamaš u Marduk aššumīya liballiṭūka. Anumma Tarībatum aṭṭardakkum. Ištēn šiqil kaspam itti aḫīka amra[m]-ma šūbilam. Ina annītim atḫūtka [l]ūmur.*

Speak to Ibbi-Sîn whom Marduk keeps in good health; thus Attâ. May Šamaš and Marduk keep you in good health for my sake. I have herewith sent you Tarībatum. From your brother (or, a brother of yours) find and send me one shekel of silver. Let me see/experience your brotherly attitude in this matter.

5. *[A]na Šamaš-magir qibī-ma; umma Sîn-muballiṭ-ma. Šamaš liballiṭka. Aššum ṭēm Igmil-Sîn mār Kukšik[ad]a ša tašpuram: ana Igmil-Sîn kiam šupur-[ma], umma attā-ma: "ṭuppam ana ṣēr bēlīya uštābil; ṭēm bēlī išapparam ašapparakkum."*

Speak to Šamaš-magir; thus Sîn-muballiṭ. May Šamaš keep you in good health. Concerning the report of Igmil-Sîn son of Kukšikada about which you wrote me: write to Igmil-Sîn as follows: "I have dispatched a tablet to my lord; I will write to you the news my lord writes to me."

6. ^{1} *[a-na]* ^{d}EN.ZU-*i-din-nam* ^{2} *[qí]-bí-ma* ^{3} *um-ma ḫa-am-ur-ra-pí-ma* ^{4} *aš-šum* ^{Id}EN.ZU-*ra-bi ša it-ti* ^{I}*nu-úr-eš*$_{4}$*-t[ár]* ^{5} *ta-aṭ-ru-da-aš-šu* ^{6} ^{Id}EN.ZU-*ra-bi šu-a-ti* ^{7} *a-na ma-aḫ-ri-ia ú-še-ri-bu-nim-ma* ^{8} *aš-šum i-din-*^{d}EN.ZU ^{9} *ú-lam-mi-da-an-ni* ^{10} *a-nu-um-ma* ^{d}EN.ZU-*ra-bi šu-a-ti* ^{11} *a-na ṣe-ri-ka aṭ-ṭar-dam* ^{12} ^{I}*i-din-*^{d}E[N.ZU] ^{13} *ù* ^{lú}*ši-i-bi ša i-qá-ab-bu-kum* ^{14} *a-na ma-aḫ-ri-ia* ^{15} *ṭú-ur-dam.*

[Ana] Sîn-iddinam [qi]bī-ma; umma Ḫammurapī-ma. Aššum Sîn-rabi ša itti Nūr-Ešt[ar] taṭrudaššu: Sîn-rabi šuāti ana maḫrīya ušēribūnim-ma aššum Iddin-Sîn ulammidanni. Anumma Sîn-rabi šuāti ana ṣērīka aṭṭardam. Iddin-S[în] u šībī ša iqabbûkum ana maḫrīya ṭurdam.

Speak to Sîn-iddinam; thus Ḫammurapi. Concerning Sîn-rabi whom you sent to me with Nūr-Eštar: said Sîn-rabi was brought in before me and informed me about Iddin-Sîn. I have herewith sent said Sîn-rabi to you. Send before me Iddin-Sîn and the witnesses he mentions to you.

LESSON TWENTY-FIVE

C.

1. AGA ^{d}INANNA
2. *tu-kúl / ku-ul-ti*
3. *i-ša-(ak-)kán / ka-an*
4. GÌR.PAD.DU ZAG
5. ÁB.GUD.HI.A UM.MI.A
6. ÍD KÚR
7. (É.)Ì.DUB (ŠE.)NUMUN
8. EME KÚR
9. *ú-ták / ta(-ak)-ki-il / il$_5$*

D.

1. *nuwattaršu*
2. *ūteddissi*
3. *napištašu / balāssu / bulussu urrikā*
4. *wuššurū*
5. *mārī mādūtim uwallissum*
6. *hurāṣam ṭābam uhhuz*
7. *ahī / idī lummissu(m)*
8. *nišū bēlī kâta ulliā(ka)*
9. *uwatterāšu*
10. *ellet / ebbet; ullulet / ubbubet*
11. *ilam kaspam tuhhazī*
12. *lā tunnašīšunūti*
13. *nūtellīšunūti*
14. *ul uwaššerāšu*
15. *rubûm mulli rēšī bīt ilim* (or, *rubûm ša rēšī bīt ilim ullû*)
16. *šum(i) iltim muwallitti kalîšunu lulli* (or, *šum(i) iltim ša kalâšunu uwallidu lulli*)
17. *suhhur kišādīya ul ele*ʾʾ*i / elê*
18. *kīma niāti*
19. *kīma kunūti u kīma yâti*
20. *ana kâšim*

E.

1. PN warad nadīt Šamaš ana mīnim takla? ul mār awīlim šū; warad nadīt Šamaš wuššer-ma nadīt Šamaš šarram lā imahhar; ana awīlim ul walid; ummašu amat nadīt Šamaš; ana mīnim ana rēdî tašṭuršu? Why did you (ms) detain PN the slave of the nadītum of Šamaš? He is not a member of the awīlum class; release the slave of the nadītum of Šamaš, lest the nadītum of Šamaš approach the king. He was not born to an awīlum; his mother is the slave of a nadītum of Šamaš. Why did you assign him to the rēdûms?
2. PN ša eqelšu ana PN2 imqutu kiam iqbīkum umma šū-ma: "ū lū yâti *itti eqlim ana* PN$_2$ *liddinūninni ū lū pūh eqlīya liddinūnim."* PN whose field "fell" to PN$_2$ said to you (ms) as follows: "Either I should be given to PN$_2$ along with the field or a substitute field should be given me."
3. *kâta u ahāka mannum uwaššerkunūtī-ma ina bīt abīni tattašbā-ma ilikni tuhtalliqā? šumi ilīkunu u mutakkilīkunu ša kâta u ahāka ana bīt abīni irdû lihliq.* Who released your (ms) brother and you, that you (pl) have taken up residence in our father's estate and destroyed our *ilkum*? May the name of your (pl) god and your supporter, who led your brother and you to our father's estate, perish.
4. *lū šalmāta šulumka šupram; aššum eqlim ša idi bītīka: mišil eqlim yâšim u mišil eqlim ana kâšum; u aššum êm kêm ša ašpurakkum: âm ana mamman la tanaddin.* Be (ms) well; send me (news of) your well-being. Concerning the field beside your house: half of the field is mine and half of the field is yours. And concerning the grain of yours, about which I wrote you: do not give the grain to anyone.
5. *šumma lupputātunu mār šiprīkunu ṭurdānim-ma ṣuhārkunu lilqe.* If

you (pl) are delayed, send me your messenger to take your servant.

6. *Adad ša šumšu ullû zēr(i) šarrūtim ša lemnim šâtu lidīm-ma liḫalliq*. May Adad, whose name is exalted, judge and destroy the royal seed of that evil one (m).
7. *ina mārī* PN *zikarim u sinništim mamman lā igerreanni u mamman kaspam lā issiranni*. Among the children of PN, male and female, no one may sue me and no one may press me for payment.
8. *ina qibīt šarrim zikaram ayyamma ina ālim šâtu idūkū / idukkū*. By the command of the king they (m) killed/will kill some male in that town.
9. *aḫātī kiam ulammidanni umma šī-ma: "inanna bītī ḫulluq; mīnum šubtī?"* My sister informed me as follows: "Now my house is destroyed; what is my home?"
10. *ummiānni ul imūt bulṭam ikšud inanna liātīni ša nukallimūka u âm ša ina našpakim nišpuku īteršanniāti*. Our money lender did not die; he regained (his) health. Now he has asked us for our cattle that we showed you (ms) and the grain that we stored in the granary.
11. *nakrū ina tībim šuāti eṣmētim ša ḫīrtīya išberū u mārīni ussirū-ma ina ṣabtūtīšunu imnû-ma šubatni iqqurū*. In that attack the enemy broke my wife's bones; they also took our children captive and included them among their prisoners and destroyed our residence.

F. 1 *šumma awīlum awīlam ubbir-ma nērtam elīšu iddī-ma lā uktīššu, mubbiršu iddâk*. If a man accused a man and laid (a charge of) murder against him but has not convicted him, his accuser will be executed.

47 *šumma errēšum aššum ina šattim maḫrītim mānaḫātīšu lā ilqû eqlam erēšam iqtabi* (or, *"eqlam errišam" iqtabi*), *bēl eqlim ul uppas; errēssū-ma eqelšu irriš-ma ina ebūrim kīma riksātīšu âm ileqqe*. If a tenant farmer, because he did not receive (the wages of) his labors in the previous year, has said he would plow the field (again) (or, has said, "I will plow the field (again)'), the owner of the field will not object; that very tenant farmer of his may plow his field, and he will receive grain at the harvest according to his contract(s).

121 *šumma awīlum ina bīt awīlim âm išpuk ina šanat ana ištēn kur êm ḫamšat qa âm idī našpakim inaddin*. If a man stored grain at a man's estate, he will give five *qûm* of grain as the (rental) cost of the granary per year for each kor of grain.

226 *šumma gallābum balum bēl wardim abbutti wardim lā šêm ugallib, ritti gallābim šuāti inakkisū*. If a barber shaved the hair of a slave that was not his without the slave-owner's permission, that barber's hand will be cut off.

254 *šumma aldâm ilqē-ma liātim ūtenniš, ta*[*š*]*na âm ša imḫuru irīab*. If he took a store of barley and so weakend the cattle, he will replace the grain he got doubly.

2 *šum-ma a-wi-lum ki-iš-pí e-li a-wi-lim id-di-ma la uk-ti-in-šu ša e-li-šu ki-iš-pu na-du-ú a-na* ^{d}ÍD *i-il-la-ak* ^{d}ÍD *i-ša-al-li-a-am-ma šum-ma* ^{d}ÍD *ik-ta-ša-sú mu-ub-bi-ir-šu* É*-sú i-tab-ba-al šum-ma a-wi-lam šu-a-ti* ^{d}ÍD *ú-te-eb-bi-ba-aš-šu-ma iš-ta-al-ma-am ša e-li-šu ki-iš-pí id-du-ú id-da-ak ša* ^{d}ÍD *iš-li-a-am* É *mu-ub-bi-ri-šu i-tab-ba-al*.

šumma awīlum kišpī eli awīlim iddī-ma lā uktīššu, ša elīšu kišpū nadû ana Id illak; Id išalliam-ma šumma Id iktašassu mubbiršu bīssu itabbal; šumma awīlam šuāti Id ūtebbibaššū-ma ištalmam, ša elīšu kišpī iddû iddâk; ša Id išliam bīt mubbirīšu itabbal. If a man laid a charge of witchcraft against a man but has not convicted him, the one against whom the witchcraft charge was laid will go to the River; he will dive into the River, and if the River has defeated him, his accuser will take away his estate; if the River has cleared that man and he has come out alright, the one who laid the witchcraft charge against him will be executed; the one who dove into the River will take away the estate of his accuser.

G. 1. *šumma šīrum ina šumēl ubānim kīma ṭulīmim šakin, māt nakrim tusannaq; ašar ištēn tupaḫḫarši.* If the flesh is situated on the left of the finger like the spleen, you (ms) will control the enemy land; you will gather it into one place.

2. *šumma bāb ekallim sunnuq, i[n]a kakkim nakrum ummānam ussar; ūmam rēqam šatammū ekallam usannaqū.* If the palace gate is closed, the enemy will enclose the army by weapon; the clerks will control the palace some time.

3. *šumma immerum ina libbi lišānīšu šīrum napiḫ-ma ana imittim u šumēlim [k]apiṣ, ayyumma ana šarrim itebbē-ma ussaršū-ma [idâk]šu.* If (a piece of) flesh is visible/swollen within the sheep's tongue and is curled to the right and the left, someone will rise up against the king, take him captive and kill him.

4. *šumma izbum šinnāšu waṣâ, šarrum um[ūšu] gamrū; ina kussīšu šanûm uš[š]ab.* If the anomaly's teeth are protruding, the king's days are over; on his throne another will sit.

5. *šum-ma na-ap-la-aš-tum re-sa ip-ṭú-ur i-na re-eš* A.ŠÀ-*im um-ma-na-am i-lu-ša i-zi-bu-ši i-na* gišTUKUL-*im mi-qí-it-ti a-li-ik pa-ni um-ma-ni-ia.*

šumma naplaštum rēssa ipṭur, ina rēš eqlim ummānam ilūša izzibūši; ina kakkim miqitti ālik pānī ummānīya. If the top of the lobe became loose, its gods will abandon the army at (its) destination; the downfall of the leader of my army by weapon.

H. 1. *Ṣillī-Ištar u Irībam-Sîn tappûtam īpušū. Ana tazkītim dayyānī ikšudū-ma, ana bīt Šamaš īrubū-ma ina bīt Šamaš ummiānam īpulū-ma, ištēn wardum Luštamar-Šamaš išteat amtum Lišlimam zītti Irībam-Sîn; ištēn wardum Ibši-(i)na-ilim išteat amtum Geštinanna-lamassī zītti Ṣillī-Ištar. Zīzū. Ina bītim Šamaš u Sîn izkurū. Aḫum ana aḫim ubbibū. Aḫum aḫam lā iturrū lā igerrû; eli mimma ša aḫum ana aḫim irgumū mimma ul īšû.*

Ṣillī-Ištar and Irībam-Sîn had formed a partnership. Having approached the judges for a dissolution, they entered the Šamaš temple, and in the Šamaš temple they paid the money lender. One male slave, Luštamar-Šamaš (and) one female slave, Lišlimam, are Irībam-Sîn's share; one male slave, Ibši-(i)na-ilim (and) one female slave, Geštinanna-lamassī, are Ṣillī-Ištar's share. They have made the division. In the temple they swore (an oath) by Šamaš and Sîn. They cleared one another; they will not sue one another again; they have no claim to whatever they might have demanded of one another. (Witnesses. Date.)

I. 1. *Ana awīlim ša Marduk uballaṭ[ūš]u qibī-ma; umma Nanna-ibila-mansum-ma. Šamaš u Marduk dāriš ūmī aḫī kâta liballiṭūka. Lū šalmāta. Aššum (ištēn) pān šittā sât ḫamšat qa (êm) ša maḫrīka ēzibu: ištēt sât ḫamšat qa âm ruddī-ma (ištēn) pān erbet(ti) sât âm mullī-ma ana Šallurum idin. Ana zērim ḫašiḫ. Lā takallāšu; arḫiš idiššu. Idam lā tušaršâm-ma lā tašapparam.*

Speak to the man whom Marduk keeps healthy; thus Nanna-ibila-mansum. May Šamaš and Marduk keep you, my brother, healthy forever. Be well. Concerning the 85 *qûm* that I left with you: add 15 *qûm* of grain and give the full 100 *qûm* of grain to Šallurum. He is in need of seed grain. Do not withold it; give it quickly. Do not raise objections by writing to me.

2. [1] *a-na ip-qú-*^{d}IŠKUR [2] *qí-bí-ma* [3] *um-ma ri-im-*^{d}EN.ZU-EN.ḪAL.MAḪ-*ma* [4] *aš-šum* ⸢*ṣa-ab*⸣*-rum* [5] *ù* ^{d}EN.ZU-*ḫa-zi-ir* [6] *ṣú-ḫa-ru-ú iu-ú-tu-un* [7] *mi-im-ma i-na qá-ti-šu-nu-ú* [8] *ú-ul ṣa-bi-it* [9] *wa-ar-ka-sú-nu pu-ru-us-ma* [10] *wu-še-er-šu-nu-ti.*

Ana Ipqu-Adad qibī-ma; umma Rīm-Sîn-Enḫalmaḫ-ma. Aššum Ṣabrum u Sîn-ḫāzir: ṣuḫārû yûttun; mimma ina qātīšunu ul ṣabit. Warkassunu purus-ma wuššeršunūti.

Speak to Ipqu-Adad; thus Rīm-Sîn-Enḫalmaḫ. Concerning Ṣabrum and Sîn-ḫāzir: the servants are mine; nothing was found (lit., seized) in their possession. Look into their situation and then release them.

LESSON TWENTY-SIX

C.
1. GÌR NA.RU-*ia*
2. MURUB$_4$ ZÉ
3. ^{d}INANNA *li-ner / ne-er / né-er-šu*
4. *ú-tir / ti(-ir)-ru*
5. *uk-ta(-aṣ)-ṣir / ṣi-ir / ṣí-ir*
6. KA ÍD
7. (ŠE.)NUMUN Ú *li-ter / te-er*
8. ÁB.GUD.ḪI.A É.GI$_4$/GI.A
9. KASKAL LUGAL

D.
1. *inūma / ūm / kīma ana dūr ālim tarkabu, mīnam / minâm tešme?*
2. *lāma terḫatam taqiššu / taqīšu / tašarraku / tašruku // adi terḫatam lā taqiššu / taqīšu / tašarraku / tašruku, ul taḫḫassi.*
3. *inūma / ūm / kīma eṭlum šū irabbû, mātam kalâša ukannaš.*
4. *ištu / kīma šībī wuššuru, utammāšu.*
5. *ina īdû narâka ul unakker.*
6. *inūma / ūm / kīma īteliam, qurribāniššu.*
7. *apāl ummiānīšu ul ilē.*
8. *zikarī mādūtim uwallid.*

E.
1. *kīma tīdû ebūrum qerub itti ṣuḫārīya alkam-ma warkat abīni i nizūz.* As you (ms) know, the harvest is near; come with my servant that we may divide our father's inheritance.
2. *ana rēš warḫim šipram šuāti igammarū.* They (m) will finish that work at the beginning of the month.
3. *šumma nēmettani ištēn manā kaspam imaṣṣi ana dayyānī i nillik-ma kīma qibītīšunu i nīpuš.* If our tax amounts to one mina of silver, let us go to the judges and act according to their command.
4. *am-mīnim purussâm ša asîm lā tugammeram-ma lā tašpuram.* Why did you (ms) not write to me fully about the case of the physician?
5. *anumma ṭuppī ina qāt aḫīya kīma aqbûkum aštaprakkum kunukkīšu šalmūtim aḫī kullim-ma wuššeršū-ma lisniqam.* I have now sent you (ms) my tablet in my brother's care, as I promised you. Show my brother his documents intact, and release him that he may come here.
6. *kīma eṭlum šū lā ṣeḫrū-ma rabû lū tīde; kīma awīlê aḫḫīšu eqlam u karānam apulšu; kīma tātaplūšu meḫer ṭuppīya šupram.* Know (ms) that said youth is not young but grown up; pay him a field and an orchard like his *awīlum* brothers; when you have paid him, send me a copy of my tablet.
7. *inūma mār(ū)ka kaspam ana awīlim iddinu ina maḫrīya iddin; u anāku awâtim īde. šumma ana bīt ilim išapparūninni apālam ul eleʾʾi; atta kīma teleʾʾû epuš. šumma ina êm ša tašāmu kaspam tīšu kunkaššū-ma ana yâšim idnam-ma itti kaspim yêm lumnūšu.* When your (ms) son gave the man the silver, he gave (it) in my presence; so I myself know the situation (matters). If I am sent to the temple, I will not be able to pay/answer; you do what you can (as you are able). If you have silver (left) from the grain you purchased, give it to me under seal that I may include it with my own silver.

8. *am-mīnim kīma ša ummān nakrim iṭeḫḫûkum tapallaḫ?* Why are you (ms) afraid, as if the enemy army were approaching you?
9. *ištu ina ālim wašbāku mamman ul utammianni.* Since I have been resident in the city, no one has adjured me.
10. *kīma ašpurakkum liātim aṭarradakkum; aḫka lā tanaddi; ṭēmam gamram šupram-ma liātim luṭrudakkum.* As I wrote you (ms) I will send you cattle; do not be negligent; send me a complete report that I may send you the cattle.
11. *kīma ṭuppī tammaru eleppam puṭram-ma liṣbatanni u adi pānīya tammaru immerātim lā tapaššar.* As soon as you (ms) see my tablet, dispatch a boat to get me; and until you see me in person (see my face), do not sell the sheep.
12. *ištu allikam ina ālim šuāti anāku; eli ayyimma âm ul īšu; ištu inanna ḫamšat ūmī wardī âm ubbalakkum; libbaka mimma lā imarraṣ. u ṭēm* PN *idnam amuršū-ma ṭēmāšu šupram; kīma tātamrūšu kiam qibīšum umma attā-ma: "bēlka ṭēmka lilmad."* Since I came I have been in this city; I am owed grain by no one; five days from now my slave will bring grain to you (ms); do not be upset. Further, give me PN's report; find him and send me his report; as soon as you have found him, speak to him as follows: "you lord would know your report."
13. *nīnu bītam anniam lāma bēlni urradam ištu ešrā šanātim niṣbat; inanna awīlû aḫûtum bīt(ā)ni ibtaqrūniāti; bēlni warkatni liprus.* We took possession of this estate twenty years before our lord came down here; now foreign men have sued us for our estate; may our lord look into our case.
14. *kīma ana ālim asniqu erbet(ti) ūmī ulappit-ma tappê aṭṭardam; kiriam kullimšu.* When I came to the town I tarried four days, and so have sent my partner; show (ms) him the orchard.
15. *ištu asûm eṣemti rubêm išberu lišāššu ikkisū.* After the physician broke the prince's bone, his tongue was cut out.
16. *zikarum šū ina puḫur ālim litmā-ma inūma itammû ṭēmam šupram-ma purussâm lū īde; aḫka lā tanaddi.* That man must swear in the town assembly; when he swears send (ms) me news that I may know the decision; do not be negligent.

F. 102 *šumma tamkārum ana šamallêm kaspam ana tadmiqtim ittadim-ma ašar illiku bitiqtam ītamar, qaqqad kaspim ana tamkārim utār.* If a merchant gave silver to an agent as an advance, but he has suffered (seen) a loss wherever he went, he will return the principal of the silver to the merchant.

114–115 114 *šumma awīlum eli awīlim âm u kaspam lā īšū-ma nipûssu ittepe, ana nipûtim ištiat šalšat manā kaspam išaqqal.* 115 *šumma awīlum eli awīlim âm u kaspam īšū-ma nipûssu ippē-ma nipûtum ina bīt nēpīša ina šīmātīša imtūt, dīnum šū rugummâm ul īšu.* 114 If a man was not owed grain or silver by a man, but has distrained a pledge of his, he will weigh out one-third mina of silver for each pledge. 115 If a man was owed grain or silver by a man and distrained a pledge of his and the pledge has died of natural causes in her/his distrainer's house, that case has no claim.

170–171 170 *šumma awīlum ḫīrtašu mārī ulissum u amassu mārī ulissum, abum ina bulṭīšu ana mārī ša amtum uldūšum "mārūya" iqtabi, itti mārī ḫīrtim imtanūšunūti; warka abum ana šīmtim ittalku ina makkūr bīt abim mārū ḫīrtim u mārū amtim mitḫāriš izuzzū; aplum mār(i) ḫīrtim ina zīttim inassaq-ma ileqqe.* 171 *u šumma abum ina bulṭīšu ana mārī ša amtum uldūšum "mārūya" lā iqtabi, warka abum ana šīmtim ittalku ina makkūr bīt abim mārū amtim itti mārī ḫīrtim ul izuzzū; andurār amtim u mārīša iššakkan; mārū ḫīrtim ana mārī amtim ana wardūtim ul iraggumū; ḫīrtum šeriktaša u nudunnâm ša mussa iddinūšim ina ṭuppim išṭurūšim ileqqē-ma ina šubat mutīša uššab; adi balṭat ikkal; ana kaspim ul inaddin; warkassa ša mārīšā-ma.* 170 If a man's wife bore him children and his slave bore him children, (and) the father during his life said to the children that the slave bore him, "my children," he has included them with the children of the wife; after the father has passed on, the children of the wife and the children of the slave will share in the property of the paternal estate equally; the chief heir of the wife will take first choice of the inheritance. 171 But if the father during his life did not say to the children that the slave bore him, "my children," after the father has passed on, the children of the slave will not share with the children of the wife in the property of the paternal estate; the freedom of the slave and her children will be established; the children of the wife may not claim the children of the slave for slavery; the wife will take her dowry and the wedding gift that her husband gave her (and) registered in a document for her, and live in her husband's residence; she may use (it) as long as she is alive, (but) may not sell (it); her inheritance is her children's only.

182–184 182 *šumma abum ana mārtīšu nadīt Marduk ša Bābilim šeriktam la išrukšim kunukkam lā išṭuršim, warka abum ana šīmtim ittalku ina makkūr bīt abim šalušti aplūtīša itti aḫḫīša izâz-ma ilkam ul illak; nadīt Marduk warkassa ēma elīša ṭābu inaddin.* 183 *šumma abum ana mārtīšu šugītim šeriktam išrukšim ana mutim iddišši kunukkam išṭuršim, warka abum ana šīmtim ittalku ina makkūr bīt abim ul izâz.* 184 *šumma awīlum ana mārtīšu šugītim šeriktam lā išrukšim ana mutim lā iddišši, warka abum ana šīmtim ittalku aḫḫūša kīma emūq bīt abim šeriktam išarrakūšim-ma ana mutim inaddinūši.* 182 If a father did not give a dowry to his daughter, a *nadītum* of Marduk of Babylon and record (it) in a document for her, after the father has passed on, she receives as her share of the property of the paternal estate her one-third inheritance along with her brothers, but she will perform no *ilkum* service; a *nadītum* of Marduk may give her inheritance wherever it is pleasing to her. 183 If a father gave a dowry to his daughter, a junior wife, gave her to a husband, and wrote out a sealed document for her, after the father has passed on, she will not share in the property of the paternal estate. 184 If a man did not give a dowry to his daughter, a junior wife, and did not give her to a husband, after the father has passed on, her brothers will give her a dowry corresponding to the value of the paternal estate, and give her to a husband.

193 *šumma mār gerseqqêm ū lū mār sekretim bīt abīšu uweddī-ma abam murabbīšu u ummam murabbīssu izēr-ma ana bīt abīšu ittalak, īššu*

inassaḫū. If an attendant's son or a *sekretum*'s son, having recognized his family and hated the father who raised him and the mother who raised him, has gone to his family, his eye will be pulled out.

282 *šumma wardum ana bēlīšu "ul bēlī atta" iqtabi, kīma warassu ukāššū-ma bēlšu uzuššu inakkis.* If a slave has said to his owner, "you are not my owner," he will prove that (he is) his slave (lit., convict him, that (he is) his slave), and his owner may cut off his ear.

180 *šum-ma a-bu-um a-na* DUMU.MUNUS-*šu* LUKUR É.GI$_4$.A *ù lu sekretim* (^{mí}ZI.IK.RU.UM) *še-ri-ik-tam la iš-‹ru›-uk-ši-im wa-ar-ka a-bu-um a-na ši-im-tim it-ta-al-ku i-na* NÍG.GA É A.BA *zí-it-tam ki-ma ap-lim iš-te-en i-za-az-ma a-di ba-al-ṭa-at i-ik-ka-al wa-ar-ka-sà ša aḫ-ḫi-ša-ma.*

šumma abum ana mārtīšu nadītim kallatim ū lū sekretim šeriktam lā išrukšim, warka abum ana šīmtim ittalku ina makkūr bīt abim zīttam kīma aplim ištēn izâz-ma adi balṭat ikkal; warkassa ša aḫḫīšā-ma. If a father did not give a dowry to his daughter, a *nadītum*, a bride, or a *sekretum*, after the father has passed on, she will share in the property of the paternal estate like an individual heir and use (it) as long as she is alive; her inheritance belongs to her brothers only.

280 *šum-ma a-wi-lum i-na ma-at nu-ku-úr-tim* ÌR GEME$_2$ *ša a-wi-lim iš-ta-am i-nu-ma i-na li-ib-bu* KALAM *it-ta-al-kam-ma be-el* ÌR *ù lu* GEME$_2$ *lu* ÌR-*sú ù lu* GEME$_2$-*sú ú-te-ed-di šum-ma* ÌR *ù lu* GEME$_2$ *šu-nu* DUMU. MEŠ *ma-tim ba-lum* KUG.BABBAR-*ma an-du-ra-ar-šu-nu iš-ša-ak-ka-an.*

šumma awīlum ina māt nukurtim wardam amtam ša awīlim ištām, inūma ina libbu mātim ittalkam«-ma» bēl wardim ū lū amtim lū warassu ū lū amassu ūteddi, šumma wardum ū lū amtum šunu mārū mātim balum kaspim-ma andurāršunu iššakkan. If a man has bought a man's male or female slave in a foreign country, (and) when he has come into the country, the owner of the male or female slave has recognized his male or female slave, if those male or female slave(s) are natives of the country, their freedom will be established without any silver.

G. 1. *šumma ubān ḫašîm šaplītum ana šumēlim išḫiṭ-ma [ana?] ṣēr ḫašîm šumēlam ana pānīša īšu, šarrum erṣetam lā šattam qāssu ikaššad.* If the lower finger of the lung twitched to the left and has the left side before it toward the lung, the king will personally conquer a land not his.

2. *šumma martum laria[m] īšu, aššat šarrim zikaram ullad.* If the gall bladder has a branch, the king's wife will bear a male (child).

3. *šum-ma mar-tum* KIR(I)$_4$-*ša mu-ṣa-am la i-šu um-ma-an šar-ri-im i-na ḫa-ra-nim ṣú-mu-um i-ṣa-ab-ba-at.*

šumma martum appaša mūṣâm lā īšu, ummān šarrim ina ḫarrānim ṣūmum iṣabbat. If the tip of the gall bladder has no exit, thirst will seize the king's army on a campaign.

4. *šum-ma mar-tum ta-a-a-ra-tim i-šu-ú a-na šar-ri-im da-mi-iq.*

šumma martum tayyarātim īšu, ana šarrim damiq. If the gall bladder has coilings(?), it is good for the king.

H. 1. *Kalkal-muballiṭ mār Ayya-damqat Ayya-damqat nadīt Šamaš mārat Ilšu-ibbīšu ummašu ullilšu. Ana ṣīt šamši pānīšu iškun. Kalkal-muballiṭ adi balṭat ittanaššīšī-ma, ina warkīt ūmim mamma[n] mimma eli Kalkal-muballiṭ ul īšu; ullul. Mārū Ilšu-ibbīšu u mārū Būr-Nunu mamman ul iraggamšum. Nīš Šamaš Ayya Marduk u Ḫammurapi itmû.*

Ayya-damqat the *nadītum* of Šamaš, daughter of Ilšu-ibbīšu, his mother, freed Kalkal-muballiṭ son of Ayya-damqat; she turned his face toward the east. Kalkal-muballiṭ will support her as long as she is alive, and in the future Kalkal-muballiṭ will owe no one anything; he is set free. As for the children of Ilšu-ibbīšu and the children of Būr-Nunu, no one may lay claim against him. They swore by the life of Šamaš, Ayya, Marduk, and Ḫammurapi. Witnesses. Date.

I. 1. *Ana Šamaš-ḫāzir qibī-ma; umma Lu-Ninurtā-ma. Šamaš liballiṭka. Aššum eqlim ša mārī Iluni: awīlû napištam ul īšû. Kīma taddinū-šunūšim mamman lā unakkaršunūti. Ina qibīt bēlīya ašpurakkum.*

Speak to Šamaš-ḫāzir; thus Lu-Ninurta. May Šamaš keep you healthy. Concerning the field of the children of Iluni: the men have no livelihood. As you gave (it) to them, no one may remove them. I write (lit., wrote) to you at the command of my lord.

2. *Ana ša ḫaṭṭātim*$^{?}$ *ša Marduk uballaṭūš[u] qibī-ma; umma Sîn-mušallim-ma. Šamaš liballiṭka; lū šalmāta. eš(e)ret šiqil kaspam itti Ibni-Amurrum wakil Amurrîm muḫur-ma, ša eš(e)ret šiqil kaspim šuāti, ū lū maḫrīka ū lū ina ālim, ēma ibaššû, šām. Ṭēmam šupram-ma, ina Sippar ana puḫḫi luddim-ma, pūḫšu ina Bābilim lulqe.*

Speak to the "captain" whom Marduk keeps healthy; thus Sîn-mušallim. May Šamaš keep you healthy; be well. Get ten shekels of silver from Ibni-Amurrum the *wakil Amurrîm,* and buy something worth (lit., that of) said ten shekels of silver, either where you are or in the town, wherever there is (something) available. Send me a report so that I may give (something) in exchange in Sippar, and can get the exchange of that in Babylon.

3. ^{1} *a-na* ^{d}EN.ZU-*i-din-nam* ^{2} *qí-bí-ma* ^{3} *um-ma ḫa-am-mu-ra-pí-ma* ^{4} *i-la-a-tim ša e-mu-ut-ba-lim* ^{5} *ša le-ti-ka* ^{6} ERIN$_2$-*um* NÍG.ŠU *i-nu-úḫ-sa-mar* ^{7} *ú-ša-al-la-ma-ak-kum* ^{8} *i-nu-ma is-sà-an-qú-ni-ik-kum* ^{9} *i-na* ERIN$_2$-*im ša qá-ti-ka* ^{10} ERIN$_2$-*am lu-pu-ut-ma* ^{11} *i-la-a-tim* ^{12} *a-na šu-ub-ti-ši-na* ^{13} *li-ša-al-li-mu.*

Ana Sîn-iddinam qibī-ma; umma Ḫammurapī-ma. Ilātim ša Emutbalim ša lētīka ṣābum ša qāt Inūḫ-samar ušallamakkum. Inūma issanqūnikkum, ina ṣābim ša qātīka ṣābam luput-ma, ilātim ana šubtīšina lišallimū.

Speak to Sîn-iddinam; thus Ḫammurapi. The troop under the charge of Inūḫ-samar will bring the goddesses of Emutbalum in your authority safely to you. When they (the troop) have reached you, assign a troop from the troop in your charge to get the goddesses safely to their residence(s).

LESSON TWENTY-SEVEN

C. 1. Ì(.GIŠ) KASKAL
2. *qí-bi-it* ^{d}INANNA *ṣir / ṣi-ir / ṣí-ir-tum / tu-um*
3. ŠE.GIŠ.Ì NIN.DINGIR(.RA)
4. GÌR.PAD.DU SIPAD
5. *ki-ma* KA NA.RU-*ia*
6. U$_8$.UDU.ḪI.A *ša* AN
7. É.GI$_4$/GI.A SIPAD
8. *ner / ne-er / né-er-tum / tu-um*
9. *ter / te-er-ḫa-tum / tu-*

D. 1. *ušaklāšu.*
2. *kīma ṣābam ālam tušasḫeru*
3. *nīš ilim šuzkirīšunūti.*
4. *pilšam ina dūrim šaplîm ušapliš.*
5. *nišī epšētīšu mādātim uštešmi.*
6. *tušakkaršunūti.*
7. *lēʾûm mušakniš lemuttim* (or, *ša lemuttam ušaknašu*)
8. *adīni šubātīni ul ušakšidūniāti.*
9. *Ellil mušarbi bēlūtīya* (or, *ša bēlūtī ušarbû*)
10. *kīma būšam lā kâm tašriqu, appaka u lišākka nušakkas.*
11. *mimma ul tušelqeanni.*
12. *ḫīrtašu ina bulṭīša akalam ušelqēši / ušamḫarši.*
13. *ēma šamaššammū šuddunū / ēma šamaššammī ušaddanū*
14. *narkabtam eššetam ḫurāṣam tuḫḫaz.*
15. *ūtatteršu.*

E. 1. *iṣam mala maṣû ana bēltīya eleppam uštarkib.* I have loaded the ship for my lady with as much wood as there is.
2. *Adad ilum rabûm zēr šarrim ša bītam šâtu ušalpatu liḫalliq.* May Adad the great god destroy the seed of the king who desecrates that house.
3. *dayyānam ša dīššu īnû šarrum ušetbīšu.* The king removed the judge who had changed his verdict.
4. *adi allakam mimma lā taraggam; šāpirum šamaššammī ul ipqidam; ana pānīya ṭēmam ṣabat-ma kasap šamaššammīya šušqilšu; šīmam ašammam-ma allakakkum.* Do not contest anything before I come; the governor has not provided me with sesame; before my arrival take action and have him weigh out the silver for my sesame; I will make the purchase and then come to you.
5. *ēm Šamaš iqabbianniāšim i nillik.* We will go wherever Šamaš tells us.
6. *ana ša maḫrīšunu allikam-ma kaspī ušaddinūšunūti ītaplūninni.* Because I went to them and collected my silver from them, they have satisfied my claim.
7. *aššum ana bīt aḫīka alākam taškunam ṭēmī ul ašpurakkum-ma aššumīka imēram ul ašām; u imērū ištu libbi mātim īlûnim-ma ina bīt aḫīya šunu; lāma imērī iddinū alkam-ma šām.* Because you (ms)

made a trip to your brother's house I did not send you my report or buy a donkey for you; but donkeys have come up from the center of the land and are at my brother's house; before the donkeys are sold, come and buy (some).

8. *rēʾiam ša tašpuram rebiat kaspim nuštamḫer.* We handed one-fourth of the silver over to the shepherd whom you (ms) sent.
9. *ūm mārum šū libbi abīšu uštamriṣu abūšu ina aplūtīšu inassaḫšu.* When that son upsets his father, his father may disinherit him (remove him from his inheritance).
10. *ina ālim annîm ištēn šiqil kaspum mimma ul šuddun.* In this town not even one shekel of silver was collected.
11. *šumma immerum šēpšu itruṣ lemuttum tībum kašdum ina mātim ibašši.* If the sheep extended its foot, evil: there will be a successful attack in the country.

F. 52 *šumma errēšum ina eqlim âm ū lū šamaššammī lā uštabši, riksātīšu ul inni.* If a tenant farmer has not produced barley or sesame in a field, he will not alter his contracts.

127 *šumma awīlum eli entim ū aššat awīlim ubānam ušatriṣ-ma lā uktīn, awīlam šuāti maḫar dayyānī inaṭṭûšu; u muttassu ugallabū.* If a man pointed a finger at an *entum*-priestess or a man's wife and has not convicted (her), that man will be beaten in the presence of the judges; and half his hair will be shaved.

194 *šumma awīlum mār(ā)šu ana mušēniqtim iddim-ma mārum šū in[a] qāt mušēniqtim imtūt mušēniqtum balum abīšu u ummīšu māram šaniam-ma irtakas, ukannūšī-ma aššum balum abī[š]u u ummīš[u] māram šaniam irku[s]u, tulâša inakkisū.* If a man gave his child to a wet-nurse and that child has died in the care of the wet-nurse, (and) the wet-nurse has attached/contracted another child without the knowledge of its father or mother, she will be convicted and, because she attached/ contracted another child without the knowledge of its father or mother, her breast will be cut off.

267 *šumma rēʾûm īgū-ma ina tarbaṣim pissātam uštabši, rēʾûm ḫiṭīt pissātim ša ina tarbaṣim ušabšû liātim u ṣēnī ušallam-ma ana bēlīšunu inaddin.* If a shepherd was negligent and has caused lameness? in a stable, the shepherd will make good and give to their owner the damage of the lameness? he caused in the stable (in) cattle and flocks.

179 *šum-ma* NIN.DINGIR LUKUR *ù lu sekretum*(míZI.IK.RU.UM) *ša a-bu-ša še-ri-ik-tam iš-ru-ku-ši-im ku-nu-kam iš-ṭú-ru-ši-im i-na* DUB-*pí-im ša iš-ṭú-ru-ši-im wa-ar-ka-sà e-ma e-li-ša ṭa-bu na-da-nam iš-ṭur-ši-im-ma ma-la li-ib-bi-ša uš-tam-ṣí-ši wa-ar-ka a-bu-um a-na ši-im-tim it-ta-al-ku wa-ar-ka-sà e-ma e-li-ša ṭa-bu i-na-ad-di-in aḫ-ḫu-ša ú-ul i-ba-aq-qá-ru-ši.*

šumma entum nadītum ū lū sekretum ša abūša šeriktam išrukūšim kunukkam išṭurūšim ina ṭuppim ša išṭurūšim warkassa ēma elīša ṭābu nadānam išturšim-ma mala libbīša uštamṣīši, warka abum ana šīmtim ittalku warkassa ēma elīša ṭābu inaddin; aḫḫūša ul ibaqqarūši.

If an *entum, nadītum,* or *sekretum* whose father gave her a dowry and wrote (it on) a tablet for her, (and) in the tablet that he wrote for her he wrote for her to give her inheritance wherever was pleasing to her, and gave her full discretion, after the father has passed on, she may give her inheritance wherever it is pleasing to her; her brothers will not sue her.

G. 1. *šumma šēpum war[k]assa pa[ṭ]er, šēp īrubakkum tušadda.* If the back of the "foot" is loose, you will wipe out the expedition that attacks you.

2. *šumma izbum in[a m]uḫḫīšu ziḫḫum šakin, nakrum mātam ušamqa[t]; ana muškēnim bīssu u unêtīš[u] ekallum iredde.* If the anomaly has a cyst on top, the enemy will bring down the land; the palace will lead its estate and furnishings to a *muškēnum.*

3. *[šumma] izbum qaqqassu kayyānum šakim-ma [u] šanûm ṣeḫrum ina šumēlim šakin, [m]āt nakrīka tušamqat.* If the normal head of the anomaly is in place, but a second small one is also present on the left, you will bring down your enemy's land.

4. [M]AŠ 2 KÁ É.GAL *ša-nu-um i-na i-mi-tim ša-ki-in na-ak-rum ma-tam ú-ša-da.*

[šu]mma šinā bāb(ū) ekallim šanûm ina imittim šakin, nakrum mātam ušadda. If there are two "palace gates" and the second is situated on the right, the enemy will wipe out the land.

H. 1. *Šinip manā kaspum ša Nūr-Šamaš mār Sîn-šeme eli Anum-gamil u Bēlessunu aššatīšu iršû. Iddin-Ea mār Rīš-ilum ana Malgîm Bēlessunu useppīšī-ma, Nūr-Šamaš ina Bābilim Iddin-Ea aššum Bēlessunu aššat Anum-gamil useppû iṣbassu. Sîn-iqīšam mār Ḫaniya qātāt Iddin-Ea kiššāt Bēlessunu ana šaluš(ti) manā erbet(ti) šiqil kaspim ana ištēn warḫim ilqē-ma, ana ūm ḫadānīšu Iddin-Ea awīltam ul irdeam-ma šaluš(ti) manā erbet(ti) šiqil kaspam ana Nūr-Šamaš Sîn-iqīšam uštašqil.*

Two-thirds mina of silver that Nūr-Šamaš son of Sîn-šeme incurred to the debit of Anum-gamil and Bēlessunu his wife. Iddin-Ea son of Rīš-ilum abducted Bēlessunu to Malgûm, and Nūr-Šamaš arrested Iddin-Ea in Babylon because he had abducted Bēlessunu the wife of Anum-gamil. Sîn-iqīšam son of Ḫaniya guaranteed Iddin-Ea for the debt-servitute of Bēlessunu — one-third mina four shekels of silver — for one month. On the (lit., his) appointed day Iddin-Ea did not bring the woman, and so Sîn-iqīšam has had one-third mina four shekels silver weighed out to Nūr-Šamaš.

I. 1. *Ana Šamaš-ḫāzir qibī-ma; umma Ḫammurapī-ma. Apil-Šamaš utullum kiam maḫrīya iškun, umma šū-ma: "būr kiriam ša pī nārim Lalatītim ša bēlī ana rē'î ša qātīya iddinam Arwûm ilteqe"; kiam maḫrīya iškun. Kiriam šuāti ana Arwûm mannum iddin? Ṭēm kirîm šuāti gamram pānam šuršiam-ma šupram.*

Speak to Šamaš-ḫāzir; thus Ḫammurapi. Apil-Šamaš the chief shepherd informed me as follows: "the one-*būrum* orchard at the mouth of the Lalatian river that my lord gave me for the shepherds under my authority Arwûm has taken"; thus he informed me. Who gave that orchard to Arwûm? Address yourself to, and send me, a complete report on that orchard.

2. 1 *a-na it-ti-*dUTU-*ba-la-su* 2 *qí-bí-ma* 3 *um-ma* d*Amurrum*(MAR.TU)-*ma-gir-ma* 4 dUTU *ù* dAMAR.UTU *li-ba-al-li-ṭú-ka* 5 I*ša-lim-pa-li-iḫ-*dUTU *x x* 6 *a-na ṣe-ri-ka aṭ-ṭar-dam* 7 ŠE-*e ša* BÀD-*ḫa-am-mu-ra-pí*ki 8 *ša i-ba-aš-šu-ú tap-pu-ut-sú* 9 *a-li-ik-ma a-na* gišMÁ *šu-ur-ki-ib* 10 *ù i-na* ŠE-*em a-ḫi-tim* 11 *ša i-ba-aš-šu-ú* 12 10 ŠE.GUR *i-di-iš-šum* 13 ŠE-*um šu-ú i-na i-ni-ka* 14 *la i-iq-qé-er.*

Ana Itti-Šamaš-balāssu qibī-ma; umma Amurrum-magir-ma. Šamaš u Marduk liballiṭūka. Šalim-paliḫ-Šamaš ... ana ṣērīka aṭṭardam. Ê ša Dūr-Ḫammurapi ša ibaššû tappûssu alik-ma ana eleppim šurkib. U ina êm aḫītim ša ibaššû eš(e)ret kur âm idiššum. Ûm šū ina īnīka lā iqqer.

Speak to Itti-Šamaš-balāssu; thus Amurrum-magir. May Šamaš and Marduk keep you well. I have sent Šalim-paliḫ-Šamaš the ... to you. Help him load on the ship my grain that is in Dūr-Ḫammurapi. Further, of the additional payment of grain that there is, give him ten kor of grain; said grain should not seem too costly in your eyes.

LESSON TWENTY-EIGHT

C. 1. NA$_4$.ḪI.A KASKAL
2. A.RÁ 3-*šu*
3. KA SIPAD
4. KUR.MEŠ (or KUR.KUR) LUGAL
5. ŠE.Ì.GIŠ
6. U$_8$.UDU.ḪI.A NIN.DINGIR(.RA) *ad-di(-in / iš)-šim / ši-im*
7. Ú KUR(-*i-im*)
8. NA.RU KÚR *aq-qúr / qú-ur / qú-ú*

D. 1. *kīma qibītīka / awātīka šamaššammī u abnī / abnātim uštābil.*
2. *rēʾûm ṣēnī u liātim ša ina tarbaṣim ibaššiā lišākil.*
3. *išdī dūrānī annûtim rabîš udannin.*
4. *šarrāqam lemnam ša šikaram u šamnam ša pašāš ilim itbalu ana maḫar / pānī rubêm ušēribū.*
5. *entum nišī rapšātim kīma šarratum aḫāssa zikaram uldu ušešmī-ma kalûšina iḫdâ.*
6. *dayyānum dīn idīnu lā inni / unakkar.*
7. *am-mīnim ina karānīšu tušēlîšu / tušēṣîšu?*
8. *ušetteqšu.*
9. *šarrum ša ina šarrī šūturu anāku.*
10. *eqlētim anniātim lā tušeṣṣeā.*
11. *qīšātum šūrudā.*
12. *têrtam ušēpiš.*
13. *arḫiš šūšibaššināti; lā tulappat.*

E. 1. *kīma tīdû nišū rabiān āl pāṭīka ittasḫā-ma ana kīdim uštēṣiāšu.* As you (ms) know the people have removed the mayor of a town of your district and sent him outside.
2. *inūma bāʾerum qāssu ušatriṣū-ma lētī imḫaṣu, šinnī iddi; inanna eṣemti idīšu ina qablīša ešteber.* When the fisherman stretched out his hand and struck my cheek, he knocked out my tooth; now I have broken the bone of his arm in the (lit. its) middle.
3. *ša baqrī maḫrûtim šalšat šiqil kaspam išteat sūtum ša ana ekallim lā umallû ušašqalūšu.* For the previous claim they will make him weigh out one-third shekel of silver for each seah that he did not deliver to the palace.
4. *mala libbīša imaṣṣī-ma ēma libbaša ṭābu karānam inaddin.* She may do what she wants and give the orchard wherever her heart pleases.
5. *aššum dīnam ušāḫizūkā-ma dīnī lā tešmû-ma tēgû, kīma ṭuppī anniam tātamru ana Bābilim ana maḫrīya alkam-ma arḫiš sinqam.* Since I/he/she/they (m) granted you (ms) a hearing and yet you have not heeded my judgment, but have been negligent, as soon as you have seen this tablet of mine, come to me in Babylon, and get here quickly.
6. *šumma izbum ullânum-ma šīpātim naši, ūmū šarrim gamrū; nakerka ummākka ina kakkī ušamqat.* If the anomaly has wool already, the days of the king are over; your (ms) enemy will bring down your army with weapons.

7. *eqlam anniam mala maṣû ana epēšim u wašābim* PN *itti* PN2 *bēl eqlim ana qabê* PN3 *ušēṣi*. At the command of PN3, PN rented this field as far as it extends for building and inhabiting, from PN2, the owner of the field.

F. 15 *šumma awīlum lū warad ekallim lū amat ekallim lū warad muškēnim lū amat muškēnim abullam uštēṣi, iddâk*. If a man let a male or female slave whether of the palace or of a *muškēnum* escape through the city gate, he will be executed.

55–56 55 *šumma awīlum atappašu ana šiqītim ipte aḫšu iddī-ma eqel itêšu mê uštābil, âm kīma itêšu imaddad*. 56 *šumma awīlum mê iptē-ma epšētim ša eqel itêšu mê uštābil, ana būrim eš(e)ret kur âm imaddad*. 55 If a man opened his off-take for irrigation, (but) was negligent and flooded his neighbor's field with water (lit., caused his neighbor's field to carry water, or, sent water onto ...), he will measure out grain in accord with his neighbor(s). 56 If a man released (opened) water and flooded the work of his neighbor's field with water, he will measure out ten kor of grain per *būrum*.

112 *šumma awīlum ina ḫarrānim wašim-ma kaspam ḫurāṣam abnam ū bīš qātīšu ana awīlim iddim-ma ana šībultim ušābilšu awīlum šū mimma ša šūbulu ašar šūbulu lā iddim-ma itbal, bēl šībultim awīlam šuāti ina mimma ša šūbulū-ma lā iddinu ukāššū-ma awīlum šū adi ḫamšīšu mimma ša innadnūšum ana bēl šībultim inaddin*. If a man was living in transit (?) and gave a man silver, gold, (precious) stone(s), or small possessions, and had him deliver (them) on consignment, (and) that man did not give something that was to be dispatched where it was to be dispatched, but kept it himself (carried it away), the owner of the consignment will convict that man concerning anything that was to be dispatched but that he did not give, and then that man will give the owner of the consignment up to five times anything was given to him.

154 *šumma awīlum mārassu iltamad, awīlam šuāti ālam ušeṣṣûšu*. If a man has known his daughter, that man will be made to leave the city.

238 *šumma malāḫum elep awīlim uṭebbī-ma uštēliašši, kaspam / kasap mišil šīmīša inaddin*. If a sailor sank a man's boat, but has refloated it (lit., has brought it up), he will give half its value in silver.

251 *šumma alap awīlim nakkāp[ī-ma] kīma nakkāpû bābtašu ušēdīšum-ma qarnīšu lā ušarrim alpam lā usanniq-ma alpum šū mār awīlim i[kk]ip-ma u[šta]mīt mišil [ma]nā kaspam i[n]addin*. If a man's ox was prone to goring and his neighborhood had made known to him that it was prone to goring, yet he had not trimmed its horns, (and) did not control the ox so that said ox gored and has caused the death of a member of the *awīlum* class, he will give half a mina of silver.

151–152 151 *šum-ma* MUNUS *ša i-na* É *a-wi-lim wa-aš-ba-at aš-šum be-el ḫu-bu-ul-lim ša mu-ti-ša la ṣa-ba-ti-ša mu-sà úr-ta-ak-ki-is* DUB-*pa-am uš-te-zi-ib šum-ma a-wi-lum šu-ú la-ma* MUNUS *šu-a-ti i-iḫ-ḫa-zu ḫu-bu-ul-lum e-li-šu i-ba-aš-ši be-el ḫu-bu-ul-li-šu aš-ša-sú ú-ul i-ṣa-ba-tu ù šum-ma* MUNUS *ši-i la-ma a-na* É *a-wi-lim i-ir-ru-bu ḫu-bu-ul-lum e-li-ša i-ba-aš-ši be-el ḫu-bu-ul-li-ša mu-sà ú-ul i-ṣa-ba-tu*.

152 *šum-ma iš-tu* MUNUS *ši-i a-na* É *a-wi-lim i-ru-bu e-li-šu-nu ḫu-bu-ul-lum it-tab-ši ki-la-la-šu-nu* DAM.GÀR *i-ip-pa-lu.*

151 *šumma sinništum ša ina bīt awīlim wašbat aššum bēl ḫubullim ša mutīša lā ṣabātīša mussa urtakkis ṭuppam uštēzib, šumma awīlum šū lāma sinništam šuāti iḫḫazu ḫubullum elīšu ibašši, bēl ḫubullīšu aššassu ul iṣabbatū; u šumma sinništum šī lāma ana bīt awīlim irrubu ḫubullum elīša ibašši, bēl ḫubullīša mussa ul iṣabbatū.* 152 *šumma ištu sinništum šī ana bīt awīlim īrubu elīšunu ḫubullum ittabši kilallāšunu tamkāram ippalū.* 151 If a woman living in a man's house has contracted (with) her husband to make out a tablet so that a creditor of her husband may not seize her, if that man owed a debt before he married that woman, his creditors will not seize his wife; and if that woman owes a debt before she enters the man's house, her creditors will not seize her husband. 152 If after that woman entered the man's house they have incurred a debt (a debt has come about against them), the two of them will pay the merchant.

G. 1. *šumma ina rēš ubānim nēkemtum ina libbi nēkemtim. nakrum qerbiš ikkimka.* 'If there is a "loss" within a "loss" at the top of the finger, the enemy will take you (ms) away in close combat(?).

2. *šumma amūtum bāb ekallim martam ubānam īšu u naṣrapti imittim naplaštam ikšudam u ṣibtum ana kakkim itūr naplaštam iṭṭul, ina tāḫāzim nakrum ummānam uḫapparam; tībum rabûm ummānam ikaššadam.* If the liver has a palace gate, gall bladder, (and) finger, and the right crucible reached the lobe, and the "increase" returned to the weapon (and) faced the lobe, the enemy will surround(?) the army in battle; a great attack will defeat the army.

3. *šumma martum mû[š]a ana kīdim ḫalṣū, rabiāna ina ālīšu ušeṣṣûšu.* If the gall bladder's liquid is squeezed out, the mayor will be made to leave his town.

4. *šumma martum kīma zibbat ḫumuṣṣīrim dannat, nakrum šallatam ušeṣṣe.* If the gall baldder is hard like a mouse's tail, the enemy will take plunder out.

5. *šumma izbum ullânum-ma imittašu ša imitti nasḫat, āl pāṭīka nakrum iṣabbat.* If the anomaly's right shoulder is already removed, the enemy will seize a border town of yours (ms).

6. *šum-ma pa-da-nu-um ša-ki-in i-lum ki-bi-is a-wi-lim ú-še-še-er.*

šumma padānum šakin, ilum kibis awīlim ušeššer. If the path is in place, the god will direct aright the man's steps.

7. *šum-ma a-mu-tum na-ap-la-aš-tam pa-da-nam* KÁ É.GAL-*li-im mar-tam i-šu ù i-na ú-ba-nim e-le-nu-um ni-di* ^{giš}GU.ZA-*im i-ki-im a-mu-ut* ^{d}*lu-ḫu-ši-im ša a-wi-lum i-na bu-ul-ṭì-šu mi-tu.*

šumma amūtum naplaštam padānam bāb ekallim martam īšu u ina ubānim elēnum nīdi kussîm īkim, amūt Luḫuššim ša awīlum ina bulṭīšu mītu. If a liver has a lobe, a path, a palace gate, (and) a gall bladder, and absorbed the *nīdi kussîm* into the finger besides, the omen of Luḫuššum, by which a man is dead while healthy.

8. *šum-ma mar-tum i-ši-is-sà a-na e-le-nu-um* SAG-*ša a-na ša-ap-la-nu-um šar-ru-um i-na a-li-šu pi-il*$_5$-*ša-am i-pa-la-aš-ma uṣ-ṣí.*

šumma martum išissa ana elēnum rēšūša ana šaplānum, šarrum ina ālīšu pilšam ipallaš-ma uṣṣi. If the gall bladder's bottom is on top and its top is underneath, the king will make a breach in his town and leave.

H. 1. *Šeššet parasrab manā šalāšat šiqil kaspam itti Awīl-ilim Sîn-illat Itūr-kīnum Ilšu-bāni Annum-pīša waraḫ Bibbulum ilqû. Waraḫ Lismim išaqqalū. Ušetteqū-ma ištēn šalšat manā kaspam išaqqalū.*

Sîn-illat, Itūr-kīnum, Ilšu-bāni, (and) Annum-pīša received six and five-sixth minas, three shekels of silver from Awīl-ilim in the month of Bibbulum. In the month of Lismum they will weigh it out. If they let (the date) pass by, they will weigh out one and one-third minas of silver.

2. *Šeššet iku eqlam kankallam i[n]a Taškun-Ešt[ar] i[t]ā Idd[in]-S[în] u itā D[am]iqti itti Ilšu-bā[nî] Šamaš-idd[inam] mār Annum-pīša eqlam ana erbe šanātim ušēṣi. Erbe šanātim e[ql]am i[p]ettē-[ma] ikk[al]. Šattam [ḫamuštam ana biltim] i[rrub]. ...*

A six-*iku* unplowed field in Taškun-Eštar bordering on Iddin-Sîn and bordering on Damiqtu(m) Šamaš-iddinam son of Annum-pīša rented (as a field) from Ilšu-bānî for four years. For four years he may open (plow) and use the field. The fifth year it will become liable for rent payment. ... Witnesses.

I. 1. *[Ana] Šamaš-ḫāzir [q]ibī-ma; umma Ḫammurapī-ma. Aššum ša tašpuram umma attā-ma: "Pītum ša [B]inâ [i]ttesker; mû ana Edena [g]ummurū. Bēlī ana Gimil-Marduk u Imgur-Akšak lišpuram-ma, ṣābam apšitâšunu liškunū-ma, pītam šuāti lidanni[n]. U erṣet mātim ša qātīšunu lišērišū." Ša tašpuram. Ana Gimil-Marduk u Imgur-Akšak udanninam-ma aštapram, ṣābam apšitâšunu išakkanū-ma, [pītam š]a Binâ udannanū. U erṣetam ša mātim ša išapparū ušerrešū.*

Speak to Šamaš-ḫāzir; thus Ḫammurapi. Concerning what you wrote me, "The opening at (lit., of) Binâ has become silted up; water toward the Edena canal is cut off. My lord should write to Gimil-Marduk and Imgur-Akšak to assign their agreed part of the work force to fortify that opening. Further, they should have the district of the country under their authority cultivated." (That is) what you wrote me. I have written forcefully to Gimil-Marduk and Imgur-Akšak to assign their agreed part of the work force to fortify the opening at Binâ. Further, they are to have the district of the country that they oversee cultivated.

2. *Ana Sîn-iddinam qibī-ma; umma Ḫammurapī-ma. Sēkirī ša ana šiprim epēšim esḫūn[i]kkum mimma š[i]pram lā tušeppessunūti; šūpušum-ma lišēpišū. U ina rēš namkūrim ša mušēpišīšunu usuḫšunūti.*

Speak to Sîn-iddinam; thus Ḫammurapi. Do not direct (lit., cause) the canal workers who are assigned to you to do the work to any work; they should be doing the directing (lit., they should certainly cause to be done). Further, remove them from the list of workers available to their director.

3. *Ana awīlê ša Marduk uballaṭūšunūti qibī-ma; umma wakil tamkārī u dayyānī-ma. Šamaš u Marduk [d]āriš ūmī liballiṭūkunūti. Aššum aplūt nadīt Šamaš ša Narām-ilīšu aḫi Ibbi-Šamaš ilqû-ma Dūrû itti Ibbi-Šamaš idīnū: awâtīšunu nīmur-ma ana pī ṭuppātim ša aplūti [š]a Ibbi-Šamaš našû dīnam ana Ibbi-Šamaš nigmur. U aššum Dūrû ana lā awātīšunu idīnū, ana pī ṭuppi ṣimdatim kīma ša lā šuniam ibqurū šērtam īsirūšunūšim. U ana lā târim-ma lā baqārim kanīkam nušēzibšunūti. Kanīkam šuāti šimeā.*

   Speak to the men whom Marduk keeps healthy; thus the overseer of the merchants and the judges. May Šamaš and Marduk keep you healthy forever. Concerning the inheritance of the *nadītum* of Šamaš that Narām-ilīšu the brother of Ibbi-Šamaš took and over which the Dūrites went to court with Ibbi-Šamaš: We looked at their statements and on the basis of the inheritance documents that Ibbi-Šamaš has we made a judgment for Ibbi-Šamaš. Further, because the Dūrites went to court for what was not their affair, on the basis of the decree document that/because they had laid claim to what was not theirs, a penalty was imposed on them. Further, we had them make out a sealed document concerning not making another claim (lit., for not returning and not claiming). Heed that sealed document.

4. [1] *a-na* ^{d}UTU-*ḫa-zi-ir* [2] ^{Id}EN.ZU-*mu-ša-lim* [3] *ù tap-pé-e-šu-nu* [4] *qí-bí-ma* [5] *um-ma ḫa-am-mu-ra-pí-ma* [6] *a-nu-um-ma* 13 LÚ.MEŠ *we-du-tim* [7] NÍG.ŠU *nu-úr-*^{d}UTU [8] *aṭ-ṭar-dam* [9] *a-na pí-i i-si-iḫ-ti-šu-nu* [10] A.ŠÀ-*am ar-ḫi-iš ap-la-šu-nu-ti-ma* [11] *ṭú-ur-da-ni-iš-šu-nu-ti* [12] *ša-at-tum la i-iz-zi-ib-šu-nu-ti-ma* [13] *ne-me-et-tam* [14] *la i-ra-aš-šu-ú.*

   Ana Šamaš-ḫāzir Sîn-mušallim u tappêšunu qibī-ma; umma Ḫammurapī-ma. Anumma šalāššeret awīlê wēdûtim ša qāt Nūr-Šamaš aṭṭardam. Ana pī isiḫtīšunu eqlam arḫiš aplāšunūtī-ma ṭurdāniššunūti. Šattum lā izzibšunūtī-ma nēmettam lā iraššû.

   Speak to Šamaš-ḫāzir, Sîn-mušallim, and their associates; thus Ḫammurapi. I have herewith sent thirteen important men who are under the authority of Nūr-Šamaš. Satisfy their claim to a field quickly, in accordance with their assignment, and then send them to me. The year must not pass them by, that they may have no cause for complaint.

LESSON TWENTY-NINE

C. 1. 5 GUN KUG.BABBAR
2. A.RÁ KASKAL AN(*-nim*)
3. (lú)MÁŠ.ŠU.GÍD.GÍD *a-na šim / ši-im-tim / ti-im il-lik / li-ik*
4. NA$_4$.MEŠ GIŠ.TIR
5. É.GI$_4$/GI.A ŠITIM
6. *ú-ul ib-qúr / qú-ur / qú-úr*
7. U$_8$.UDU.ḪI.A (lú)MÁŠ.ŠU.GÍD.GÍD
8. *ú-ter / te(-er)-ru*
9. *uš-mat / ma-at*

D. 1. *terraššu.*
2. *kunnat.*
3. *ušmattūka.*
4. *bītum ša tukallu*
5. *emāšu uštadīk.*
6. *māram utterrā.*
7. *ītariq / īteriq.*
8. *mutēr kīttim*
9. *dannātīka lā tušmād.*
10. *lū ušaklilši.*
11. *unaʾʾissu / ušāḫissu / ulammissu / maḫrīšu aškun.*
12. *awâtūya libbaša mādiš / rabîš uṭibbā.*
13. *ubarrūšu.*
14. *am-mīnim alpīya tureqqā / tušreqqā.*
15. *alāk ṣābim uwaʾʾer.*

E. 1. *kīma rabiānum uwaʾʾeranni eleppam ša bārîm ušrīq-ma bilassa ana ṣērīšu ušābil.* As the mayor instructed me I unloaded (emptied) the diviner's boat and dispatched its contents to him.

2. *am-mīnim aššum wardim šuāti awâtim tušmiddam-ma tašpuram?* Why did you (ms) write me so many things/words about that slave?

3. *aššum eš(e)ret kur êm ša bēlī ina ālim šâti ukinnam uznāya kīma Marduk ana bēlīya kâta ibaššiā bēlī liqbiam ēma bēlī eš(e)ret kur âm ukinnu ašappakšu.* Concerning the ten kor of grain that my lord assigned in that town, my attention is (ears are) (directed) to you my lord as (to) Marduk. May my lord command me; wherever my lord has assigned the ten kor of grain I will store it.

4. *ina šīm annîm libbašu ṭūb.* His heart is satisfied with this price.

5. *ina kakkim ša ilim âm mala ina eqel itinnim libirrū-ma itinnum mišilšu lilqe.* However much grain is in the house builder's field should be ascertained with the divine weapon, so that the house builder may take his half.

6. *šumma ina rēš martim kakkum šakin Adad ummākka ina ḫarrānim iraḫḫiṣ.* If a weapon is situated at the top of the gall bladder, Adad will inundate your (ms) army on a campaign.

7. *išteat narkabtam šuklultam ana emīya uštābil.* I have dispatched one completed chariot to my father-in-law.

F. 27–29 27 *šumma lū rēdûm ū lū bāʾerum ša ina dannat šarrim turru war[k]īšu eqelšu u kirīšu ana šanîm iddinū-ma ilikšu ittalak šumma i[t]tūram-ma āl(ā)šu iktašdam eqelšu u kirīšu utarrūšum-ma šū-ma ilikšu illak.* 28 *šumma lū rēdûm ū lū bāʾerum ša ina dannat šarrim tu[r]ru māršu ilkam alākam ileʾʾi eqlum u kirûm innaddiššum-ma ili[k a]bīšu il[la]k.* 29 *šumma māršu ṣeḫer-[m]a ilik abīšu alākam lā ileʾʾi šalušti eqlim u kirîm ana ummīšu inna*[*d*]*dim-ma ummašu urabbāšu*. 27 If, after the departure of either a *rēdûm* or a *bāʾerum* who was taken captive in royal military service, his field or orchard was given to another and he has performed his *ilkum*-service, if he has come back and reached his town, his field or orchard will be returned to him and he himself will perform his *ilkum*-service. 28 If the son of either a *rēdûm* or a *bāʾerum* who was taken captive in royal military service is able to perform the *ilkum*-service, the field or orchard will be given to him to perform his father's *ilkum*-service. 29 If his son is (too) young and cannot perform his father's *ilkum*-service, one-third of the field or orchard will be given to his mother and his mother will raise him.

30–31 30 *šumma lū rēdûm ū lū bāʾerum eqelšu kirīšu u bīssu ina pānī ilkim iddī-ma uddappir šanûm warkīšu eqelšu kirīšu u bīssu iṣbat-ma šalāš šanātim ilikšu ittalak šumma ittūram-ma eqelšu kirīšu u bīssu irriš ul innaddiššum; ša iṣṣabtū-ma ilikšu ittalku šū-ma illak*. 31 *šumma šattam ištiat-ma uddappir-ma ittūram eqelšu kirīšu u bīssu innaddiššum-ma šū-ma ilikšu illak* 30 If either a *rēdûm* or a *bāʾerum* abandoned his field, orchard, or house on account of the *ilkum*-service and has gone away, (and) after his departure another took over his field, orchard, or house and has performed his *ilkum*-service for three years, if he has returned and wants his field, orchard, or house, it will not be given to him; it is the one who took over and has performed his *ilkum*-service who will perform (it). 31 If it is only for a single year that he has gone away, and he has returned, his field, orchard, or house will be given to him and he is the one who will perform his *ilkum*-service.

44 *šumma awīlum eqel kankallim ana šalāš šanātim ana teptītim ušēṣī-ma aḫšu iddī-ma eqlam lā iptete, ina rebūtim šattim eqlam mayyarī imaḫḫaṣ imarrar u išakkak-ma ana bēl eqlim utār; u ana būrim eš(e)ret kur âm ima*[*dd*]*ad*. If a man rented an unworked field for three years for cultivation, but was negligent and has not opened the field, in the fourth year he will plow, hoe, and harrow the field and return (it) to the owner of the field; he will also measure out ten kor of grain per *būrum*.

45 *šumma awīlum eqelšu ana biltim ana errēšim iddim-ma u bilat eqlīšu imtaḫar, warka eqlam Adad irtaḫiṣ ū lū bibbulum itbal, bitiqtum ša errēšim-ma*. If a man gave his field to a tenant farmer for rent and has also received the rent for his field, (and) afterwards Adad has inundated the field or else a flood has carried (it) off, the loss is the tenant farmer's only.

R/75e *šumma awīlum âm u kaspam itti tamk*[*ārim i*]*lqē-ma âm u kaspam ana turrim lā īšu bīšam-ma īšu, mimma ša ina qātīšu ibaššû maḫar šībī kīma ubbalu ana tamkārīšu inaddin; tamkārum ul uppas; imaḫḫar*. If a man received grain or silver from a merchant and does not have grain or silver to return, (but) does have property (or, has only property), whatever there is in his possession he will give to his merchant, before witnesses when(ever) he brings (it); the merchant will not object; he will accept (it).

153 *šumma aššat awīlim aššum zikarim šanîm mussa ušdīk, sinništam šuāti ina gašīšim išakkanūši*. If a man's wife had her husband killed because of another man, that woman will be impaled.

224–225 224 *šumma asi alpim ū lū imērim lū alpam ū lū imēram simmam kabtam īpuš-ma ubtalliṭ, bēl alpim ū lū imērim šuduš/ šeššat kaspam ana asîm idīšu inaddin.* 225 *šumma alpam ū lū imēram simmam kabtam īpuš-ma uštamīt, rebiat*? (*ḫamšat*?) *šīmīšu ana bēl alpim ū lū imērim inaddin.* 224 If an ox or donkey physician treated either an ox or a donkey for a serious wound and has healed (it), the owner of the ox or donkey will give the physician one-sixth (shekel of) silver as his wages. 225 If he treated either an ox or a donkey for a serious wound and has killed (it), he will give the owner of the ox or donkey one-fourth? (-fifth?) of its value.

228–229 228 *šumma itinnum bītam ana awīlim īpuš-ma ušaklilšum, ana ištēn mūšar bītim šinā šiqil kaspam ana qīštīšu inaddiššum.* 229 *šumma itinnum ana awīlim bītam īpuš-ma šipiršu lā udannim-ma bīt īpušu imqut-ma bēl bītim uštamīt, itinnum šū iddâk.* 228 If a house builder built a house to completion for a man, he will give as his fee two shekels of silver for each *mūšarum* of the house. 229 If a house builder built a house for a man but did not secure/fortify his work so that the house he built collapsed and caused the death of the house owner, that house builder will be executed.

245 *šumma awīlum alpam īgur-ma ina mēgûtim ū lū ina maḫāṣim uštamīt, alpam kīma alpim ana bēl alpim irīab.* If a man rented an ox and caused its death, through negligence or through hitting (it), he will pay back ox for ox to the owner of the ox.

162–163 162 *šum-ma a-wi-lum aš-ša-tam i-ḫu-uz* DUMU.MEŠ *ú-li-súm-ma* MUNUS *ši-i a-na ši-im-tim it-ta-la-ak a-na še-ri-ik-ti-ša a-bu-ša ú-ul i-ra-ag-gu-um še-ri-ik-ta-ša ša* DUMU.MEŠ-*ša-ma.* 163 *šum-ma a-wi-lum aš-ša-tam i-ḫu-uz-ma* DUMU.MEŠ *la ú-šar-ši-šu* MUNUS *ši-i a-na ši-im-tim it-ta-la-ak šum-ma ter-ḫa-tam ša a-wi-lum šu-ú a-na* É *e-mi-šu ub-lu e-mu-šu ut-te-er-šum a-na še-ri-ik-ti* MUNUS *šu-a-ti mu-sà ú-ul i-ra-ag-gu-um še-ri-ik-ta-ša ša* É *a-bi-ša-ma.*

162 *šumma awīlum aššatam īḫuz, mārī ulissum-ma sinništum šī ana šīmtim ittalak, ana šeriktīša abūša ul iraggum; šeriktaša ša mārīšā-ma.* 163 *šumma awīlum aššatam īḫuz-ma mārī lā ušaršīšu, sinništum šī ana šīmtim ittalak, šumma terḫatam ša awīlum šū ana bīt emīšu ublu emūšu utteršum, ana šerikti sinništim šuāti mussa ul iraggum; šeriktaša ša bīt abīšā-ma.* 162 If a man married a wife, she bore him children, and then that woman has passed on, her father will not lay claim to her dowry; her dowry belongs to her children alone. 163 If a man married a wife but she did not cause him to get children, (and) that woman has passed on, if his father-in-law has returned to him the bride-price that that man brought to his father-in-law's house, her husband will not lay claim to the dowry of that woman; her dowry belongs to her father's house alone.

173–174 173 *šum-ma* MUNUS *ši-i a-šar i-ru-bu a-na mu-ti-ša wa-ar-ki-im* DUMU.MEŠ *it-ta-la-ad wa-ar-ka* MUNUS *ši-i im-tu-ut še-ri-ik-ta-ša* DUMU.MEŠ *maḫ-ru-tum ù wa-ar-ku-tum i-zu-uz-zu.* 174 *šum-ma a-na mu-ti-ša wa-ar-ki-im* DUMU.MEŠ *la it-ta-la-ad še-ri-ik-ta-ša* DUMU.MEŠ *ḫa-wi-ri-ša-ma i-le-qú-ú.*

173 *šumma sinništum šī ašar īrubu ana mutīša warkîm mārī ittalad, warka sinništum šī imtūt šeriktaša mārū maḫrûtum u warkûtum izuzzū.* 174 *šumma ana mutīša warkîm mārī lā ittalad, šeriktaša*

mārū ḫāwirīšā-ma ileqqû. 173 If that woman, wherever she entered, has born children to her later husband, after that woman has died, her earlier and later children will share her dowry. 174 If she has not born children to her later husband, only the children of her first husband will get her dowry.

G. 1. *[šumma ina bāb e]kallim ū rēš martim qûm ṣabit, rākib imēri nakram utār*. If a filament is held in the palace gate or the top of the gall bladder, a donkey-rider will send back / take captive the enemy.

2. *šumma kakki imittim kīma sikkatim izziz, kabtum ša libbi bēlīšu uṭabbu ibbašši*. If the weapon of the right side stands like a peg, a noble who pleases his lord will appear.

3. *šum-ma mar-tum ši-ši-ta-am ú-ka-al a-na be-el im-me-ri-im mu-ur-ṣa-am ú-ka-al*.

šumma martum šišītam ukāl, ana bēl immerim murṣam ukāl. If the gall bladder contains a membrane, it holds disease for the owner of the sheep.

4. *šum-ma li-ib-bi li-ša-nim wa-ru-uq e-ri-iš-ti* KUG.SIG$_{17}$.

šumma libbi lišānim waruq, erišti ḫurāṣim. If the center of the tongue is yellow, desire for gold.

H. 1. *x eqlum ... itā* PN *u itā* PN$_2$ ... *y bītum ina gagîm idi bīt* PN$_3$ *išteat amtum* PN$_4$ *bušûša warkassa ištu pê adi ḫurāṣim-ma ša Munawwirtum nadīt Šamaš mārat Nanna-mansum ana Ipqu-ilīša mārat* PN$_6$ *mārīša iddinu. Adi Munawwir[tum] balṭ[at], eqlam bītam amtam qāssā-ma ukā[l]. Ištu ilūša iqterû[ši] ša [Ipqu-ilīšā]-ma*.

x field ... bordering on PN and bordering on PN$_2$, ... y house in the *gagûm* beside the house of PN$_3$, one female slave, PN$_4$, her property, her inheritance, from chaff to gold are what Munawwirtum the *nadītum* of Šamaš daughter of Nanna-mansum gave to Ipqu-ilīša daughter of PN$_6$ her child. As long as Munawwirtum is alive, she alone retains personal possession of the field, house, (and) slave. After her god(s) have summoned her, they belong to Ipqu-ilīša alone.

2. *Ištēn kur âm [itti] Bēletum mārat Zababa-nāṣir Passalum ilqe. Ana ūm ebūrim [a]na našpak [ilq]û âm utār*.

Passalum received one kur of grain from Bēletum daughter of Zababa-nāṣir. On the day of the harvest he will return the grain to the granary he borrowed from.

I. 1. *Ana Sîn-[iddinam] qibī-[m]a; umma Ḫammurapī-ma. Kušabkī ana šikir maqqarī ana qāt qurqurrī ina Bad-Tibira u ēma ibaššû līmurūnikkum-ma, 7200 kušabkī šīḫūtim ... likkisūnikkum-ma ... ina našpakim itadd[iam-ma] ... ana Bābilim liblūnim. Ina kušabkī, ša inakkisū, iṣam, ša ina qištīšu mītu, lā inakkisū; iṣam warqam-ma likkisū. Arḫiš kušabkī šunūti liblūnim-ma, qurqurrū lā iriqqū*.

Speak to Sîn-iddinam; thus Ḫammurapi. Thorn trees for chisel handels are to be found for you for the possession of the wood/metal-workers in Bad-Tibira and wherever they may be; 7200 full-grown thorn trees ... should be cut down for you; ... that you may put (them) into a cargo-boat to be brought to Babylon. Among the thorn trees that are to be cut down wood that is dead in its thicket must not be cut down; green wood only should be cut. Said thorn trees should be brought quickly, lest the wood/metal-workers become idle.

2. *Ana awīlim qibī-ma; umma Ibni-Amurrum-ma. Šamaš u Marduk dāriš ūmī liballiṭūka. Lū šalmāta, lū balṭāta. Ilum nāṣirka rēška ana damiqtim likīl. Ana šulmīka ašpuram; šulumka maḫar Šamaš u Marduk lū dāri. Qīš-Amurrim mārka kiam išpuram, umma šū-ma: "našpakum ina nēreb bāb Iddin-Eštar patiḫ-ma ûm leqi. Amtam ussir-ma umma amtum-ma: 'x âm šinīšu ... ilqe.' "*

   Speak to the man; thus Ibni-Amurrum. May Šamaš and Marduk keep you healthy forever. Be well, be healthy. May the god who protects you treat you well. I wrote you about your well-being; may your well-being be lasting before Šamaš and Marduk. Your son Qīš-Amurrim wrote me as follows: "The granary at the entrance to the gate of Iddin-Eštar was broken into and grain was taken. I pressed a slave woman, and the slave woman (said): 'He took x grain twice ...' "

3. *Ana bēlī[ya] qibī-[m]a; umma Adrakatum amatkā-ma. Aššum kaspim ša Iddin-Sîn irgumam-ma bēlī dīnam ušāḫizūnêti: akšudam-ma awīlû mūdû awātim, ša ina rēš Mut-bisir izzizzū, ul wašbū; itti Sumu-ṭābi illikū, u adīni awātam ul asniq. Inanna bēlī aššum kaspim šâtu išpuram-m[a], ana našparti bēlīya aplaḫ-ma šeššet šiqil kaspam kišdāt mārīya ša ittīya wašbū ašqul; šapiltum erbet(ti) šiqil kaspum. Lillikam-ma itti mārī Mut-Bisir lisniq. Šanītam, aššum bītīya: elīya Iddin-Annu qaqqadam iršī-ma, u ina bītīya ušēṣûninnī-ma, šâtu ušēribūšu. Šumma libbi bēlīya, libbī ana marāṣim bēlī lā inaddin; bītī literrūnim. U šumma abī u ummī eqlam u kirêm ul inḫilūninni, itti bēlīyā-ma erriš; bēlī lišāḫiz-ma eqlam u kirêm liwašširūnim Bēlī ...*

   Speak to my lord; thus Adrakatum, your servant. Concerning the silver about which Iddin-Sîn sued me and my lord granted us a hearing: I arrived/succeeded, but the men who know the matter, who are in the service of Mut-bisir, are not in residence; they went with Sumu-ṭābi, and I have not yet gone into the matter. Now my lord wrote me about said silver, and I respected my lord's message and weighed out six shekels of silver, assets of my children who live with me; the remainder is four shekels of silver. Let him come and go into (it) with Mut-Bisir's children. Moreover, concerning my house: Iddin-Annu got the better of me, and I was evicted from my house, and he was allowed to move in. If it pleases my lord, may my lord not cause me grief (lit., give my heart to becoming ill); may my house be returned to me. Even though my father and mother did not hand over the field and orchard to me, it is only my lord that I can ask; may my lord give instruction that the field and orchard be released to me. My lord ...

4. [1] *a-na ka-ak-ka-bi* [2] *qí-bí-ma* [3] *um-ma* ^{f}*i-ni-ib-ši-na-ma* [4] *i-na* ⸢*pa*⸣*-ni-tim še-le-bu-um as-sí-in-nu* [5] *te-er-tam id-di-[na]m-ma aš-pu-ra-kum* [6] *i-na-an-na* 1 ^{f}*qa-ma-tum* [7] *ša* ^{d}*d[a-gan] ša ter-qa*^{ki} [8] *[i]l-li-ka-am-ma* [9] ⸢*ki*⸣*-a-aṃ iq-bé-e-em* [10] *[u]m-ma ši-i-*⸢*ma*⸣ [11] *sa-li-ma-tum ša* LÚ *èš-*

n[un-na^{ki}] ^{12} *da-aṣ-tum-ma* ^{13} *ša-pa-al* IN.NU.DA *mu-ú* ^{14} *i-il-la-ku ù a-na še-tim* ^{15} *ša ú-qa-aṣ-ṣa-ru a-ka-am-mi-is-sú* ^{16} *a-al-šu ú-ḫa-al-la-aq* ^{17} *ù ma-ak-ku-ur-šu* ^{18} *ša iš-tu aq-da-mi* ^{19} [*l*]*a šu-ul-pu-ut ú-ša-al-p*[*a-a*]*t* ^{20} *an-ni-tam iq-bé-e-em* ^{21} *i-na-an-na pa-ga-ar-ka* ^{22} *ú-ṣú-ur ba-lum te-er-tim* ^{23} *a-na li-ib-bi a-lim*$^{[ki]}$ ^{24} *la te-er-ru-u*[*b*].

Ana Kakkabī qibī-ma; umma Inibšinā-ma. Ina pānītim Šēlebum assinnu têrtam iddi[*na*]*m-ma ašpurakkum. Inanna išteat qammatum ša D*[*agan*] *ša Terqa* [*i*]*llikam-ma kiam iqbêm,* [*u*]*mma šī-ma: "Salīmātum ša awīl Ešn*[*unna*] *dāṣtum-ma; šapal tibnim mû illakū. U ana šētim ša uqaṣṣaru akammissu, ālšu uḫallaq, u makkūršu ša ištu aqdamī* [*l*]*ā šulput ušalp*[*a*]*t.*" *Annītam iqbêm. Inanna pagarka uṣur; balum têrtim ana libbi ālim lā terru*[*b*].

Speak to Kakkabī; thus Inibšina. Previously Šēlebum the *assinnum* gave me an oracle and I wrote to you. Now a certain *qammatum* of Dagan of Terqa came and said as follows to me: "The alliance of the man of Ešnunna is mere deception; beneath the straw water runs. But I will gather him into the net I am putting together, I will destroy his city, and I will desecrate his property, which since ancient times has been undesecrated." This she said to me. Now guard yourself; do not go into the center of town without an oracle.

LESSON THIRTY

C. 1. GUN ḪÉ.GÁL
2. Ú GIŠ.TIR
3. NU.MU.SU (lú)MÁŠ.ŠU.GÍD.GÍD
4. BARAG AN(*-nim*)
5. U8.UDU.ḪI.A NA.GADA
6. SILA.MEŠ *ù* KASKAL.MEŠ
7. KISLAḪ ŠITIM

D. 1. *šarrum alākam iqbiam* or *šarrum alākī iqbi(am)* or *ana/aššum alākim uwaʾʾeranni*.
2. *dâkšu ul eleʾʾi/elê*.
3. *itinnum ina epēš/banê bītim ligmur* (or *bītam ina epēšim/banêm* or *ina bītim epēšim/banêm*).
4. *pānī(ya) ana nabêšu aškun*.
5. *biltam ana kullim mugrā* (or *ana kulli biltim* or *ana biltim kullim*).
6. *aššum sanāq/kašād emīya u raḫāṣ eqlētīya ašpurakkim* (or, less often, *aššum emīya sanāqim/kašādim-ma eqlētīya raḫāṣim ašpurakkim*).
7. *awâtīšu ina šemêm / ina šemê awâtīšu / ina awâtīšu šemêm*.

E. 1. *ana lā ereb ṣābim ana ālim amguršunūti*. I agreed with them (m) about the soldiers not entering the town.
2. *bārûm ina uniāt almattim šarāqim būr*. The diviner was shown to have stolen the widow's furnishings.
3. *nāqidī aššum ṣēnī šināti šullumim uwaʾʾeršunūti*. I/she/he commanded the shepherds to keep those flocks healthy.
4. *bēlī bītam nadānam ušāḫissunūtī-ma bītam ul iddinū*. My lord instructed them (m) to give the house, but they have not given the house.
5. *aklam mimma ana dannatim ana šūrubim ul addiššum*. I did not give him any food to take into the fortress.
6. *bēlī awātam lišpuram-ma ša qabê bēlīya lūpuš*. May my lord send me a message that I may do what my lord commands.
7. *inanna abī* PN *liṭrudam-ma ša šullum mātim i nīpuš; u aššum wardī ša maḫar abīya wašbū abī liṭrudaššunūti u ṣābam ša ṭarādim abī liṭrud*. Now my father should send PN that we may do what is necessary to make the land safe; further, concerning the slaves who live with my father: my father should send them; further, my father should send the troops that can be sent.
8. *aššum iṣṣī ša bēlī ana* PN *ana turrim išpuram iṣṣī šunūti utēršum-ma mimma ul iqbi ana iṣṣīšu ḫadûm-ma ḫadi*. Concerning the timbers that my lord ordered me to give back to PN: I gave those timbers back to him and he has said nothing; he is quite happy with his timbers.
9. *šalšat šiqil kaspam eli* PN *īšu bulṭam ina kašādim* PN *kaspam ippalanni*. PN owes me one-third shekel of silver; when PN regains (his) health, he will pay me the silver.
10. *eqlam šâtu aššum ḫubullī apālim ana bēl ḫubullīya addin*. I gave that field to my creditor(s) to pay the debts.

F. 8 *šumma awīlum lū alpam lū immeram lū imēram lū šaḫâm ū lū eleppam išriq šumma ša ilim šumma ša ekallim, adi šalāšāʾīšu inaddin; šumma ša muškēnim, adi ešrīšu irīab; šumma šarrāqānum ša nadānim lā īšu, iddâk.* If a man stole either an ox or a sheep or a donkey or a pig or a boat, if it belonged to the god or the palace, he will give up to thirty-fold; if it belonged to a *muškēnum*, he will give back up to ten-fold; if the thief in question does not have what must be given (or, anything to give) he will be executed.

113 *šumma awīlum eli awīlim âm ū kaspam īšū-ma ina balum bēl êm ina našpakim ū lū ina maškanim âm ilteqe, awīlam šuāti ina balum bēl êm ina našpakim ū lū ina maškanim ina êm leqêm ukannūšū-ma âm mala ilqû utār; u ina mimma šumšu mala iddinu ītelli.* If a man was owed grain or silver by a man and has taken grain from a granary or from a threshing-floor without the consent of the owner of the grain, that man will be convicted of taking the grain from the granary or from the threshing-floor without the consent of the owner of the grain, and will return however much grain he took; moreover he will forfeit whatever amount he had given.

144 *šumma awīlum nadītam īḫuz-ma nadītum šī amtam ana mutīša iddim-ma mārī uštabši awīlum šū ana šugītim aḫāzim pānīšu ištakan, awīlam šuāti ul imaggarūšu; šugītam ul iḫḫaz.* If a man married a *nadītum* and that *nadītum* gave her husband a slave and has (thereby) produced children, (but) that man has decided to marry a junior wife, that man will not be permitted; he will not marry a junior wife.

177 *šumma almattum ša mārūša ṣeḫḫerū ana bīt(im) šanîm erēbim pānīša ištakan, balum dayyānī ul irrub; inūma ana bīt(im) šanîm irrubu, dayyānū warkat bīt mutīša pānîm iparrasū-ma bītam ša mutīša pānîm ana mutīša warkîm u sinništim šuāti ipaqqidū-ma ṭuppam ušezzebūšunūti; bītam inaṣṣarū u ṣeḫḫerūtim urabbû; uniātim ana kaspim ul inaddinū; šayyāmānum ša unūt mārī almattim išammu ina kaspīšu ītelli; makkūrum ana bēlīšu itâr.* If a widow whose children are very young has decided to enter the house of another man, she will not enter without the consent of the judges; when she enters the house of another man, the judges will investigate the circumstances of her previous husband's estate, and assign the estate of her previous husband to her future husband and that woman, and have them make out a document; they will look after the estate and raise the young children; they will not sell the furnishings; the buyer who buys the furnishings of the widow's children will forfeit his silver; the property will return to its owner.

207–208 207 *šumma ina maḫāṣīšu imtūt, itammā-ma šumma mār awīlim, mišil manā kaspam išaqqal.* 208 *šumma mār muškēnim, šalšat manā kaspam išaqqal.* 207 If in striking him he has killed him, he will take an oath, and if (it was) a member of the *awīlum* class, he will weigh out one-half mina of silver; 208 if a member of the *muškēnum* class, he will weigh out one-third mina of silver.

209–211 209 *šumma awīlum mārat awīlim imḫaṣ-ma ša libbīša uštaddīši, ešret šiqil kaspam ana ša libbīša išaqqal.* 210 *šumma sinništum šī imtūt, mārassu idukkū.* 211 *šumma mārat muškēnim ina maḫāṣim ša libbīša uštaddīši, ḫamšat šiqil kaspam išaqqal.* 209 If a man struck a man's daughter and has caused her to have a miscarriage, he will weigh out ten shekels of silver for her foetus. 210 If that woman has died, his daughter will be executed. 211 If he has caused the daughter of a commoner to have a miscarriage through striking (her), he will weight out five shekels of silver.

250 *šumma alpum sūqam ina alākīšu awīlam ikkip-ma uštamīt, dīnum šū rugummâm ul īšu.* If an ox, while walking along the street, gored a man and has killed him, such a case has no grounds for legal action.

42 *šum-ma a-wi-lum* A.ŠÀ *a-na er-re-šu-tim ú-še-ṣi-ma i-na* A.ŠÀ ŠE *la uš-tab-ši i-na* A.ŠÀ *ši-ip-ri-im la e-pé-ši-im ú-ka-an-nu-šu-ma* ŠE *ki-ma i-te-šu a-na be-el* A.ŠÀ *i-na-ad-di-in.*

šumma awīlum eqlam ana errēšūtim ušēṣī-ma ina eqlim âm lā uštabši, ina eqlim šiprim lā epēšim ukannūšū-ma âm kīma itêšu ana bēl eqlim inaddin. If a man rented a field for cultivation but has not produced any grain in the field, he will be convicted of not working the field and will give the owner of the field grain corresponding to his neighbors.

168 *šum-ma a-wi-lum a-na* DUMU-*šu na-sa-ḫi-im pa-nam iš-ta-ka-an a-na da-a-a-ni* DUMU-*i a-na-sà-aḫ iq-ta-bi da-a-a-nu wa-ar-ka-sú i-pár-ra-su-ma šum-ma* DUMU *ar-nam kab-tam ša i-na ap-lu-tim na-sa-ḫi-im la ub-lam a-bu-um* DUMU-*šu i-na ap-lu-tim ú-ul i-na-sà-aḫ.*

šumma awīlum ana mārīšu nasāḫim pānam ištakan, ana dayyānī "mārī anassaḫ" iqtabi, dayyānū warkassu iparrasū-ma šumma mārum arnam kabtam ša ina aplūtim nasāḫim lā ublam, abum mār(ā)šu ina aplūtim ul inassaḫ. If a man has decided to disinherit his son, has said to the judges, "I will disinherit my son," the judges will investigate his circumstances and if the son has not committed (lit., brought) a crime serious enough for disinheriting, the father will not disinherit his son.

261 *šum-ma a-wi-lum* NA.GADA *a-na* ÁB.GUD.ḪI.A *ù* U$_8$.UDU.ḪI.A *re-em i-gur* 8 ŠE.GUR *i-na* MU.1.KAM *i-na-ad-di-iš-šum.*

šumma awīlum nāqidam ana liātim ū ṣēnī rêm/reʾêm īgur, samānat kur âm ina išteat šattim inaddiššum. If a man hired a shepherd to tend cattle or flocks, he will give him eight kor of grain per year.

G. 1. *šumma naplaštum kīma ḫarrānim, šarrum kabtūtīšu idâk-ma bišâšunu u makkūršunu ana bītāt ilānī izâz.* If the lobe is like a road, the king will kill his nobles and divide their possessions and their property among the temples.

2. *šumma naplaštum ana kakkim itūr-ma nīram iṭṭul, tībi lemuttim ana bī[tim] ite[bbe].* If the lobe went back to the weapon and faced the yoke, an attack of evil will arise against the house.

3. *šumma bāb ekallim maškaššu īzim-ma ina šumēlim šakin, mātam lā kattam q[ātka] ikaššad; šumma bāb ekallim maškaššu īzim-ma ina imittim šakin, erṣetka nakrum itabbal; šumma bāb ekallim ina maškanīšu la ibaššī-ma ina warkat amūtim šakin, māt nakrim biltam inaššiakku.* If the palace gate has left its place and is situated on the left, you (ms) will personally conquer a land not your own; if the

palace gate has left its place and is situated on the right, the enemy will carry off your land; if the palace gate in not in its place and is situated at the rear of the liver, the land of the enemy will carry tribute to you.

4. *šumma bāb ekallim kayyānum kayyānum ina imittim šakin, kabtu kīma bēlīšu imaṣṣi.* If the palace gate is situated on the right completely normally, a noble will be equal to his lord.
5. *šumma ina ‹i›šid martim piṭrum šakim-ma ana zumrīša ṭuḫḫu, awīlum ina lā lamādīšu maruštum imaqqutaššum.* If a fissure is situated at the base of the gall bladder and is brought near its body, difficulty will befall the man without his knowing.
6. *[šumma ṭ]ulīmum šārtam laḫim, mā[r a]lmattim kussiam iṣabbat.* If the spleen is covered with hair, a widow's son will seize the throne.
7. *šumma ina mu[ḫ]ḫi nīri kakkum / kakkū šinā imittam u šumēlam šaknū, qarrādū ya'ūtun u ša nakrim iš[t]ē[n]iš imaqqutū.* If above the yoke two weapons are situated, on the right and the left, warriors of mine and of the enemy will fall together.
8. *šumma sebe šēpētum*$^{?}$*, rabûm kabtum ana mātīka iṭeḫḫeakkum.* If (there are) seven feet$^{?}$, an important noble will approach your (ms) country (on your behalf).
9. *[šumma] naplaštum rēssa rapaš, ilum rēš awīlim inašši.* If the top of the lobe is wide, the god will exalt the man.
10. DIŠ *a-na pa-ni da-na-nim* ^{giš}TUKUL *ša-ki-im-ma e-li-iš iṭ-ṭù-ul ma-ar ši-ip-ri-im we-du-um i-ṭe*$_4^!$*-ḫe-a-am.*

    šumma ana pānī danānim kakkum šakim-ma eliš iṭṭul, mār šiprim wēdum / wēdûm iṭeḫḫeam. If the weapon is situated before the "strength" and faces upward, a solitary/important messenger will approach.
11. DIŠ KÁ É.GAL *ri-iq-ma a-na li-bi-šu ši-ta ú-ba-na-tu-ka i-ru-ba* É.GAL-*am da-an-na-tum i-ṣa-ba-at.*

    šumma bāb ekallim rīq-ma ana libbīšu šittā ubānātūka irrubā / īrubā, ekallam dannatum iṣabbat. If the palace gate is empty and two of your (ms) fingers will go/went in, hardship/famine will seize the palace.

H. 1. *Bīt kankallim mala maṣû itā Sîn-bānî ... u itā Adad-bānî ... bīt Marduk-kūn-dārum itti Marduk-kūn-dārum bēl bītim Kūdanna ana epēšim u wašābim ana šalāš šanātim ušēṣi. Ana qabê Warad-ilīšu u Apil-Amurrim.*

   Kūdanna rented a house on unworked ground, as far as it extends, beside Sîn-bānî ... and beside Adad-bānî ..., the house of Marduk-kūn-dārum, from Marduk-kūn-dārum the owner of the house, for three years, for working and inhabiting. At the command of Warad-ilīšu and Apil-Amurrim.

2. *Ištēn immeram šīm šuduš šiqil kaspim ša Sîn-iddinam sirāšûm mār Ēṭirum ana Warad-Kūbi mār-ši[prim] mār Ubarrum ana šipri epēšim kīma idīšu iddinūšu.*

   One sheep worth one-sixth shekel of silver that Sîn-iddinam the brewer, the son of Ēṭirum, gave to Warad-Kūbi the messenger, the son of Ubarrum, as his wages for doing work/plowing.

3. [1] *iš-tu* ITI *Ṭebētim*(AB.È.A) [2] UD.18.KAM [3] [If]*ši-nu-nu-tum lā nāṭiltam* (IGI.NU.[TUK]) [4] *a-na na-ru-tim a-ḫa-zi-im* [5] *a-na ma-aḫ-ri-ia* [6] *ub-lu-ni-iš.*

   Ištu waraḫ Ṭebētim ūmam šamāššeriam Šinunūtum lā nāṭiltam ana nārūtim aḫāzim ana maḫrīya ublūniš.

   From the month of Ṭebētum, eighteenth day, the blind Šinunūtum was brought to me to learn the musician's craft.

I. 1. *Ana Lu-Bau qibī-ma; umma Aḫum-ma. Aššum ipir Iataratim nadānim lū ašpurakkum. Ana mīnim lā taddin? Ipir Iataratim i[n]a ma[t]i tanaddi[n]? I[d]in! Šumma lā [t]addin, a[š]apparam-ma ipir [š]attīša ina bītīka tanaddin. Šan[ī]tam amtam ša itti Bēlâ ana Iataratim idin.*

   Speak to Lu-Bau; thus Aḫum. I wrote indeed to you about giving Iataratum's barley ration. Why have you not given (it)? When will you give Iataratum's barley ration? Give (it)! If you do not give (it), I will write/order that you give her annual barley ration from your estate. Moreover, give the woman slave who is with Bēlâ to Iataratum.

2. *Ana awīlim [q]ibī-ma; umma Iškur-mansum-ma. Šamaš u Marduk dāriš ūmī liballiṭūka. Lū šalmāta, lū balṭāta. Ilum n[ā]ṣirka rēška ana damiqtim likīl. Ana šulmīka ašpuram; šul[um]ka maḫar Šamaš u Marduk lū dāri. Aššum šamaššammī nasāḫim i[n]a qibīt awīlim bēlīya u Ilšu-bāni aḫīka iššiakkū i[l]likūnim. Kīma ra[bût]īka eš(e)ret ṣābū [š]a [q]āt[īk]a ana ištēn ūmim tappûtam lillikū.*

   Speak to the boss; thus Iškur-mansum. May Šamaš and Marduk keep you healthy forever. Be well, be healthy. May the god who protects you treat you well. I wrote about your well-being; may your well-being be constant before Šamaš and Marduk. The land agents came here, at the command of my lord the boss and your brother Ilšu-bāni, in order to remove the sesame. In accord with your high position may ten workers under your authority help (them) for one day.

3. *Ana bēlīya qibī-ma umma Iaqim-Addu waradkā-ma. [Ū]m ṭuppī annêm ana ṣēr bēlīya ušābilam awīlû ša bazaḫatim kašād Ṣūra-Ḫammu ubarrūnim, ummāmi: "Ṣūra-Ḫammu ana Ḫuḫrî iktašdam. Bēlšunu u Iawṣi-Il ša bēlīya ālik idīšu ittīšū-ma illakūnim. U meat ṣābum ittīšu illakam." Kašāssu ubarrūnim-ma [qātam] ana [q]ātim ana ṣēr [bēlīya] ašpuram.*

   Speak to my lord; thus your servant Iaqim-Addu. The day I dispatched this tablet of mine to my lord, the men of the outpost were guaranteeing to me the arrival of Ṣūra-Ḫammu: "Ṣūra-Ḫammu has reached Ḫuḫrû. Bēlšunu and Iawṣi-Il, (subjects) of my lord who march at his side, are coming with him too. Further, a troop of one hundred is coming with him." Since they were guaranteeing his arrival I wrote immediately to my lord.

J. ^{1} *a-na* ^{d}AMAR.UTU ^{2} *be-li-im* ^{3} *ra-bi-im* ^{4} *na-di-in* ḪÉ.GÁL ^{5} *a-na ì-lí* ^{6} *be-el* É.SAG.ÍL ^{7} *ù* É.ZI.DA ^{8} *be-lí-šu* ^{9} *ḫa-am-mu-ra-pí* ^{10} *na-bi-ù* ^{11} AN-*nim* ^{12} [*še*]-*mu* ^{13} ^{d}EN.LÍL ^{14} [*mi*]-*gi*$_{4}$-*ir* ^{15} ^{d}UTU ^{16} SIPAD *na-ra-am* ^{17} ^{d}AMAR. UTU ^{18} LUGAL *da-núm* ^{19} LUGAL KALAM ^{20} *šu-me-ri-im* ^{21} *ù ak-ka-di-im* ^{22} LUGAL *ki-ib-ra-tim* ^{23} *ar-ba-im* ^{24} *ì-nu* ^{d}EN. LÍL ^{25} KALAM *ù ni-šì* ^{26} *a-na be-li-im* ^{27} *id-di-nu-šum* ^{28} *ṣe-er-ra-sí-na* ^{29} *a-na qá-ti-šu* ^{30} *ú-ma-al-li-ù* ^{31} *a-na* ^{d}AMAR.UTU ^{32} DINGIR *ba-ni-šu* ^{33} *in bar-sí-pa*^{ki} ^{34} URU *na-ra-mi-šu* ^{35} É.ZI.DA ^{36} BARAG-*šu el-lam* ^{37} *ib-ni-šum.*

Ana Marduk, bēlim rabîm, nādin ḫegallim ana ilī, bēl Esagil u Ezida, bēlīšu,

Ḫammurapi, nabiu Anim, [šē]mû Ellil, [mi]gir Šamaš, rēʾûm narām Marduk, šarrum dannum, šar(ri) māt Šumerîm u Akkadîm, šar(ri) kibrātim arbaʾim,

inu Ellil mātam u nišī ana bêlim iddinūšum, ṣerrassina ana qātīšu umalliu,

ana Marduk, ilim bānīšu, in Barsipa, ālim narāmīšu, Ezida, parakkašu ellam, ibnīšum.

For Marduk, the great lord, the giver of abundance to the gods, the lord of Esagil and Ezida, his lord

Ḫammurapi, the called of An, the one who hears Enlil, the favorite of Šamaš, the beloved shepherd of Marduk, the mighty king, the king of the land of Sumer and Akkad, the king of the four regions,

when Enlil gave him the land and the people to rule, handed their lead-rope to him,

he built for Marduk, the god who created him, in Borsippa, his beloved city, Ezida, his holy throne-dais.

LESSON THIRTY-ONE

C. 1. NÍG.KAS7 NA.GADA
2. GUN BARAG.MEŠ
3. A.MEŠ ḪÉ.GÁL
4. NU.MU.SU ŠITIM
5. SANGA ^{d}UTU
6. KAR ÍD
7. SILA ZIMBIR^{ki}
8. A.RÁ KISLAḪ NUN
9. A.GÀR *ù* GIŠ.TIR
10. 2 GUN ZÚ.LUM(.MA)

D. 1. *abnum iššaqil.*
2. *nišī ina naplusīka*
3. *šangûm ittaṭrad / ittašpar.*
4. *emūka irreddeam.*
5. *nasḫerīm!*
6. *liātum immaniā.*
7. *ṣīt pīšu / qibīssu ul iššemi / iššami.*
8. *dayyānū ul innaṣrū.*
9. *šamaššammū ibbašû.*
10. *tarbaṣum ibbani.*
11. *suluppū illeqqû.*
12. *ṣāb(ū)ka / ummākka ittankis.*
13. *šubassa illawi / issaḫer.*
14. *aplum innassaḫ / innadda.*
15. *nešmiā / našmiā!*
16. *bābum muppetûm*
17. *nagmurum*
18. *šum(ū)šu ayy-iššaṭram.*
19. *eṣmētūšu iššebberā.*
20. *naddi / nandi!*
21. *ittamgarū.*
22. *rabiānum iḫḫabit.*
23. *išātum ina kārim innapiḫ.*
24. *šum(ū)ša linnabi / lizzaker.*
25. *numāssa issappaḫ.*
26. *ugārī ittarḫiṣ.*
27. *išdum ippaṭṭar.*

E. 22–24 22 *šumma awīlum ḫubtam iḫbut-ma ittaṣbat, awīlum šū iddâk.* 23 *šumma ḫabbātum lā ittaṣbat, awīlum ḫabtum mimmâšu ḫalqam maḫar ilim ubār-ma ālum u rabiānum ša ina erṣetīšunu u pāṭīšunu ḫubtum iḫḫabtu mimmâšu ḫalqam iribbūšum.* 24 *šumma napištum, ālum u rabiānum ištēn manā kaspam ana nišīšu išaqqalū.* 22 If a man committed a robbery and has been caught, that man will be executed. 23 If the robber has not been caught, the robbed man will establish his missing property before the god and the town and mayor in whose region and district the robbery was committed will replace his missing property for him. 24 If a life (was lost), the town and mayor will weight out one mina of silver to his people.

25 *šumma ina bīt awīlim išātum innapiḫ-ma awīlum ša ana bullîm illiku ana numāt bēl bītim īššu iššī-ma numāt bēl bītim ilteqe, awīlum šū ana išātim šuāti innaddi.* If fire broke out in a man's house and a man who went to extinguish (it) cast his eye on the house owner's furnishings and has taken the house owner's furnishings, that man will be thrown on that fire.

32. [*š*]*umma lū rēdiam ū lū bāʾeram ša ina ḫarrān šarrim turru tamkārum ipṭuraššū-ma ālšu uštakšidaššu, šumma ina bītīšu ša paṭārim ibašši, šū-ma ramāššu ipaṭṭar; šumma ina bītīšu ša paṭārīšu lā ibašši, ina bīt il(i) ālīšu ippaṭṭar; šumma ina bīt il(i) ālīšu ša paṭārīšu lā ibašši, ekallum ipaṭṭaršu. Eqelšu kirīšu u bīssu ana*

ipterīšu ul innaddin. If a merchant ransomed either a *rēdûm* or a *bāʾerum* who was taken captive on a royal campaign, and allowed him to reach his town, if there is enough in his estate to ransom him, he will ransom himself; if there is not enough in his estate to ransom him, he will be ransomed through the temple of his town; if there is not enough to ransom him in the temple of his town, the palace will ransom him. His field, orchard, and estate will not be sold as his ransom price.

49 *šumma awīlum kaspam itti tamkārim ilqē-ma eqel epšētim ša êm ū lū ša šamaššammī ana tamkārim iddin, "eqlam eriš-ma âm ū lū šamaššammī ša ibbaššû esip, tabal," iqbīšum, šumma errēšum ina eqlim âm ū lū šamaššammī uštabši, ina ebūrim âm ū šamaššammī ša ina eqlim ibbaššû bēl eqlim-ma ileqqē-ma âm ša kaspīšu u ṣibassu ša itti tamkārim ilqû u mānaḫāt erēšim ana tamkārim inaddin.* If a man received silver from a merchant and gave the merchant a field prepared for barley or for sesame, (and) said "cultivate the field and collect and take for yourself the barley or sesame that grows," if a cultivator produced barley or sesame in the field, at harvest time it is the owner of the field who will receive the barley or sesame that grow in the field, and then he will give the merchant the barley (worth the amount) of his silver and its interest that he received from the merchant, as well as the maintenance amounts of the cultivating.

53–54 53 *šumm[a aw]īlum an[a kār eqlī]šu du[nnun]im aḫšu i[ddī-m]a kār [eqlīšu] lā ud[annim-ma] ina kā[rīšu] pītum itt[epte] u ugāram mê uštābil, awīlum ša ina kārīšu pītum ippetû âm ša uḫalliqu irīab.* 54 *šumma âm riābam lā ileʾʾi šuāti u bišāšu ana kaspim inaddinū-ma mārū ugārim ša êšunu mû ublū izuzzū.* 53 If a man neglected to fortify the embankment of his field and did not fortify his embankment, so that an opening has been made in his embankment and has brought water onto the land, the man in whose embankment the opening was made will replace the grain he destroyed. 54 If he is not able to replace the grain, he and his property will be sold and the "sons of the land" whose grain the water carried away will divide (the amount).

66 *šumma awīlum kaspam itti tamkārim ilqē-ma tamkāršu īsiršū-ma mimma ša nadānim lā ibaššīšum, kirīšu ištu tarkibtim ana tamkārim iddim-ma "suluppī mala ina kirîm ibbaššû ana kaspīka tabal," iqbīšum, tamkārum šū ul immaggar; suluppī ša ina kirîm ibbaššû bēl kirîm-ma ileqqē-ma kaspam u ṣibassu ša pī ṭuppīšu tamkāram ippal-ma suluppī watrūtim ša ina kirîm ibbaššû bēl kirîm-ma il[eqqe].* If a man received silver from a merchant and his merchant pressed him but there was nothing for him to give (so that) he gave the merchant his orchard after pollination and said to him, "take however many dates grow in the orchard as your silver," that merchant will not agree; it is the orchard owner who will get the dates that grow in the orchard, and then he will pay the merchant the silver and its interest according to his document, and the orchard owner himself will receive the excess dates that grow in the orchard.

105 *šumma šamallûm ītegī-ma kanīk kaspim ša ana tamkārim iddinu lā ilteqe, kasap lā kanīkim ana nikkassim ul iššakkan.* If an agent has been careless and has not received a receipt for silver he gave to a merchant, the silver without a receipt will not be put on an account.

109 *šumma sābītum sarrūtum ina bītīša ittarkasū-ma sarrūtim šunūti lā iṣṣabtam-ma ana ekallim lā irdeam, sābītum šī iddâk.* If criminals have conspired in an innkeeper's establishment and she has not arrested and conducted those criminals to the palace, that innkeeper will be executed.

117–118 117 *šumma awīlam e'iltum iṣbassū-ma aššassu mār(ā)šu u mārassu ana kaspim iddin ū lū ana kiššātim ittandin, šalāš šanātim bīt šayyāmānīšunu ū kāšišīšunu ippešū; ina rebūtim šattim andurāršunu iššakkan.* 118 *šumma wardum ū lū amtum ana kiššātim ittandin, tamkārum ušetteq, ana kaspim inaddin; ul ibbaqqar.* 117 If financial difficulty has seized a man and he sold his wife, his son, and his daughter, or he has been sold into debt servitude, they will work in the house of their buyer or debt-exactor for three years; in the fourth year their freedom will be established. 118 If a male or female slave was sold for debt servitude, a merchant may take (him/her) along (or, may let the period elapse) and sell (him/her); it will not be contested.

141 *šumma aššat awīlim ša ina bīt awīlim wašbat ana waṣêm pānīša ištakam-ma sikiltam isakkil bīssa usappaḫ mussa ušamṭa, ukannūšī-ma, šumma mussa ezēbša iqtabi, izzibši; ḫarrāšša uzubbûša mimma ul innaddiššim; šumma mussa lā ezēbša iqtabi, mussa sinništam šanītam iḫḫaz; sinništum šī kīma amtim ina bīt mutīša uššab.* If a man's wife who was living in the man's house has decided to leave and has been acquiring property illegally, squandering her own house, (and) belittling her husband, she will be convicted and, if her husband has ordered her divorce, he may divorce her; her travel provisions, her divorce payment, nothing will be given to her; if her husband has not ordered her divorce, her husband may (nevertheless) marry another woman; the aforesaid woman will dwell in her husband's house as a slave.

202 *šumma awīlum lēt awīlim ša elīšu rabû imtaḫaṣ, ina puḫrim ina qinnāz alpim (ištēn) šūši immaḫḫaṣ.* If a man has struck the cheek of a man who is of higher rank than he, he will be struck with an ox whip sixty times in the assembly.

17–19 17 *šum-ma a-wi-lum lu* ÌR *lu* GEME2 *ḫal-qá-am i-na ṣe-ri-im iṣ-ba-at-ma a-na be-lí-šu ir-te-de-a-aš-šu* 2 GÍN KUG.BABBAR *be-el* ÌR *i-na-ad-di-iš-šum.* 18 *šum-ma* ÌR *šu-ú be-el-šu la iz-za-kar a-na* É.GAL *i-re-ed-de-šu wa-ar-ka-sú ip-pa-ar-ra-ás-ma a-na be-lí-šu ú-ta-ar-ru-šu.* 19 *šum-ma* ÌR *šu-a-ti i-na bi-ti-šu ik-ta-la-šu wa-ar-ka* ÌR *i-na qá-ti-šu it-ta-aṣ-ba-at a-wi-lum šu-ú id-da-ak.*

17 *šumma awīlum lū wardam lū amtam ḫalqam ina ṣērim iṣbat-ma ana bēlīšu irtedeaššu, šinā šiqil kaspam bēl wardim inaddiššum* 18 *šumma wardum šū bēlšu lā izzakar, ana ekallim ireddēšu; warkassu ipparras-ma ana bēlīšu utarrūšu.* 19 *šumma wardam šuāti ina bītīšu iktalāšu warka wardum ina qātīšu ittaṣbat, awīlum šū iddâk.* 17 If a man captured an escaped male or female slave in the hinterland and has conducted him to his owner, the slave's owner will give him two shekels of silver. 18 If said slave has not named his owner, he will conduct him to the palace; the circumstances of his case will be investigated and he will be returned to his owner. 19 If he has kept that slave in his house (and) later the slave has been caught in his possession, that man will be executed.

265 *šum-ma* SIPAD *ša* ÁB.GUD.ḪI.A *ù lu* U8.UDU.ḪI.A *a-na re-em in-na-ad-nu-šum ú-sa-ar-ri-ir-ma ši-im-tam ut-ta-ak-ki-ir ù a-na* KUG.BABBAR *it-ta-di-in ú-ka-an-nu-šu-ma* A.RÁ 10-*šu ša iš-ri-qú* ÁB.GUD.ḪI.A *ù* U8.UDU.ḪI.A *a-na be-lí-šu-nu i-ri-a-ab.*

šumma rēʾûm ša liātum ū lū ṣēnum ana reʾêm/rêm innadnūšum usarrir-ma šimtam uttakkir u ana kaspim ittadin, ukannūšū-ma adi ešrīšu ša išriqu liātim ū ṣēnam ana bēlīšunu iriāb. If a shepherd who was given cattle or flocks to tend made false claims and changed the brand (or, falsely changed the brand), and also sold (them), he will be convicted and will repay to their owner up to ten times what he stole in cattle and flocks.

F. 1. *šumma naplaštum kīma nalbattim-ma u šīlum ina libbīša, ālam šarrum ilawwi; iṣṣabbat-ma innaqqar.* If the lobe is like a brick-mold and there is also a hole in it, the king will surround a city; it will be captured and torn down.

2. *šumma erbe naplasātum, qablum ina lib*[*bi*] *māti i*[*bbašši*]. If (there are) four lobes, warfare will occur in the land.

3. *šumma izbum muštinnam lā īšu, mīlum ina nārim ipparrasam; zinnū ina šamê iššaqqalū.* If the anomaly has no urethra, the flood will be kept away in the river; rain will be removed from the sky.

4. *šumma izbum pānī barbarim šakin, mūtānū dannūtum ibbaššû-ma aḫum ana bīt aḫim ul irrub.* If the anomaly has the face of a wolf, severe plague will arise, so that one will not enter another's house.

5. *šum-ma mar-tum in-na-as-ḫa-am-ma i-na ba-ab* É.GAL-*im ik-tu-un šar-ra-am ú-ka-aš-ša-du-šu-ú-ma i-na pa-ṭi-šu i-da-an-ni-in.*

šumma martum innasḫam-ma ina bāb ekallim iktūn, šarram ukaššadūšū-ma ina pāṭīšu idannin. If the gall bladder was removed and has become fixed in the palace gate, the king will be driven out, but he will become strong in his border region(s).

6. *šum-ma mar-tum i-na qá-ab-li-ša na-ak-sà-at gi-li-it-tum i-na ma-a-tim ib-ba-aš-ši.*

šumma martum ina qablīša naksat, gilittum ina mātim ibbašši. If the gall bladder is cut in its middle, terror will occur in the land.

G. 1. *x bītum epšum ṭēḫi bīt Awīl-ilim u ṭēḫi bīt Ilī-u-Šamaš rēssu rebītum rēssu šanûm bīt Kiš-abī pūḫ y bītim epšim ša Dan-erēssa enet Zababa mārat Manium u Ip*[*qu*]*-Erra rēʾi laḫrātim, ša ana Emeteursag ša Zababa illeqû, ina qabê šarrim Zababa-m*[*ub*]*alliṭ rabiān Kiš Munawwirum šakkanakkum Munawwirum nāgirum u šībūt Kiš iddinūšunūšim.*

x built house (plot) adjoining the house of Awīl-ilim and adjoining the house of Ilī-u-Šamaš, its frontage the plaza and its other frontage the house of Kiš-abī, as substitute for the y built house (plot) of Dan-erēssa the high priestess of Zababa, daughter of Manium, and Ipqu-Erra the ewe-herder, which was taken for the Emeteursag of Zababa, by the king's command Zababa-muballiṭ the mayor of Kiš, Munawwirum the governor, Munawwirum the herald, and the elders of Kiš gave them. (Witnesses. Date.)

2. *x kur suluppum šukunnê kiri Tarībum ša ana Ilī-iddinam iššaknu; Waraḫsamnam suluppam imaddad.*

   x kor of dates is the estimated yield of the orchard of Tarībum that is fixed for Ilī-iddinam; he will measure out the dates in Waraḫsamnum.

H. 1. *Ana Marduk-mušallim Sîn-iddinam u Awīl-Sîn qibī-ma; umma Ammī-ditānā-ma. Awīlû šūt pīḫatim ša ina Šaga wašbū kiam išpurūnim, umma šunū-ma: "x kur ûm ana kurummat ṣāb birti Šaga u aḫiātim ša waraḫ Kislīmim iḫḫaššeḫ"; kiam išpurūnim. Ana awīlê šūt pīḫatim ša ina Šaga wašbū aššum inūma tašapparāšunūšim babbilī ana maḫrīkun[u šapārim] ittašpa[r]. Šuprā; ba[bbilī] ana maḫrīkunu l[išpurūnim]-ma ina êm ša q[ātīkunu] x [kur âm] ana kurummat ṣāb birti Šaga [u aḫiātim] ša waraḫ Kislīmim šumḫirāš[unūti]. Bārû ša maḫrīk[unu] warkatam liprus[ū-ma] ina têrētim šalmāt[im] âm šuāti ana Šaga šūbilā.*

   Speak to Marduk-mušallim, Sîn-iddinam, and Awīl-Sîn; thus Ammī-ditāna. The officials who are resident in Šaga wrote to me as follows: "x kor of grain for the food allowance of the troop of the Šaga fort and outlying regions will be needed for the month of Kislīmum'; thus they wrote me. The officials who are resident in Šaga have been commanded to send you bearers when you write to them. Write that they send bearers to you that you may hand over to them, from the grain in your charge, x kor of grain for the food allowance of the troop of the Šaga fort and the outlying regions for the month of Kislīmum. The diviners with you should look into the matter that you may dispatch said grain to Šaga under favorable omens.

2. *[Ana Sîn-iddinam qibī]-ma; [umm]a Ḫammurapī-ma. Šattum dirigâm īšu; warḫum ša irrubam (warḫum) Elūlum-šanûm liššaṭer; u ašar igisûm ina (warḫim) [Tašrīt]im ūmam 25 ana Bābilim sanāqum iq[qab]û ina (warḫim) Elūlim-šanîm ūmam 25 ana Bābilim lisniqam.*

   Speak to Sîn-iddinam; thus Ḫammurapi. The year has an extra month; the month that is coming up should be registered as Second-Elūlum; further, wherever tax was ordered to come to Babylon on the 25th of Tašrītum it should (now) come to Babylon on the 25th of Second-Elūlum.

3. ^{1} *a-na a-wi-lim ša* ^{d}AMAR.UTU ^{2} *ú-ba-al-la-ṭú-šu* ^{3} *qí-bí-ma* ^{4} *um-ma aš-ta-mar-*^{d}IŠKUR*-ma* ^{5} ^{d}UTU *ù* ^{d}AMAR.UTU *da-ri-iš* UD*-mi* ^{6} *li-ba-al-li-ṭú-ka* ^{7} *a-wi-lu-ú nukaribbātum*(NU.^{giš}KIRI$_6$.MEŠ) DUMU.MEŠ ZIMBIR^{ki} ^{8} *aš-šum ṣe-eḫ-ḫe-ru-ti-šu-nu* ^{9} *ša iḫ-li-qú-ma iṣ-ṣa-ab-tu* ^{10} *iq-bu-nim-ma* ^{11} *aš-šum ki-a-am* DUB*-pí ú-ša-bi-la-kum* ^{12} *a-wi-le-e šu-nu-ti* ^{13} *aṭ-ṭar-da-kum* ^{14} *si-ik-mi-šu-nu* ^{15} *mu-ḫu-ur-ma* ^{16} *ma-ḫa-ar* ^{d}UTU ^{17} *li-ik-ru-bu-ni-kum.* ^{18} *Ṣú-ḫa-re-e-šu-nu* ^{19} *wu-uš-še-er-šu-nu-ši-im* ^{20} *pu-uṭ-ṭe*$_4$*-er-šu-nu-ti* ^{21} KÁ.DINGIR.RA^{ki} *la i-ka-aš-ša-du* ^{22} *aš-šu-mi-ia an-ni-tam e-pu-sú-nu-ši.*

   Ana awīlim ša Marduk uballaṭūšu qibī-ma; umma Aštamar-Adad-ma. Šamaš u Marduk dāriš ūmī liballiṭūka. Awīlû nukaribbāt mārū Sippar aššum ṣeḫḫerūtīšunu ša iḫliqū-ma iṣṣabtū iqbûnim-ma aššum kiam ṭuppī ušābilakkum. Awīlê šunūti aṭṭardakkum; sikmīšunu muḫur-ma maḫar Šamaš likrubūnikkum. Ṣuḫārêšunu wuššeršunūšim; puṭṭeršunūti; Bābilim lā ikaššadū. Aššumīya annītam epussunūši.

Speak to the man whom Marduk keeps healthy; thus Aštamar-Adad. May Šamaš and Marduk keep you healthy forever. The men, gardeners (who are) citizens of Sippar, spoke to me about their retainers who escaped and were captured, and therefore I have dispatched my tablet to you. I have sent those men to you; accept their payment that they may invoke blessings for you before Šamaš. Release their servants to them; free them; they (the men) must not come to Babylon. Do this for them for my sake.

I. *Inu Šamaš, bēlum rabium ša šamāʾi u erṣetim, šarrum ša ilī, Ḫammurapi, rubâm, migiršu, iâti, in pānīšu namrūtim ḫadîš ippalsanni, šarrūtam dārītam palê ūmī arkūtim išrukam, išid mātim, ša ana bêlim iddinam, ukinnam, nišī Sippar u Bābilim šubat nēḫtim šūšubam in pīšu ellim ša lā nakār iqbiu, dūr Sippar epēšam, rēšīšu ullâm rabîš lū uwaʾʾeranni,*
inūmīšu Ḫammurapi, šarrum dannum, šar Bābilim, naʾdum, šēmû Šamaš, narām Ayya, muṭīb libbi Marduk bēlīšu, anāku, in emūqīn ṣīrātim ša Šamaš iddinam, in tibût ummān mātīya, uššī dūr Sippar in eperī kīma šadîm rabîm rēšessunu lū ulli; dūram ṣīram lū ēpuš.

When Šamaš, great lord of heaven and earth, king of the gods, joyfully looked upon me, Ḫammurapi, the prince, his favorite, with his shining face, bestowed on me perpetual kingship, a reign of long days, established for me the foundation of the land that he had given me to rule, commanded with his pure unchanging word that the people of Sippar and Babylon be made to dwell in security, greatly commissioned me to build the wall of Sippar, to raise its top,
at that time I, Ḫammurapi, the mighty king, king of Babylon, the pious, who obeys Šamaš, beloved of Ayya, who pleases the heart of his lord Marduk, with the outstanding strength that Šamaš gave me, with a levy of the army of my land, verily raised the foundation of the wall of Sippar with earth like a great mountain (and) its peak, verily made the outstanding wall.

LESSON THIRTY-TWO

B.

1. *innemmidū*
2. *ninnabbit*
3. *iṣṣūrū iššāmū / iṣṣūrātum iššāmā*
4. *iššalil*
5. *iddâk*
6. *ittenpeš / ittenpuš*
7. *iddekkeā*
8. *iqqiššā*
9. *ittangarū*
10. *ibbablam*
11. *inūma / ūm iwwaldu*
12. *innenneā*

C.

1. PN *aḫāt* PN$_2$ *itti* PN$_3$ *abīšina* PN$_4$ *ana aššūtim īḫussi* PN *kussi aḫātīša ana bīt Marduk inašši mārū mala waldū u iwwalladū mārūšinā-ma.* PN$_4$ took PN sister of PN$_2$ from PN$_3$ their father in marriage. PN will carry her sister's chair to the temple of Marduk; however many children are born and will be born are their children only.
2. *Ana Sîn-iddinam qibī-ma; umma Ḫammurapī-ma.* PN *kiam iqbiam, umma šū-ma: "ṣāb našpakim ša bēlī īsiḫam adīni ul iddinūnim-ma našpakam ul ēpuš." Kiam iqbiam. Am-mīnim ṣāb našpakim ana* PN *lā innadim-ma našpakum lā innepuš? Ūm ṭuppī anniam tammaru ṣāb našpakim* PN *apul-ma našpakam ša qātīšu līpuš. Arḫiš ṣāb našpakim ul tappalšū-ma pīḫatum šī ina muḫḫīka iššakkan.* Speak to Sîn-iddinam; thus Ḫammurapi. PN spoke to me as follows: "The cargo boat gang that my lord assigned me has not yet been given to me and so I have not yet made up the cargo boat." Thus he said to me. Why has the cargo boat gang not been given to PN, so that the cargo boat has not been made up? When you see this tablet of mine, pay PN the cargo boat gang that he may make up the cargo boat under his authority. If you do not pay him the cargo boat gang quickly that responsibility will be upon you.
3. *Aššum šīpātim qatnātim ša tērišanni: inanna kasap šīpātim šināti iššaqil-ma šīpātum iššāmā.* Concerning the fine wool that you (ms) requested of me: now the silver for that wool was weighted out and the wool was purchased.
4. *Am-mīnim bāʾerū ša maḫrīka uššabū-ma rīqū? Am-mīnim kiam lā tašpuram, umma attā-ma: "ḫarrānum inneppeš"?* Why are the *bāʾerum*-troops who are with you (ms) sitting around idle? Why have you not written to me as follows: "An expedition is being made"?
5. *Inanna ana šar mātim šâti aššum ittīšu nenmudim aštapar.* I have now written to the king of that land about joining forces with him.
6. *Ina waṣêni warkat numātīni išālūniāti.* As we left they (m) asked us about the disposition of our vessels.
7. *iṣṣūrātum ina ugārim ittanmarā.* Birds have been seen in the meadow.

D. 5 *šumma dayyānum dīnam idīn, purussâm iprus, kunukkam ušēzib, warkānum-ma dīššu īteni, dayyānam šuāti ina dīn idīnu enêm ukannūšū-ma rugummâm ša ina dīnim šuāti ibbaššû adi šinšerīšu inaddin; u ina puḫrim ina kussi dayyānūtīšu ušetbûšū-ma ul itâr-ma itti dayyānī ina dīnim ul uššab.* If a judge adjudicated a decision, rendered a verdict, had a sealed document deposited, (and) later on changed his decision, that judge will be convicted of changing the decision he adjudicated and will give up to twelve times the fine that was in force in that judgment; further, he will be removed from his judicial seat in the assembly, and will not longer sit with the judges in decision(s).

9–12 9 *šumma awīlum ša mimmûšu ḫalqu mimmâšu ḫalqam ina qāti/qātī awīlim iṣṣabat, awīlum ša ḫulqum ina qātīšu ṣabtu "nādinānum-mi iddinam; maḫar šībī-mi ašām" iqtabi, u bēl ḫulqim "šībī mūde ḫulqīyā-mi lublam" iqtabi, šayyāmānum nādin iddinūšum u šībī ša ina maḫrīšunu išāmu itbalam u bēl ḫulqim šībī mūde ḫulqīšu itbalam, dayyānū awâtīšunu immarū-ma šībū ša maḫrīšunu šīmum iššāmu u šībū mūde ḫulqim mūdûssunu maḫar ilim iqabbû-ma nādinānum šarrāq; iddâk; bēl ḫulqim ḫuluqšu ileqqe; šayyāmānum ina bīt nādinānim kasap išqulu ileqqe.* 10 *šumma šayyāmānum nādin iddinūšum u šībī ša ina maḫrīšunu išāmu lā itbalam, bēl ḫulqim-ma šībī mūde ḫulqīšu itbalam, šayyāmānum šarrāq iddâk; bēl ḫulqim ḫuluqšu ileqqe.* 11 *šumma bēl ḫulqim šībī mūde ḫulqīšu lā itbalam, sar; tuššam-ma idke; iddâk.* 12 *šumma nādinānum ana šīmtim ittalak, šayyāmānum ina bīt nādinānim rugummê dīnim šuāti adi ḫamšīšu ileqqe.* 9 If a man whose property is missing has seized his missing property in a(nother) man's possession, (and) the man in whose possession the missing property was seized has said, "A seller sold to me; I bought before witnesses," and the owner of the stolen property has said, "Let me produce witnesses who recognize my stolen property," (and) the buyer has produced the seller who sold to him and the witnesses before whom he bought and the owner of the stolen property has produced the witnesses who recognize his stolen property, the judges will consider their words and if the witnesses before whom the purchase was made and the witnesses who recognize the stolen property say what they know before the god then the seller is a thief; he will be executed; the owner of the stolen property will receive his stolen property; the buyer will receive the silver he weighed out from the seller's estate. 10 If the buyer has not produced the seller who sold to him and the witnesses before whom he bought, but the owner of the stolen property has produced witnesses who recognize his stolen property, the buyer is a thief; he will be executed; the owner of the property will receive his stolen property. 11 If the owner of the property has not produced witnesses who recognise his stolen property he is a liar; he raised only slander; he will be executed. 12 If the seller has passed on, the buyer will receive up to five times the fine for that judgment from the seller's estate.

58 *šumma ištu ṣēnū ina ugārim īteliānim kannū gamartim ina abullim ittaḫlalū rēʾûm ṣēnī ana eqlim iddī-ma eqlam ṣēnī uštākil, rēʾûm eqel ušākilu inaṣṣar-ma ina ebūrim ana būrim šūši kur âm ana bēl eqlim imaddad.* If, after a flock has come up from a meadow, the "termination pennants"? have been hung from the city gate, (yet) the shepherd let the flock go to a field (i.e., put the flock out to pasture), and allowed the flock to use the field, the shepherd will look after the field he allowed to be used and will measure out sixty kor of grain per *būrum* to the owner of the field at harvest time.

61–62 61 *šumma nukaribbum eqlam ina zaqāpim lā igmur-ma nidītam īzib nidītam ana libbi zīttīšu išakkanūšum.* 62 *šumma eqlam ša innadnūšum ana kirîm lā izqup, šumma abšinnum, bilat eqlim ša šanātim ša innadû nukaribbum ana bēl eqlim kīma itêšu imaddad; u eqlam šipram ippeš-ma ana bēl eqlim utār.* 61 If a gardener did not finish planting a field and left an uncultivated plot, the uncultivated plot will be placed toward his share. 62 If he did not plant a field that was given to him as an orchard, if (it was) a cultivated field, the gardner will measure out to the owner of the field produce of the field for the years that it was left fallow according to his neighbors; further, he will work and return the field to the field's owner.

137 *šumma awīlum ana šugītim ša mārī uldūšum ū lū nadītim ša mārī ušaršûšu ezēbim pānīšu ištakan, ana sinništim šuāti šeriktaša utarrūšim; u muttat eqlim kirîm u bīšim inaddinūšim-ma mārīša urabba; ištu mārīša urtabbû ina mimma ša ana mārīša innadnu zīttam kīma aplim ištēn inaddinūšim-ma mutu libbīša iḫḫassi.* If a man has decided to divorce a junior wife who bore him children or a *nadītum* who provided him with children, that woman's dowry will be returned to her; further half of the field, orchard, and property will be given to her so that she may raise her children; after she has raised her children she will be given a share like (that of) an individual heir from whatever was given to her children, and then the man of her heart may marry her.

159 *šumma awīlum ša ana bīt emīšu biblam ušābilu terḫatam iddinu ana sinništim šanītim uptallis-ma ana emīšu "māratka ul aḫḫaz" iqtabi, abi mārtim mimma ša ibbablūšum itabbal.* If a man who had dispatched a marriage-gift to his father-in-law's estate and given the bride-price has become attracted to another woman and said to his father-in-law "I will not marry your daughter," the daughter's father will keep for himself whatever was brought to him.

176 *u šumma warad ekallim ū lū warad muškēnim mārat awīlim īḫuz-ma inūma īḫuzūši qadum šeriktim ša bīt abīša ana bīt warad ekallim ū lū warad muškēnim īrum-ma ištu innemdū bītam īpušū bīšam iršû warkānum-ma lū warad ekallim ū lū warad muškēnim ana šīmtim ittalak mārat awīlim šeriktaša ileqqe; u mimma ša mussa u šī ištu innemdū iršû ana šinīšu izuzzū-ma mišlam bēl wardim ileqqe mišlam mārat awīlim ana mārīša ileqqe.* And if a palace slave or a *muškēnum*'s slave married a daughter of an *awīlum* and when he married her she entered the house of the palace slave or *muškēnum*'s slave with a dowry from (lit., of) her father's estate and afterward, after they were joined, made a home, (and) acquired property, the palace slave or the *muškēnum*'s slave passed on, the *awīlum*'s daughter will receive her dowry; further, whatever her husband and she acquired after they were joined will be divided in two, and the slave's owner will receive half (and) the *awīlum*'s daughter will receive half for her children.

188–189 188 *šumma mār ummiānim māram ana tarbītim ilqē-ma šipir qātīšu uštāḫissu, ul ibbaqqar.* 189 *šumma šipir qātīšu lā uštāḫissu, tarbītum šī ana bīt abīšu itâr.* 188 If a member of a guild adopted a son to raise and has taught him his craft, he will not be contested. 189 If he has not taught him his craft, said adopted child will/may return to his paternal estate.

134–136 134 *šum-ma a-wi-lum iš-ša-li-il-ma i-na* É-*šu ša a-ka-li-im la i-ba-aš-ši aš-ša-sú a-na* É *ša-ni-im i-ir-ru-ub* MUNUS *ši-i ar-nam ú-ul i-šu*. 135 *šum-ma a-wi-lum iš-ša-li-il-ma i-na* É-*šu ša a-ka-li-im la i-ba-aš-ši a-na pa-ni-šu aš-ša-sú a-na* É *ša-ni-im i-te-ru-ub-ma* DUMU. MEŠ *it-ta-la-ad i-na wa-ar-ka mu-sà it-tu-ra-am-ma* URU-*šu ik-ta-áš-dam* MUNUS *ši-i a-na ḫa-wi-ri-ša i-ta-ar* DUMU.MEŠ *wa-ar-ki a-bi-šu-nu i-il-la-ku*. 136 *šum-ma a-wi-lum* URU-*šu id-di-ma it-ta-bi-it wa-ar-ki-šu aš-ša-sú a-na* É *ša-ni-im i-te-ru-ub šum-ma a-wi-lum šu-ú it-tu-ra-am-ma aš-ša-sú iṣ-ṣa-ba-at aš-šum* URU-*šu i-ze-ru-ma in-na-bi-tu aš-ša-at mu-na-ab-tim a-na mu-ti-ša ú-ul i-ta-ar*.

134 *šumma awīlum iššalil-ma ina bītīšu ša akālim lā ibašši, aššassu ana bīt šanîm irrub; sinništum šī arnam ul īšu*. 135 *šumma awīlum iššalil-ma ina bītīšu ša akālim lā ibašši, ana pānīšu aššassu ana bīt šanîm īterum-ma mārī ittalad, ina warka mussa ittūram-ma āl(ā)šu iktašdam, sinništum šī ana ḫāwirīša itâr; mārū warki abīšunu illakū*. 136 *šumma awīlum āl(ā)šu iddī-ma itta(ʾ)bit, warkīšu aššassu ana bīt šanîm īterub, šumma awīlum šū ittūram-ma aššassu iṣṣabat, aššum āl(ā)šu izērū-ma innābitu, aššat munnabtim ana mutīša ul itâr*. 134 If a man was taken captive and there is not enough to eat in his house, his wife may enter another's house; that woman will have no guilt. 135 If a man was taken captive and there is not enough to eat in his house, (and) therefore (or, before his return) his wife has entered another's house and has born children, (and) later her husband has returned and reached his town, that woman will return to her first husband; the children will follow their father. 136 If a man abandoned his town and has fled, (and) after his departure his wife has entered another's house, if that man has returned and seized his wife, because he despised his town and fled, the fugitive's wife will not return to her husband.

E. 1. *šumma šittā naplasātum ṣellūšina nenm[udū], sunqum ina mātim i[bb]ašši*. If the sides of the two lobes are joined, famine will appear in the land.

2. *šumma martum nasḫat-ma [in]a bāb ekallim [...]at, [nu]kurtum iššakkan*. If the gall bladder is removed and [...]ed in the palace gate, war will happen.

3. *šumma ubān iṣṣurim imittam u šumēlam nawer, atta u nakrum tannammarā*. If the "finger" of the "bird" is bright on the right and the left, the enemy and you will meet.

4. *šumma izbum pānī nēšim šakin, šarrum [d]annum ibbaššī-ma mātam šâti unnaš*. If the anomaly has the face of a lion, a mighty king will appear and weaken that land.

5. *šumma izbum kīma barbarim bibbum ina mātim ibba[š]ši*. If the anomaly is like a wolf, plague will appear in the land.

6. *šumma izbum ina irtīšu petī-ma u daltum ša ši[...] šaknat-[m]a ippette u i‹nne›ddil, mātum šī innandi; [ḫ]arrānātūša ippeḫḫeā*. If the anomaly is open in its chest and also the door of the ... is in place and opens and closes, that land will be overthrown; its roads will be open.

7. DIŠ *qí-na-tum i-mi-tam pa-ar-sà-at ru-bu-ú ú-la in-né-mi-du.*

   šumma qinnatum imittam parsat, rubû ula innemmidū. If the buttocks are divided on the right, the princes will not join forces.

8. *šum-ma mar-tum* SAG-*ša da-ma-am la-pi-it* SUKKAL.MAḪ *im-ma-ḫa-aṣ šum-ma mar-tum qá-ab-la-ša da-ma-am la-ap-ta* MÁŠ.ŠU.GÍD.GÍD.

   šumma martum rēšūša damam lapit, sukkalmaḫḫum immaḫḫaṣ; šumma martum qablāša damam laptā, bārûm. If the top of the gall bladder is smeared with blood, the chief minister will be struck; if the middle of the gall bladder is smeared with blood, the diviner.

F. 1. *Išteat amtam Mutī-bāštī šumša Sîn-pilaḫ ana Šaddašu aššatīšu iqīš. Mārū Sîn-pilaḫ ul iraggamūšim. Ištu ūm ṭup[p]um innezbu, ‹mārū› mala Mutī-bāštī ulladu ša Šaddašū-ma. Saniq-pīša mārat Šaddašu.*

   Sîn-pilaḫ gave his wife Šaddašu a slave named Mutī-bāštī. The children of Sîn-pilaḫ will not contest against her. From the day the tablet is deposited, however many children Mutī-bāštī bears belong only to Šaddašu. Saniq-pīša is the daughter of Šaddašu.

2. *Parasrab manā kaspum libbi/libbu ištēn manā kaspim ša itti Imlik-Sîn ana ḫamšā agrī innadnu ša ana ḫarrān šarrim innagrū, ezub tibût ṣāb Iddin-Ea u Ištar-īnāya.*

   Five-sixths mina silver from the one mina of silver that was given by Imlik-Sîn for fifty hirelings, who were hired for the royal campaign; except for the levy of the troops of Iddin-Ea and Ištar-īnāya.

G. 1. *Ana [T]arību[m] qibī-ma; umma Iddin-yatum-ma. Šamaš liballiṭka. Šulpae-bāni mār bīt ṭuppim kiam ulammid, umma šū-ma: "Bīt abim ul īšū-ma ana bīt sekretim ana mārūtim ērub. Bīt ana mārūtim ērubu ana ṣīt ekallim uštēṣû." [ṭup]pi bēlīya ana bītim nadānim [i]llikak-kūnūšim-[m]a am-mīni lā innapil-ma udabbab? ū lū bīt ana mārūtim īrubu literrūšum ū lū bītam mali bītim idiššum-ma lā uda[bb]ab.*

   Speak to Tarībum; thus Iddin-yatum. May Šamaš keep you well. The military scribe Šulpae-bāni made known as follows: "I have no paternal estate, and so I entered the house of a *sekretum* in adoption. The house I entered in adoption has been leased on a palace lease." My lord's tablet (instructing you) to give a house came to you, so why was he not satisfied, so that he complains? Either the house he entered in adoption should be returned to him, or give him a house as large as (that) house so that he may not complain.

2. *Ana Marduk-nāṣir u Šamaš-ḫāzir qibī-ma; umma Ḫammurapī-ma. Anumma ṭuppi isiḫti kiriātim ša ana šandanakkī izzuz[z]ā [u]štābilakkunūšim. [Ana p]ī ṭuppātim šināti [kiriāt]im zūzāšunūšim.*
   Speak to Marduk-nāṣir and Šamaš-ḫāzir; thus Ḫammurapi. I have herewith dispatched to you the certificate of assignment of the orchards that were distributed to the administrators. Distribute the orchards to them according to these documents.

3. *Ana awīlim qibī-ma; umma Ipqu-Šalā-ma. Šamaš u Marduk dāriš ūmī liballiṭūka. Lū šalmāta; lū balṭāta. Ilum nāṣirka rēš damiqtīka likīl. Ana šulmīka ašpuram; šulumka maḫar Šamaš u Marduk lū dāri. Šinā maškī ana parās ‹w›arkatim uštābilakku. Aḫī atta kīma rabûtīka warkatam purus tukkil-ma, liātim dannātim lissuḫānim. Rēḫet liātīya šuātu ša ina maḫrīka innezzibā: adi ašapparam-ma ileqqûnim aḫī atta nīdi aḫim lā taraššīšināšim. Ana ša ašpurakkum lā tuštaʾʾa. Šumma liātum dannātum mitḫāriš alākam adi maḫrīya ilaʾʾâ, warkatam tukkil purus-ma, mitḫāriš-ma lissuḫānim.*

Speak to the man; thus Ipqu-Šala. May Šamaš and Marduk keep you well forever. Be healthy; be well. May the god who protects you do well by you. I wrote concerning your health; may your health be ever before Šamaš and Marduk. I have dispatched to you two hides to check into. You, my brother, in accord with your high station, check into it carefully, so that they (f) transfer strong cattle to me. As for that remainder of my cattle that are being left with you: until I write for them (m) to take (them), you, my brother, must not be negligent about them (the cattle). Do not be idle about what I wrote to you. If strong cattle can come to me together, look carefully into the matter so that they (f) may in fact transfer (them) to me together.

H. *Ša ištu ūm ṣiātim šarrū in šarrī manāma lā īpušū ana Šamaš bēlīya rabîš lū ēpussum. Dūrum šū "In-qibīt-Šamaš-Ḫammurapi māḫirī ayy-irši" šumšu. In palêya damqim, ša Šamaš ibbiu, Sippar āl ṣiātim ša Šamaš ṣābšu in tupšikkim ana Šamaš lū assuḫ. Nāršu lū eḫre; ana erṣetīšu mê dārûtim lū aškun. Nuḫšam u ḫegallam lū ukammer. Ana nišī Sippar rīštam lū aškun; ana balāṭīya lū ikarrabā. Ša ana šīr Šamaš bēlīya u Ayya bēltīya ṭābu lū ēpuš. Šumī damqam ūmišam kīma ilim zakāram ša ana dār lā immaššû in pī nišī lū aškun.*

What from ancient times no kings among the kings had done, I verily did greatly for my lord Šamaš. The name of this wall is "By-the-command-of-Šamaš-may-Ḫammurapi-have-no-rivals." In my good reign, which Šamaš summoned, I verily removed the workers of Sippar from corvée duty for Šamaš in Sippar, the ancient city of Šamaš. Verily I dug its canal; I verily set up (a) continual water (supply) for its districts. I verily heaped up prosperity and abundance. I verily brought about joy for the people of Sippar, so that they invoke blessings for my life. I verily did what is pleasing to my lord Šamaš and my lady Ayya. I verily placed in the people's mouths the daily invoking of my good name like a god('s), which will not be forgotten forever.

LESSON THIRTY-THREE

C. 1. KUN GUD
2. NÍG.KAS7 SANGA
3. ZÚ.LUM(.MA).MEŠ NUN
4. A.GÀR NU.MU.SU
5. KAR ZIMBIR^{ki}
6. KISLAḪ NA.GADA

D. 1. *nimtagar*
2. *atlakā*
3. *šaman* (or, *šamnum ana*) *piš-šuš abīya*
4. *ittaʾʾidū*
5. *am-mīnim tamtaḫḫaṣā*
6. *tiṣbutā*
7. *aštāl*
8. *imtaḫrū*
9. *ītawâ*
10. *ittīša ittatīl*
11. *taṣṣabbatā*
12. *ina bītīki tētellî*

E. 35–37 35 *šumma awīlum liātim u ṣēnī ša šarrum ana rēdîm iddinu ina qāti rēdîm ištām, ina kaspīšu ītelli.* 36 *eqlum kirûm u bītum ša rēdîm bāʾerim ū nāši biltim ana kaspim ul innaddin.* 37 *šumma awīlum eqlam kiriam ū bītam ša rēdîm bāʾerim ū nāši biltim ištām, ṭuppašu iḫḫeppe u ina kaspīšu ītelli; eqlum kirûm ū bītum ana bēlīšu itâr.* 35 If a man has purchased from a *rēdûm* cattle or flocks that the king gave to the *rēdûm*, he will forfeit his silver. 36 A field, orchard, or house of a *rēdûm*, *bāʾerum* or tenant will not be sold for silver. 37 If a man has purchased a field, orchard, or house of a *rēdûm*, *bāʾerum* or tenant, his tablet will be broken and he will also forfeit his silver; the field, orchard, or house will return to its owner.

57 *šumma reʾûm ana šammī ṣēnī šūkulim itti bēl eqlim lā imtagar-ma balum bēl eqlim eqlam ṣēnī uštākil, bēl eqlim eqelšu iṣṣid, reʾûm ša ina balum bēl eqlim ṣēnī ušākilu elēnum-ma ana būrim ešrā kur âm ana bēl eqlim inaddin.* If a shepherd did not come to an agreement with the owner of a field to feed a flock herbage, but has fed the flock on the field without the field owner's consent, the field owner will harvest his field (and) the shepherd who fed the flock without the field owner's consent will give the field owner twenty kor of grain per *būr* in addition.

64 *šumma awīlum kirīšu ana nukaribbim ana rukkubim iddin nukaribbum adi kiriam ṣabtu ina bilat kirîm šittīn ana bēl kirîm inaddin; šaluštam šū ileqqe.* If a man gave his orchard to a gardener for pollination, the gardener, as long as he holds the orchard, will give two thirds of the yield of the orchard to the owner of the orchard, (while) he himself will receive one third.

116 *šumma nipûtum ina bīt nēpīša ina maḫāṣim ū lū ina uššušim imtūt, bēl nipûtim tamkāršu ukām-ma šumma mār awīlim māršu idukkū, šumma warad awīlim šalušti manā kaspam išaqqal; u ina mimma šumšu mala iddinu ītelli.* If a pledge has died in her/his distrainer's house through beating or through mistreatment, the owner of the pledge will convict his merchant, and if it was an *awīlum*'s offspring, they will execute his offspring, if it was an *awīlum*'s slave, he will weigh out one third mina of silver; and he will also forfeit whatever he had given.

129–132 129 *šumma aššat awīlim itti zikarim šanîm ina itūlim ittaṣbat, ikassûšunūtī-ma ana mê inaddûšunūti; šumma bēl aššatim aššassu uballaṭ u šarrum warassu uballaṭ.* 130 *šumma awīlum aššat awīlim ša zikaram lā īdû-ma ina bīt abīša wašbat ukabbilšī-ma ina sunīša ittatīl-ma iṣṣabtūšu, awīlum šū iddâk; sinništum šī ūtaššar.* 131 *šumma aššat awīlim mussa ubbiršī-ma itti zikarim šanîm ina utūlim lā iṣṣabit, nīš ilim izakkar ana bītīša itâr.* 132 *šumma aššat awīlim aššum zikarim šanîm ubānum elīša ittariṣ-ma itti zikarim šanîm ina utūlim lā ittaṣbat ana mutīša Id išalli.* 129 If an *awīlum*'s wife has been caught lying with another man, they will be bound and thrown into the water; if the wife's lord wishes to spare his wife, the king may also spare his servant. 130 If an *awīlum* immobilized and had intercourse with an *awīlum*'s wife who had not known a man and who was living in her father's house, and he has been caught, that *awīlum* will be executed; that woman will be released. 131 If a man's wife was accused by her husband but was not caught lying with another man, she will take an oath and return to her house. 132 If a finger has been pointed at an *awīlum*'s wife on account of another man but she has not been caught lying with another man, she will dive into the River for her husband.

142–143 142 *šumma sinništum mussa izēr-ma "ul taḫḫazannī" iqtabi, warkassa ina bābtīša ipparras-ma šumma naṣrat-ma ḫiṭītam lā īšu u mussa waṣī-ma magal ušamṭāši, sinništum šī arnam ul īšu; šeriktaša ileqqē-ma ana bīt abīša ittallak.* 143 *šumma lā naṣrat-ma waṣiat bīssa usappaḫ mussa ušamṭa, sinništam šuāti ana mê inaddûši.* 142 If a woman detested her husband and has said, "you will not have me," her circumstances will be investigated in her district, and if she has been vigilant and has no fault, but her husband goes out and treats her very badly, that woman has no offense; she may take her dowry and go off to her father's house. 143 If she has not been vigilant and goes out, squanders her estate, (and) treats her husband badly, that woman will be cast into the water.

155–157 155 *šumma awīlum ana mārīšu kallatam iḫīr-ma māršu ilmassi šū warkānum-ma ina sūnīša ittatīl-ma iṣṣabtūšu, awīlam šuāti ikassûšū-ma ana mê inaddûšu.* 156 *šumma awīlum ana mārīšu kallatam iḫīr-ma māršu lā ilmassī-ma šū ina sūnīša ittatīl, mišil manā kaspam išaqqalšim-ma u mimma ša ištu bīt abīša ublam ušallamšim-ma mutu libbīša iḫḫassi.* 157 *šumma awīlum warki abīšu ina sūn ummīšu ittatīl, kilallīšunu iqallûšunūti.* 155 If a man chose a bride for his son and the son has known her, (and) he himself has later had intercourse with her and has been caught, that man will be bound and thrown into the water. 156 If a man has chosen a bride for his son and his son has not known her, (and) he himself has had intercourse with her, he will weigh out for her half a mina of silver; and also whatever she brought from her father's estate he will restore to her and the husband she wishes may marry her. 157 If a man has had intercourse with his mother after the death of his father, they will both be burned.

165–166 165 *šum-ma a-wi-lum a-na* IBILA-*šu ša i-in-šu maḫ-ru* A.ŠÀ ^{giš}KIRI$_6$ *ù* É *iš-ru-uk ku-nu-kam iš-ṭur-šum wa-ar-ka a-bu-um a-na ši-im-tim it-ta-al-ku i-nu-ma aḫ-ḫu i-zu-uz-zu qí-iš-ti a-bu-um id-di-nu-šum i-le-qé-*

ta-al-ku i-nu-ma aḫ-ḫu i-zu-uz-zu qí-iš-ti a-bu-um id-di-nu-šum i-le-qé-ma e-le-nu-um-ma i-na NÍG.GA É A.BA *mi-it-ḫa-ri-iš i-zu-uz-zu.* 166 *šum-ma a-wi-lum a-na* DUMU.MEŠ *ša ir-šu-ú aš-ša-tim i-ḫu-uz a-na* DUMU-*šu ṣe-eḫ-ri-im aš-ša-tam la i-ḫu-uz wa-ar-ka a-bu-um a-na ši-im-tim it-ta-al-ku i-nu-ma aḫ-ḫu i-zu-uz-zu i-na* NÍG.GA É A.BA *a-na a-ḫi-šu-nu ṣe-eḫ-ri-im ša aš-ša-tam la aḫ-zu e-li-a-at zi-it-ti-šu* KUG.BABBAR *ter-ḫa-tim i-ša-ak-ka-nu-šum-ma aš-ša-tam ú-ša-aḫ-ḫa-zu-šu.*

165 *šumma awīlum ana aplīšu ša īššu maḫru eqlam kiriam ū bītam išruk kunukkam išṭuršum, warka abum ana šīmtim ittalku inūma aḫḫū izuzzū qīšti abum iddinūšum ileqqē-ma elēnum-ma ina makkūr bīt abim mitḫāriš izuzzū.* 166 *šumma awīlum ana mārī ša iršû aššātim īḫuz ana mārīšu ṣeḫrim aššatam lā īḫuz warka abum ana šīmtim ittalku inūma aḫḫū izuzzū ina makkūr bīt abim ana aḫīšunu ṣeḫrim ša aššatam lā aḫzu eliāt zīttīšu kasap terḫatim išakkanūšum-ma aššatam ušaḫḫazūšu.* 165 If a man gave a field, an orchard, or a house to his heir who pleased him and wrote out a sealed document for him, after the father has gone to his fate, when the brothers take shares, he will take the bequest his father gave him and in addition they will divide the property of the father's estate equally. 166 If a man got wives for the sons he had (but) did not get a wife for his youngest son, after the father has gone to his fate, when the brothers take shares, they will set up out of the father's property bride-price silver as an additional sum to his share for their young brother who does not have a wife, and obtain a wife for him.

F.

1. *šumma ina išdī naplaštim kakkum/kakkū šinā imittam u šumēlam ittaṭ[lū], ana šarrim ayyimma ana salīmim taša[ppar-ma] salīmšu teleqqēšu.* If at the base of the lobe two weapons faced each other on the right and left, you (ms) will send to some king for peace, and receive his peace from him.
2. *[šumma] kakkum šakim-[ma ṣ]īt rēšim iṭṭul u piṭru ana pānīšu paṭir, [mā]ri šipri maḫrûm bussurat ḫadêm našīkum.* If the weapon was in place and faced the *ṣīt rēšim,* and also a fissure is loosened in front of it, the first messenger has for you (ms) news for rejoicing.
3. *šumma martum u ubānum šitnunā, puḫrum ula imtaggar.* If the gall bladder and the finger are equal, the assembly will not come to an agreement.
4. *šumma ina ṣēr birītim kakkum šinā ittaṭlū, šarrānū ina puḫrim innammarū.* If upon the border two weapons faced each other, kings will meet in the assembly.
5. *šumma kakki/kakkū imittim šalāštum ittaṭlū, šarram ina libbi ekallīšu ussarūšū-ma idukkūšu; šanûm šumšu: bārûm ašar illaku imaqqut.* If three weapons on the right side faced each other, the king will be taken captive in his palace and killed; another interpretation of it: the haruspex will fall wherever he goes.
6. *šumma tiše šētum, atta u nakerka taṣṣabbatā-ma aḫum aḫ[a]m ušamqat.* If there are nine *šētum,* your (ms) enemy and you will quarrel and one will fell the other.

7. *šumma izbum qaqqassu ana ḫallīšu kamis-ma itti zibbatīšu tiṣbut, awīlum ṣeḫēr bītīšu u unêtīšu īnāšu immarā.* If the head of the malformed foetus is bent down toward its crotch/hind legs and connected with its tail, the man's eyes will see the decrease of his household and his utensils.

8. *šumma rē[š] libbim qâ saḫer, nīš ilim šarram ṣabit.* If the top of the heart is surrounded with thread, an oath (lit., life of a god) holds the king.

9. B[E] KÁ É.GAL *ma-aš-ka-an-šu i-zi-im-ma a-na e-le-nu-um i-te-li-a-am* LÚ KÚR-*ka ú-ṣe-ḫe-er-ka pi-a-am ma-ṭi-a-am ta-ša-ka-an-šu.*

   šum[ma] bāb ekallim maškaššu īzim-ma ana elēnum īteliam, nakerka uṣeḫḫerka; piam maṭiam tašakkaššu. If the palace gate left its location and came upward besides, your (ms) enemy will diminish you; you will speak humbly to him.

10. *šum-ma mar-tum ip-lu-uš-ma it-ta-ṣí a-wi-lum it-ta-aṣ-ṣí.*

   šumma martum ipluš-ma ittaṣi, awīlum ittaṣṣi. If the gall bladder broke through and protruded, the man will depart.

G. 1. *Gimillum mār Appali itti ramānīšu Ina-Esagil-zērum mār Warad-ilīšu ana ikkarūtim adi paṭār erēšim īgur-ma idi / idī ištēn warḫim ištēn šiqil kaspam išaqqal. ... Alpī urāq-ma kasap inītim išaqqal. Ina šalšim warḫim qātam iṣabbat. [Alpī] inappuš inassaḫ inaddi ittallak, ina idīšu ītelli; ina libbi idīšu ištēn šiqil kaspam maḫir.*

   Gimillum son of Appalu, on his own, hired Ina-Esagil-zērum son of Warad-ilīšu for plowing until the end of the planting, and will pay as the wages of one month one shekel of silver. ... If he keeps the oxen idle he will pay the hire-rate silver. In the third month he will give assistance. If he relaxes concerning the oxen, moves on, drops (the work), (or) goes away, he will forfeit his wages; from his wages he may have one shekel of silver.

2. *Šinā ṣubātū ša labšat; šittā paršīgātum ‹ša› aprat; ištēn eršum; šalāš kussiātum; ištēt šiqqatum ša erbet qa šamnam maliat; ištēn pišannum garru ša erbe sât akalam malû: mimma annîm ša Ātanaḫ-ilī abūša mār Ṣillī-Šamaš ana Ṣiḫar-ṭilluk egītim mārtīšu iddinū-ma ana bīt Zimer-Šamaš ana Warad-Ulmaššītum mārīšu ušēribu. Ḫamšat šiqil kaspam terḫassa ina qāti Zimer-Šamaš Ātanaḫ-ilī abūša maḫir. Libbašu ṭāb. Ṣiḫar-ṭilluk ana Warad-Ulmaššītum mutīša "ul mu[tī atta]" iq[abbī-ma ana kaspim inaddi]šši; u [Warad-Ulmaššītum] ana [Ṣiḫar-ṭilluk aššatīšu] "ul [aššatī atti]" i[qabbī-ma] šittīn manā [kaspam išaqqal]. Nīš Šamaš Marduk [u Ammī-ṣaduqa] šarrim itmû.*

   Two garments that she is wearing; two caps that she wears on her head; one bed; three chairs; one basin filled with four liters of oil; one round basket filled with four seahs of food: All this is what her father Ātanaḫ-ilī, the son of Ṣillī-Šamaš, gave to his daughter Ṣiḫar-ṭilluk the *egītum* and presented to the house of Zimer-Šamaš for his son Warad-Ulmaššītum. Ātanaḫ-ilī is in receipt of five shekels of silver from Zimer-Šamaš as her bride-price. His heart is satisfied. Should Ṣiḫar-ṭilluk say to Warad-Ulmaššītum her husband, "you are not my husband," he may sell her; and should Warad-Ulmaššītum say to Ṣiḫar-ṭilluk his wife, "you are not my wife," he will pay two-thirds of a mina of silver. They swore by the life of Šamaš, Marduk, and Ammī-ṣaduqa.

H. 1. *Ana Amat-Kallatim qibī-ma; umma Šamaš-mušēzib-ma. Šamaš u Marduk liballiṭūki. Aššum eqlim, ša atti u Narāmtani tiṣbutātina, ana Mār-Sippar ṭuppī u ṭuppi Tappatum udanninam-ma uštābilam. Adi allakam, eqlam ul izuzzakkināšim; ina alākīya ana dayyān‹ī› Sippar uṭaḫḫākinātī-ma awâtīkina immarū-ma ekallam ikaššadū-ma ḫibiltaki ugammarakkim. Aplūtum ṣeḫertum u rabītum ina Sippar ul ibašši.*

Speak to Amat-Kallatim; thus (says) Šamaš-mušēzib. May Šamaš and Marduk keep you alive. Concerning the field about which Narāmtani and you are quarreling, I have forcefully dispatched my tablet and Tappatum's tablet to Mār-Sippar. Until I come, he will not divide the field for you (pl); upon my coming I will present you (pl) to the judges of Sippar so that they can investigate your (pl) case and approach the palace, and it can settle your (sg) damage(s) for you. The institution of the younger and older heir does not exist in Sippar.

2. *Ana Šamaš-ḫāzir qibī-ma; umma Sîn-iddinam-ma. Šamaš u Marduk liballiṭūka. Šamaš-ḫāzir kiam ulammidanni, umma šū-ma: "Pāna inūma ana rēdīka allaku, šinā būr eqlam ṣabtāku; inanna aššum ana biltim [ilqû]ninni, eqlī Wardīya ibtaqranni." Kiam iqbiam. Anumma Šamaš-ḫāzir aṭṭardam; eqlum ša aššumīšu ulammidanni nadiššum? Gana ṭēmam šupram.*

Speak to Šamaš-ḫāzir; thus (says) Sîn-iddinam. May Šamaš and Marduk keep you alive. Šamaš-ḫāzir informed me thus, as follows: "Previously when I served as your *rēdûm*, I had a field of two *būr*; now because I have been seized for rent, Wardīya has brought suit against me for my field." Thus he said to me. I have herewith sent Šamaš-ḫāzir. Was the field about which he informed me given to him? Come, send me a report.

3. *Ana Nabi-ilīšu qibī-ma; umma Sîn-bēl-aplim-ma. Šamaš u Marduk liballiṭūka. Ina šitulti kullizū ištālū-ma igmilū; alpū šalā‹m›šunu ṭāb u ḫīṭam ul īšû. Ana pī sūqim taqūl-ma anniam tašpuram. Alpū ḫīṭam ul īšû; mimma lā tanazziq. Alpī kalâšunu anākū-ma ušallam; ana awātim annītim lā tanazziq. Alpū šalmū; ḫīṭam ul īšû. U mērešam erriš; meḫer ṭuppim uštābilakkum; mimma lā tanazziq. Aššum tašpuram, umma attā-ma, "Ana alpī īkka lā tanašši," aqbī-ma gimlum tiṣbut-ma ana gamālim ul ibašši.*

Speak to Nabi-ilīšu; thus (says) Sîn-bēl-aplim. May Šamaš and Marduk keep you alive. The ox-drivers pondered in deliberation and came to an agreement; the health of the oxen is good and they have no fault. You paid attention to street talk, and that (is what) you wrote to me. (But) the oxen have no fault; do not worry at all. I myself will take care of all the oxen; do not worry about this matter. The oxen are fine; they have no fault. Moreover I will plow the cultivated land; I have sent you a copy of the tablet; do not worry at all. Because you wrote, "Do not covet the oxen," I gave order that a reserve ox be engaged, but there are none to spare.

4. *Ana Yasmaḫ-[Addu] qibī-m[a]; umma Išme-Dagan aḫūkā-ma. Aššum ṭēm awīl‹ê› Turukkim, ša tašpuram, ṭēmšunu ittanakkir. Ina kiam adi inanna takītt[am] ul ašapp[arakkum]. ‹Bēl› awâtīšu[nu], ša ana salīm[im] ṣabt[u/ū], ittatla[k(ū)]. Iantakim Lu-Ninsuanna Water-Nanum u awīlê rabbûtim-ma iḫakkû, u kiam išpurūnim, ummāmi: "Ištu līṭī annûtim lā tanaddinam, urram ū lū ullītiš ašar atlukim nittallak." Ašrānum lišpu[rū] u ašar atlukim [l]ittal[kū]. [...] lū ī[de] [Ina ḫ]alṣi[m], [š]a [w]ašbāt, ṭēmka lū ṣabit.*

Speak to Yasmaḫ-Addu; thus (says) your brother Išme-Dagan. Concerning the situation of the men of Turukkum, about which you wrote me, their situation keeps changing. Therefore until now I have not been sending you confirmation. Their adversary(ies), who was/were engaged in peace (negotiations), has/have left. They were awaiting Iantakim, Lu-Ninsuanna, Water-Nanum, and the noblemen, and wrote thus to me: "Since you will not give (up) these hostages, tomorrow or the day after we will depart to wherever possible." Let them send there that they may depart to wherever possible. ... let me know. In the fortress that you inhabit be ready for action (lit., let your action be taken).

I. 1. *[i]ltam zumrā rašubti ilātim*
2. *litta*ʾʾ*id bēlet nišī rabīt Igigi*
3. *Eštar zumrā rašubti ilātim litta*ʾʾ*id*
4. *bēlet iššī rabīt Igigi*

Sing of the goddess, most awesome of goddesses;
Let her be praised, the lady of the people, great one of the Igigi.
Sing of Eštar, most awesome of goddess; let her be praised;
The lady of the women, great one of the Igigi.

5. *šāt mēleṣim ru*ʾ*āmam labšat*
6. *za*ʾ*nat inbī mēqiam u kuzbam*
7. *Eštar mēleṣim ru*ʾ*āmam labšat*
8. *za*ʾ*nat inbī mēqiam u kuzbam*

She of joy, clothed in charm,
Endowed with attractiveness, appeal?, and allure;
Eštar of joy, clothed in charm,
Endowed with attractiveness, appeal?, and allure.

9. *[š]aptīn duššupat balāṭum pīša*
10. *simtišša iḫannimā ṣīḫātum*
11. *šarḫat irīmū ramû rēšušša*
12. *baniā šimtāša bitrāmā īnāša šit*ʾ*ārā*

She is sweet of lips, her mouth is life;
At her appearance smiles bloom;
She is proud; loveliness is cast upon her;
Her features are beautiful; bright are her eyes, brilliant.

13. *iltum ištāša ibašši milkum*
14. *šīmat mimmāmi qātišša tamḫat*
15. *naplasušša bani buʾāru*
16. *bāštum mašraḫū lamassum šēdum*

The goddess — with her is (good) counsel;
The fate of all she holds in her hand.
At her glance prosperity is built;
Dignity, splendor, fortune, health.

17. *tartâm tešmê ritūmī ṭūbī*
18. *u mitguram tebêl šī-ma*
19. *ardat tattab‹lu› umma tarašši*
20. *izakkarši in-nišī inabbi šumša*

She loves understanding, love, goodness,
And it is she who rules agreement.
The young woman who was taken away acquires a mother;
She invokes her, among the people she calls her name.

LESSON THIRTY-FOUR

C.
1. GABA SANGA
2. KUN KU$_6$
3. NÍG.KAS$_7$ ZÚ.LUM(.MA).MEŠ
4. UGULA ŠITIM.MEŠ
5. A.GÀR ZIMBIR^{ki}
6. $^{(giš)}$MAR.GÍD.DA GÌR.NITA(Ḫ)$_2$
7. SUKKAL *ù* NUN

D.
1. *liktammisū*
2. *itabbi / tizakkar*
3. *iddanabbub*
4. *tattanazziqā*
5. *ittataṣṣiā*
6. *ina lā mitaggurim*
7. *nīteterrub*
8. *ētenelli*
9. *ul assanappaḫ*
10. *attanaṭṭal / addanagga*
11. *šitaʾʾalšu*
12. *ittanallakū*
13. *iḫtatabbalūniāti*
14. *attašši / attabbal / azzabbil*
15. *ana itaddunim / qitayyušim*
16. *attillam*
17. *ništenemme*
18. *tēteterrišī*
19. *šitakkunat*
20. *ītanappal*

E. 13 *šumma awīlum šū šībūšu lā qerbū, dayyānū adānam ana šeššet warḫī išakkanūšum-ma, šumma ina šeššet warḫī šībīšu lā irdeam awīlum šū sar; aran dīnim šuāti ittanašši.* If that man's witnesses are not nearby, the judges will set for him a period of six months, and if in six months he has not brought forward his witnesses, that man is a liar; he will bear the penalty of that case.

125 *šumma awīlum mimmâšu ana maṣṣarūtim iddim-ma ašar iddinu ū lū ina pilšim ū lū ina nabalkattim mimmûšu itti mimmê bēl bītim iḫtaliq, bēl bītim ša īgû-ma mimma ša ana maṣṣarūtim iddinūšum-ma uḫalliqu ušallam-ma ana bēl makkūrim irīab; bēl bītim mimmâšu ḫalqam išteneʾʾī-ma [it]ti šarrāqānīšu ileqqe.* If a man gave his property for safekeeping and where he gave (it) either through a break-in or through a burglary his property along with the property of the owner of the house has gone missing, the owner of the house who was negligent will make good and restore to the owner of the goods whatever he gave him for safekeeping and he lost; the owner of the house will look for his stolen property and get it from his thief.

148–149 148 *šumma awīlum aššatam īḫuz-ma laʾbum iṣṣabassi ana šanītim aḫāzim pānīšu ištakan, iḫḫaz; aššassu ša laʾbum iṣbatu ul izzibši; ina bīt īpušu uššam-ma adi balṭat ittanaššīši.* 149 *šumma sinništum šī ina bīt mutīša wašābam lā imtagar, šeriktaša ša ištu bīt abīša ublam u[š]allamšim-ma ittallak.* 148 If a man married a woman and a skin disease has afflicted her, (and) he has decided to marry another woman, he may marry; he may not divorce his wife whom the disease afflicted; she may live in the household he made and he will support her as long as she lives. 149 If that woman has not consented to live in her husband's house, he will restore to her the dowry that she brought from her father's house, and she may go off.

191 *šumma awīlum ṣeḫram ša ana mārūtīšu ilqûšū-ma urabbûšu bīssu īpuš warka mārī irtašī-ma ana tarbītim nasāḫim pānam ištakan, mārum šū rīqūssu ul ittallak; abum murabbīšu ina makkūrīšu šalušti aplūtīšu inaddiššum-ma ittallak; ina eqlim kirîm u bītim ul inaddiššum.* If a man set up his household with a boy whom he adopted and raised, and afterwards has acquired sons and decided to remove the foster child, that child will not go off empty-handed; the father who raised him will give him out of his property a third of his inheritance and then he will go away; he will not give him any of the field, orchard, or house.

255–256 255 *šumma liāt awīlim ana igrim ittadin ū lū zēram išriq-ma ina eqlim lā uštabši, awīlam šuāti ukannūšū-ma ina ebūrim ana būrim šūši kur âm imaddad.* 256 *šumma pīḫassu apālam lā ileʾʾi, ina eqlim šuāti ina liātim imtanaššarūšu.* 255 If he gave the man's cattle for hire or stole the seed and has not produced (anything) in the field, that man will be convicted and at the harvest he will measure out sixty kor of grain per *būr*. 256 If he is unable to meet his obligation, he will be dragged back and forth in that field by cattle.

4 *šum-ma a-na ši-bu-ut* ŠE *ù* KUG.BABBAR *ú-ṣí-a-am a-ra-an di-nim šu-a-ti it-ta-na-aš-ši.*

šumma ana šībūt êm u kaspim uṣiam, aran dīnim šuāti ittanašši. If he came forth for testimony about grain or silver, he will bear the penalty of that case.

271 *šum-ma a-wi-lum* ÁB.GUD.ḪI.A ^{giš}MAR.GÍD.DA *ù mu-úr-te-di-ša i-gur i-na* UD.1.KAM 3 ("PI"; or, NIEŠ) ŠE *i-na-ad-di-in.*

šumma awīlum liātim ereqqam u murteddīša īgur, ina ištēn ūmim šalāšat pān (or, *šalāš parsikat*) *âm inaddin.* If a man rented cattle, a wagon, and its driver, he will give three *pānum / parsiktum* (180 liters; see pages 584–85) of grain per day.

F. 1. *šumma šumēl ubānim pūṣam itaddâ[t], tibût erbîm.* If the left of the finger is completely set with white flecks, locust attack.

2. *šumma bāb ekallim šinā-ma ritkubū, sukkallum kussi bēlīšu ištenê.* If the palace gates are two and they are lying against each other, the vizier is seeking his master's throne.

3. *šumma [martum] šerʾā[nī] udduḫa[t], ummā[nu]m ina tāḫāzim imtanaqqut.* If the gall bladder is completely covered with tendons, the army will constantly fall in battle.

4. *[šumma ṭulīmu]m šeršerrī sāmūtim mali, wāšib maḫrīka [kar]ṣīka ītanakkal.* If the spleen is full of red rings, one who sits before you (ms) will continually calumniate you.

5. DIŠ *pu-ug-lum* Á.ZI *ta-ri-ik ša li-ša-ni-ia i-na ma-a-tim it-ta-na-al-la-ak.*

šumma puglum imittam tarik, ša lišānīya ina mātim ittanallak. If the radish is dark on the right, my informer will go throughout the land.

6. *šum-ma i-ir-ti* MUŠEN *i-mi-it-tam ù šu-me-lam!* *su-mu ma-du-tum i-ta-ad-du-ú ṣa-bi ù ṣa-bi na-ak-ri-im in-na-ma-ru-ma ta-ḫa-za-am ú-ul i-pe-e-šu.*

šumma irti iṣṣūrim imittam u šumēlam sūmū mādūtum itaddû, ṣābī u ṣābi nakrim innammarū-ma tāḫāzam ul ippešū. If the breast of the bird — many red spots are situated right and left, my army and the army of the enemy will meet, but will not do battle.

G. 1. *Suḫārum šilip rēmim Mār-‹Eštar mār› Atkalšim mītim: itti Šamaš-nāṣir [aḫi] ummīšu u Tarīš-mātim aššatīšu Ipqu-iltum mār Sîn-magir ana mārūtim ilqe. Ištēn šiqil kaspam u tēnīq šittā šanātim ipram piššatam lubūšam Ipqu-iltum ana Šamaš-nāṣir u Tarīš-mātim iddin, maḫrū. [Libbaš]unu ṭāb. Šamaš-nāṣir u Tarīš-[mātum] ul iturrū-ma ana Ipqu-iltum ul iraggamū. Eš(e)ret māri liršī-ma Mār-Eštar-ma apilšu rabûm. Nīš Šamaš Ayya Marduk u Ḫammu-rapi itmû.*

A child by caesarian section, Mār-Eštar son of the late Atkalšim: Ipqu-iltum son of Sîn-magir adopted (him) from Šamaš-nāṣir his maternal uncle and Tarīš-mātum his wife. Ipqu-iltum gave one shekel of silver and wet-nursing expenses for two years, barley ration, oil ration, (and) clothing to Šamaš-nāṣir and Tarīš-mātum, (and) they are in receipt (of these things). Their heart is satisfied. Šamaš-nāṣir and Tarīš-mātum will not bring suit again against Ipqu-iltum. Should he acquire ten (other) children, it is Mār-Eštar who is his eldest heir. They swore by the life of Šamaš, Ayya, Marduk, and Ḫammurapi. (Witnesses. Date.)

2. *Surratum qadu mārat irtim mārat Erišti-Ayya nadīt Šamaš ša Erišti-Ayya nadīt Šamaš ummaša udammiqūšī-ma ana mārūtīša iškunūši. [U] Erišti-Ayya nadīt Šamaš mārat Šarrum-Adad ullilši [pānī]ša ana ṣīt šamšim iškun. [Adi] Erišti-Ayya nadīt Šamaš ummaša balṭat, ittanaššīši. Ištu Erišti-Ayya nadīt Šamaš ummaša ilūša iqterûši, ellet; ša ramānīša šī; mala libbīša maṣiat. Ana warkiāt ūmī ina mārī Erišti-Ayya nadīt Šamaš mārat Šarrum-Adad u mārī Kalūmum aḫīša, zikar u sinniš, ša ibšû u ibbaššû, ana Surra-tum qadu mā[r(at) irtim] [mārat] Erišti-Ayya nadīt Šamaš [mamman lā i]raggamū.*

Surratum with a suckling baby is the daughter of Erišti-Ayya the *nadītum* of Šamaš, whom Erišti-Ayya the *nadītum* of Šamaš her mother treated kindly and adopted (or, who treated Erišti-Ayya the *nadītum* of Šamaš her mother well, and whom she [E-A] adopted). And Erišti-Ayya the *nadītum* of Šamaš the daughter of Šarrum-Adad freed her (and) set her face to the east. As long as her mother Erišti-Ayya the *nadītum* of Šamaš lives, she will take care of her. After the god(s) of her mother Erišti-Ayya the *nadītum* of Šamaš has/have summoned her, she is free; she belongs to herself; she may do what she wants. In the future no one among the children of Erišti-Ayya the *nadītum* of Šamaš, daughter of Šarrum-Adad, or among the children of her brother Kalūmum, male or female, who have appeared or who will appear, may contest against Surratum with the suckling baby, the daughter of Erišti-Ayya the *nadītum* of Šamaš. (Witnesses. Date.)

3. *Mār-erṣetim mār Ayyatīya Atkal-ana-bēlti amassa ana aššūtim u mutūtim īḫuz. Atkal-ana-bēlti ana Ayyatīya bēltīša "ul bēltī atti" iqabbī-ma ugallabši ana kaspim [in]addiš(ši). Mimma ša Ayyatīya iršû u iraššû ša Mār-erṣetim-ma. Adi balṭat kilallān ittanaššû.*

Mār-erṣetim son of Ayyatīya took her (his mother's) slave Atkal-ana-bēlti in marriage. Should Atkal-ana-bēlti say to her mistress Ayyatīya, "You are not my mistress," she may shave and sell her. Whatever Ayyatīya has acquired or will acquire belongs to Mār-erṣetim alone. As long as she lives they will both look after (her). (Witnesses.)

H. 1. *Ana Sîn-iddinam qibī-ma; umma Ḫammurapī-ma. Ilšu-ibbi tam[kā]-rum [waki]l ḫamištim kiam u[l]amm[ida]nni, umma šū-[m]a: "Šalāšā kur âm a[n]a Sîn-magir šakkanakkim addim-ma ṭuppašu našiākū-ma [i]š[tu] šalāš šanātim ētenerrissū-ma [â]m ul inaddinam"; [ki]am ulammidanni. Ṭuppašu amur-ma âm u ṣibassu Sîn-magir lišaddinū-ma ana Ilšu-ibbi idin.*

Speak to Sîn-iddinam; thus (says) Ḫammurapi. Ilšu-ibbi the merchant, the foreman of five, informed me thus, as follows: "I gave Sîn-magir the governor thirty kor of grain and have his tablet; for three years I have continually asked him for it but he will not give me the grain"; thus he informed me. Check his tablet, let the grain and its interest be collected from Sîn-magir, and give (it) to Ilšu-ibbi.

2. *Ana S[în]-i[ddinam] kā[r] Sipp[ar] u dayyānī Sippa[r] qibī-ma; umma Samsu-ilunā-m[a]. Kīma ana ugārim rabî[m] u ugār Šamkā-nim eleppēt bāʾerī ittanarrad[ā-ma] nūnī ibarr[ū] iqbû[nim]. Ištēn lāsimam aṭṭarda[m]; kīma issanqak[kum], eleppēt bāʾer[ī], ša ina ugārim rabîm u [ugār] Š[am]kānim [nūnī ibarrū] ... ... U lā itâr-ma eleppēt bāʾerī ana ugārim rabîm u ugār Šamkā[nim] [l]ā urrad.*

Speak to Sîn-iddinam, the merchant community of Sippar, and the judges of Sippar; thus (says) Samsu-ilūna. I have been told that the fishermen's boats keep going down to the great meadow and the Šamkānum meadow and catching fish. I have sent a courier; as soon as he has reached you, ... the fishermen's boats that are catching fish in the great meadow and the Šamkānum meadow. ... ... Moreover the fishermen's boats must no longer go down to the great meadow and the Šamkānum meadow.

3. *Ana Šamaš-ḫāzir qibī-ma; umma Ḫammurapī-ma. Ilī-ippalsam rēʾûm kiam ulammidanni, umma šū-ma: "Šalāšat būr eqlam, ša ina kanīk bēlīya kankam, ištu erbe šanātim Etel-pī-Marduk īkimannī-ma, âšu ilteneqqe. U Sîn-iddinam ulammid-ma ul uterrūnim." Kiam ulammidanni. Ana Sîn-iddinam aštapram; šumma kīma Ilī-ippalsam šū iqbû, šalāšat būr eqlam, ša ina ekallim kankūšum, Etel-pī-Marduk ištu erbe šanātim ilqē-ma, ikkal, elīša awātum maruštum ul ibašši. Warkat awātim šuāti damqiš pursā-ma, eqlam ša pī kanīkim, ša ina ekallim ikkankūšum, ana Ilī-ippalsam ter[r]ā. U âm, ša ištu erbe šanātim ina eqlim šuāti Etel-pī-Marduk ilteqqû, ina kakkim ša ilim birrā-ma, ana Ilī-ippalsam rēʾîm idnā. U ṭēm dīnim šuāti šuprānim.*

Speak to Šamaš-ḫāzir; thus (says) Ḫammurapi. Ilī-ippalsam the shepherd informed me thus, as follows: "Four years ago Etel-pī-Marduk took from me a field of three *būr*, which is sealed to me in a document of my lord, and he has been taking its grain. I also informed Sîn-iddinam but it has not been returned to me." Thus he informed me. I have sent a message to Sîn-iddinam; if, as this Ilī-ippalsam has said,

Etel-pī-Marduk four years ago took and has been using a field of three *būr* that is sealed to him by the palace, there is nothing more grievous than this. Investigate (pl) the circumstances of that matter well, and return the field to Ilī-ippalsam according to the document that was sealed to him by the palace. Further, establish by the divine standard the grain that Etel-pī-Marduk took from that field for four years, and give (it) to Ilī-ippalsam the shepherd. And send me a report of that case.

I. 21. *ayyum narbiaš išannan mannum*
22. *gašrū ṣīrū šūpû parṣūša*
23. *Eštar narbiaš išannan mannum*
24. *gašrū ṣīrū šūpû parṣūša.*

Which one, who can equal her greatness?
Powerful, august, illustrious are her rites;
Eštar, who can equal her greatness?
Powerful, august, illustrious are her rites.

25. *šāt in-ilī atar nazzazuš*
26. *kabtat amāssa elšunu ḫaptat-ma*
27. *Eštar in-ilī atar nazzazuš*
28. *kabtat amāssa elšunu ḫaptat-ma*

The one whose standing among the gods is preeminent,
Whose word is more honored, more powerful than they;
Eštar, whose standing among the gods is preeminent,
Whose word is more honored, more powerful than they.

29. *šarrassun, uštanaddanū siqrīša*
30. *kullassunu šâš kamsūši*
31. *nannarīša ilaqqûšim*
32. *iššū u awīlum palḫūšī-ma*

Their queen (is she), they discuss her words;
They all bow down to her;
They receive her light from her;
Women and men (lit., man) have respect for her.

33. *puḫriššun etel qabûša šūtur*
34. *ana Anim šarrīšunu malâm ašbassunu*
35. *uznam nēmeqem ḫasīsam eršet*
36. *imtallikū šī u ḫammuš*

In their assembly her speech is supreme, surpassing;
She sits with them as equal to Anum, their king;
She is wise in intelligence, knowledge, understanding;
They deliberate, she and her family head.

37. *ramû-ma ištēniš parakkam*
38. *ig-gegunnêm šubat rīšātim*
39. *muttiššun ilū nazuzzū*
40. *ipšiš pīšunu bašiā uznāšun*

They reside together on the dais,
In the temple tower, the joyful dwelling;
In front of them the gods stand,
Their ears attendant (lit., present) to their commands.

LESSON THIRTY-FIVE

C. 1. KUN MUŠEN
2. GABA SUKKAL
3. GIŠIMMAR.ḪI.A ZIMBIR^{ki}
4. KU_6 NU.MU.SU
5. UGULA NA.GADA.MEŠ
6. $^{(giš)}$MAR.GÍD.DA GÌR.NITA(Ḫ)

D. 1. *ṣābum ūtebbeb / ūtabbab / ūtallal / ūtellel / uzzakka.*
2. *uštallamū / ubtallaṭū.*
3. *tuttanarram.*
4. *nārum ša nuktallimu*
5. *lutabber-ma ešer / šilim / dimiq.*
6. *tuštaʾʾi*
7. *ul ūteddû / ūtaddû*
8. *littaʾʾid*
9. *tuttanakkal*
10. *pānūka lištannû*

E. 1. *Ellil bēlum ... ša qibīssu lā uttakkaru.* Lord Enlil ..., whose command is not changed.
2. *kussûm ḫurāṣam ūtaḫḫaz.* The throne will be overlaid with gold.
3. *kakkū nakrīya lištabbirū.* May my enemies' weapons be smashed.
4. *nādinānum ša bīšam ana* PN *iddinu u* PN_2 *ubtarrū ištu dabābšunu ina puḫrim ubtirru ana bīt ilim ana burri ilim leqēšunūti.* The seller who sold property to PN, and PN_2 will be convicted; after their speech is proved in the assembly, take (ms) them to the temple for the proving of the god.
5. *adi* PN *illikam šalāš ṣuḫārû ittīni wašbū; inanna šinā ṣuḫārû šanûtum urtaddû.* Until PN came three young men lived with us; now two additional young men were added.
6. *kīma awīlum šū lā ṣeḫrū-ma rabû ul tīdê? Kīma awīlê aḫḫīšu eqlam apulšu. Kīma lā ša šutaʾʾîm šū ul tīdê? Lā tuštaʾʾāšum.* Do you (ms) not know that that man is not young, but of age? Pay him a field corresponding to his brothers who are men. Do you not know that he is not to be neglected? Do not be negligent about him.
7. *šattam bītī u bītāt mārīya ussappaḫū.* This year my house and my children's houses are being scattered.
8. *šumma ina kīttim aḫī atta, qibī-ma šikarum ša ina bīt šarrāqim illeqû u alpum ša ina qabê aḫīya ana wardim utterru ana ṣuḫārīya lippaqdū.* If you are indeed my brother, give order that the beer that was taken from the thief's house and the ox that was returned to the slave at my brother's order be consigned to my servant.
9. *mimma ša teppušanni Adad ilka liddammiq.* May Adad your god constantly make good whatever you (ms) do for me.

F. 20 *šumma wardum ina qāt ṣābitānīšu iḫtaliq, awīlum šū ana bēl wardim nīš ilim izakkar-ma ūtaššar.* If the slave has escaped from his captor(s), that man will swear by the life of the god to the slave's owner and be released.

103 *šumma ḫarrānam ina alākīšu nakrum mimma ša našû uštaddīšu, šamallûm nīš ilim izakkar-ma ūtaššar.* If while traveling his route an enemy made him give up what he had, the agent will swear by the life of the god and be released.

G. 1. *šumma naplaštum kīma unqim, mātum ūtesser; pīša ana ištēn itâr.* If the lobe is like a ring, the land will be closed up and its voice will become unified again.

2. *šumma ina šumēl ubānim kakkum isḫur, šēpum ana māt nakrim ūtaššar.* If the weapon rotated on the left of the finger, the transport will be released to the enemy land.

3. *šumma rēš bāb ekallim ana šinîšu paṭer ..., butuqā[tum] ubtatta[qā].* If the top of the palace gate is split twice ..., the sluice channels will be cut off.

H. 1. *Warad-Sîn mār Sîn-gamil ana Ili-awīlim mār Ilī-ūrī warki Ilī-ūrī abūšu u Duššuptum ummašu imūtū aššum ištēn mūšar maškanim ša Duššuptum itti Warad-Amurrim aḫi abīšu i[š]āmu u mišil mūšar bītim ša Duššuptum itti Warad-Sîn išāmu Warad-Sîn ana Ili-a‹wī›lim irgum-ma, kiam iqbi, umma šū-ma: "Inūma bītam Duššuptum ummaka īpušu ana bītīya ... īrubam; u mišil mūšar bītum ša ittīya išāmu, bītī watar; usannaqka," iqbi. Ili-awīlim awīlê mārī bābtim mūdêšunu upaḫḫer-ma, awīlû mārū bābtīšunu awâtīšunu īmurū-ma, aššum bītum ištu ešrā šanātim šāmu, ana mala ussannaqūšu kīma [Warad]-Sîn iqbû; ana watarti bītīšu ištēn šiqil kaspam ša sebet mišil šiqil bītim ša eli ištēn mūšarim watru u ištēn šiqil kaspam ša ḫamšat mišil šiqil bītim ša eli mišil mūšarim ina sunnuqim īteru Ili-awīlim ušamgirū-ma, šinā šiqil kaspam ana Warad-Sîn iddinū. Ša watarti bītīšu apil. Libbašu ṭāb. Ana warkiāt ūmī Warad-Sîn ana Ili-awīlim ana wa‹t›arti ištēn mišil mūšar bītim ul iraggum. Nīš Marduk u Samsu-iluna šarrim.*

Warad-Sîn son of Sîn-gamil against Ili-awīlim son of Ilī-ūrī, after his father Ilī-ūrī and his mother Duššuptum had died, over a one-*mūšar* lot that Duššuptum had bought from his uncle Warad-Amurrim and a half-*mūšar* house that Duššuptum had bought from Warad-Sîn — Warad-Sîn brought suit against Ili-awīlim, and said as follows: "When your mother Duššuptum made the house, she went into my property ...; also, as for the half-*mūšar* house that she bought from me, my house is over-large; I will check it for you," he said. Ili-awīlim assembled the men from the district who know them and the men from their district considered their words and, because the house was sold twenty years ago, as far as it could be checked for him, they spoke in accord with Warad-Sîn; for the excess of his house they made Ili-awīlim agree to one shekel of silver per seven and a half "shekels" of house in excess of the one *mūšar* and one shekel of silver per five and a half "shekels" of house that exceeded the half *mūšar* upon checking, and they gave two shekels of silver to Warad-Sîn. He is paid for the excess of his house. His heart is satisfied. In future Warad-Sîn will not bring suit against Ili-awīlim for the excess of the one and a half *mūšar* of property. Oath of Marduk and King Samsu-iluna.

I. 1. *Ana Ruttum qibī-ma; umma Marduk-nāṣir-ma. Šamaš u Marduk dāriš ūmī liballiṭūki. Ûm ša ibbašû ina sūt Šamaš maḫrīki lištannī-ma likkanik. Aššum Babātim u ṣuḫārātīša ṭarādim kīma ištīššu ešrīšu aštapparakk*[*i*]*m; ul tāpul*[*ī*]*n*[*n*]*i. Ibissâki tubtaʾʾilī. Appūnā-ma ibissâm šaniam tassanaḫḫurī. Babātim Lagabītum-balāssu u Abī-liblut ṭurdīšinātī-ma luddiš. Awâtūya mati īkki imaḫḫarā? Ina lā mitaggurīya* [*ibi*]*ssâ tubtanaʾʾalī. Ša aqabbûkim: mugrīnnī-ma awâtum lā iḫḫaṭṭiā. Šumma ḫaṭītam eppuš, lā tamaggarīnni.*

Speak to Ruttum; thus Marduk-nāṣir. May Šamaš and Marduk keep you well forever. The grain that has become available should be counted by the Šamaš seah and sealed in your presence. I have been writing to you ten times if once about sending Babātum and her servants; you have not answered me. You kept enlarging your loss. Moreover, you keep looking for another loss. Send Babātum, Lagabītum-balāssu and Abī-liblut that I may *renew my efforts*. When will my words please you? By never complying with me you keep enlarging the loss. (Here is) what I say to you: comply with me, so that matters may not be missed. Do not comply only if I am doing something wrong.

2. *Ana Ruttum* [*qibī-ma*]*; umma Marduk-*[*nāṣir-ma*]*. Šamaš u Marduk* [*dāriš ūmī*] *libal*[*liṭūki*]*. Aššum êm ša ussannaqu: ana mīnim libbaki imtanarraṣ? Šattam kûm nûm; ša ana pānīki iššaknu tamtašî? Ûm ša ussannaqu ul ana kâšim. Ištu ṣeḫḫerēku awâtīki aḫḫīya aḫḫātīya u qerbūtīya ul ušešmi. Mīnum ša ana aḫātīki/aḫḫātīki u aḫḫīki "ina bubūtim amât" tašpurīm? Kī maṣi ḫiṭaṭṭî? Babātum u ṣuḫārātim kīma* [*aš*]*puram ṭurdī*[*šināti*]*. Lāma all*[*ikakkim*] *luddiš.* [...] *. Awātī lā te*[*ggî*?]*.*

Speak to Ruttum; thus Marduk-nāṣir. May Šamaš and Marduk keep you well forever. Concerning the grain that was checked: why are you always getting upset? This year what is yours is ours; have you forgotten what was put at your disposal? The grain that will be checked is not yours. Since I was young I have not made my brothers, sisters, and relatives listen to your words. (For) what (reason) did you write to your sister(s) and your brothers, "I am dying of hunger"? How often is my constant failing? Send Babātum and the servants as I wrote. Before I come to you I would *renew my efforts* [...] . Do not *neglect* my word.

3. *Ana Šū-Amurrim ša* [*Marduk*] *uballaṭūš*[*u*] *qibī-ma; umma Ilī-ummatī-m*[*a*]*. Šamaš u Marduk liballiṭūka. Mê idim-ma eqlam ša pānī apim lišqû. La tušta*ʾʾ*a, zēršunu lā iḫalliq.*

Speak to Šū-Amurrim, whom Marduk keeps well; thus Ilī-ummatī. May Šamaš and Marduk keep you well. Give water so that the field in front of the canebrake may be watered. Do not be negligent lest their seed perish.

4. *Ana Šamaš-ḫāzir qibī-ma; umma Lu-Ninurtā-ma. Šamaš liballiṭka. Pirḫum mār Mutum-ilum kiam ulammidanni, umma* [*š*]*ū-ma: "Ina bī*[*t a*]*bīya išteat ḫarrānam ina lāsimim išteat ḫarrānam ina kullizim nillak. Eqel bīt abīni ana kullizim-ma ugdammer." Ibaššî, ašar ištēm-ma gummurū? Warkatam purus-ma, šumma šittā ḫarrānātūšunu ina bīt abīšunu bāmâ zūssunūšim-ma ekallam lā udabbab.*

Speak to Šamaš-ḫāzir; thus Lu-Ninurta. May Šamaš keep you well. Pirḫum son of Mutum-ilum informed me as follows: "In my family we perform one corvée service as courier and one corvée service as ox driver. The field of our family has (now) been assigned completely to the ox driver(s)." Can it be that they are assigned completely in one area? Look into the matter, and if there are two corvée services in their family, divide (them) in half for them, so that he does not bother the palace.

5. [1] *a-na* ^{d}UTU-*ḫa-zi-ir* [2] *qí-bí-ma* [3] *um-ma ḫa-am-mu-ra-pí-ma* [4] ^{Id}EN.ZU-*iš-me-a-ni* LÚ *ku-ta-al-la*^{ki} [5] *nukaribbum*(NU.^{giš}KIRI$_6$) *ša* ^{giš}GIŠIMMAR DILMUN.NA [6] *ki-a-am ú-lam-mi-da-an-ni* [7] *um-ma šu-ma* [8] ^{Id}UTU-*ḫa-zi-ir* A.ŠÀ É *a-bi-ia* [9] *i-ki-ma-an-ni-ma* [10] *a-na* AGA.ÚS-*im* [11] *it-ta-di-in* [12] *ki-a-am ú-lam-mi-da-an-ni* [13] A.ŠÀ-*ú-um du-ru-um* [14] *ma-ti-ma in-ne-ek-ki-im* [15] *wa-ar-ka-tam pu-ru-ús-ma* [16] *šum-ma* A.ŠÀ-*um šu-ú* [17] *ša* É *a-bi-šu* [18] A.ŠÀ-*am šu-a-ti* [19] *a-na* ^{d}EN.ZU-*iš-me-a-ni* [20] *te-e-er.*

Ana Šamaš-ḫāzir qibī-ma; umma Ḫammurapī-ma. Sîn-išmeanni awīl Kutalla nukaribbum ša gišimmar Dilmun(im) kiam ulammidanni, umma šū-ma: "Šamaš-ḫāzir eqel bīt abīya īkimannī-ma ana rēdîm ittadin"; kiam ulammidanni. Eqlûm dūrum matī-ma innekkim? Warkatam purus-ma, šumma eqlum šū ša bīt abīšu, eqlam šuāti ana Sîn-išmeanni tēr.

Speak to Šamaš-ḫāzir; thus Ḫammurapi. Sîn-išmeanni, a man of Kutalla, a gardener of the Dilmun date-palm informed me as follows: "Šamaš-ḫāzir took my family field from me and has given it to a *rēdûm*"; thus he informed me. Is a permanent field ever taken away? Look into the matter, and if that field belongs to his family, return that field to Sîn-išmeanni.

J. 41. *šarrum migrašun narām libbīšun*
42. *šarḫiš it‹ta›naqqīšunūt niqiašu ellam*
43. *Ammī-ditāna ellam niqî qātīšu*
44. *maḫrīšun ušebbe lî u aslī namrāʾī.*

The king, their favorite, the beloved of their heart,
In splendor he constantly offers them his pure libation;
Ammī-ditāna sates them with his pure personal offerings:
Fattened bulls and sheep.

45. *išti Anim ḫāwerīša tēteršaššum*
46. *dāriam balāṭam arkam*
47. *mādātim šanāt balāṭim ana Ammī-ditāna*
48. *tušatlim Eštar tattadin.*

From Anum her spouse she has asked for him
Perpetual long life;
Many years of life for Ammī-ditāna
Eštar bestowed, has given.

49. *siqrušša tušaknišaššum*
50. *kibrāt erbêm ana šēpīšu*

51. *u napḫar kalîšunu dadmī*
52. *taṣṣamissunūti an-nīrīšu.*

By her word she has made bow down to him
The four quarters, at his feet;
And the totality of all habitations
She has harnessed to his yoke.

53. *bibil libbīša zamār lalêša*
54. *naṭûm-ma ana pīšu siqrī Ea ippussi*
55. *išmē-ma tanīttaša irīssu*
56. *"liblut-mi šarrašu lirāmšu ad-dāriš."*

Her desire, singing of her charm
Is fitting to his mouth; he carries out Ea's orders for her;
He heard her praise and rejoiced in him,
"May he live, may his king love him forever."

57. *Eštar ana Ammī-ditāna šarri rāʾimīki*
58. *arkam dāriam balāṭam šurkī*
59. *liblut.*

Eštar, on Ammī-ditāna the king who loves you,
Bestow long, perpetual life.
May he live.

LESSON THIRTY-SIX

C. 1. GIŠIMMAR.ḪI.A *ša a-aḫ* ^{id}BURANUN
2. UGULA $^{(lú)}$MÁŠ.ŠU.GÍD.GÍD.MEŠ *i-na* $^{(giš)}$MAR.GÍD.DA *ir-kab* / *ka-ab*
3. SUKKAL *i-na* NÁ *i-ni-il*
4. SIG_4.ḪI.A É.GAR_8
5. *a-na* UZU DINGIR *i-ṭi-ib*

D. 1. *tuštaṣabbat*
2. *uštašanna*
3. *uštamli*
4. *uštalpatū*
5. *ušteterdiā* / *uštatardiā*
6. *šutēpišā*
7. *tuštenerrebī*
8. *uštēšer*
9. *uštetēmidū*
10. *uštesṣeā*
11. *muštasḫirum*
12. *nuštatta*

E. 1. *Sābītum ana šâšum issaqqaram ana Gilgameš:*
"Gilgameš êš tadâl?
Balāṭam ša tasaḫḫuru lā tutta.
Inūma ilū ibnû awīlūtam,
Mūtam iškunū ana awīlūtim,
Balāṭam ina qātīšunu iṣṣabtū."

The innkeeper says to him, to Gilgameš:
"Gilgameš whither do you wander?
The life you seek you shall not find.
When the gods made humanity,
Death they decreed for humanity,
Life they kept in their possession."

2. *inūma Marduk ana šutēšur nišī mātim usim šūḫuzim uwa*^{ʾʾ}*eranni, kīttam u mīšaram ina pī mātim aškun, šīr nišī uṭīb.* When Marduk commissioned me to lead the people of the land aright, to instil guidance, I established truth and redress in the mouth of the land, I pleased the people.

3. *šarrum ša in šarrī šūturu anāku; awâtūya nasqā; lēʾûtī šāninam ul īšu; ina qibīt Šamaš dayyānim rabîm ša šamê u erṣetim mīšarī ina mātim lištēpi.* I am the king who is pre-eminent among kings; my words are choice; my power has no rival; by the command of Šamaš the great judge of heaven and earth may my redress be proclaimed in the land.

4. *aššum eqlētim ša* PN *ana* PN_2 *šêm-ma kamāsim u ekallim apālim lū ašpuraššum.* I wrote indeed to him about seeking and collecting the fields of PN for PN_2 and paying the palace.

5. *kiam iqbiam, umma šū-ma: "šarram atma, ištu inanna adi ḫamšāt ūmī kasapka lū anaddikkum."* He said to me as follows: "I swore by the king, I will give you your silver five days from now."

6. *aššum nakrum ušēṣianni aklī šutamṭū-ma ša akālim ul īšu; u aššum awāt ekallim ša ešmû nazqāku; ṭēmki arḫiš šuprīm-ma lā anazziq.*

Because the enemy expelled me my food is in short supply and I have nothing to eat; further I am upset because of the word from the palace that I heard; send (fs) me your report quickly that I not become (more) upset.

7. *ana* PN *aqbī-ma, ana Babilim wardam šuāti ul iṭrud* PN *kaspam irriš; kaspam šūbilaššum-ma luštamgiršū-ma wardam šuāti liṭrudakkum.* I spoke to PN but he did not send that slave to Babylon; PN wants the silver; dispatch (ms) the silver to him that I may get him to agree to send you that slave.

8. *atta u šū qaqqadātīkunu šutēmidā-ma warkatam šuāti pursā. šanītam inanna paṭārī qerub; ṣuḫārû bītam ana pānīya lištassiqū u eqlētum lū šutassuqā.* He and you (ms) must join forces and look into that matter. Moreover, my release is now imminent; the servants should prepare the house for my arrival, and the fields should also be prepared.

9. *inūma anāku u abī ina Sippar nuštātû, mādiš aḫdu; inanna mušaddinū kaspam uštanaddanūniāti u mādiš nuštamarraṣ.* When my father and I met in Sippar, I rejoiced greatly; now the tax collectors keep collecting silver from us, and we are very concerned.

10. *šumma libbaka, ṭēmka gamram šupram-ma awīlum šū kasapšu lilqē-ma lillikakkum. immerī/immerātim idiššum. u ṣuḫārum ša illikakkum itti ṣābim šutaṣbitaššu.* If you (ms) wish, send me your complete report, so that the aforementioned man may receive his silver and come to you. Give him sheep. And as for the servant who came to you, attach him to the work gang.

F. 101 *šumma ašar illiku nēmelam lā ītamar, kasap ilqû uštašannā-ma šamallûm ana tamkārim inaddin.* If he did not make a profit wherever he went, the agent will give twice the silver he received to the merchant.

120 *šumma awīlum âšu ana našpakūtim ina bīt awīlim išpuk-ma ina qarītim ibbûm ittabši ū lū bēl bītim našpakam iptē-ma âm ilqe ū lū âm ša ina bītīšu iššapku ana gamrim ittakir, bēl êm maḫar ilim âšu ubār-ma bēl bītim âm ša ilqû uštašannā-ma ana bēl êm inaddin.* If a man stored his grain as silage in a(nother) man's establishment and a deficit occurred in the storeroom, (and) either the owner of the establishment opened the granary and took the grain or he denied completely that the grain had been stored in his establishment, the owner of the grain will certify his grain before the god, and the owner of the establishment will give the owner of the grain twice the grain he received.

126 *šumma awīlum mimmûšu lā ḫali[q]-ma "mimmê ḫaliq" iqtabi, bābtašu ūtebbir, kīma mimmûšu lā ḫalqu bābtašu ina maḫar ilim ubāršū-ma mimma ša irgumu uštašannā-ma ana bābtīšu inaddin.* If a man whose property was not missing has said, "my property is missing," and has accused his district, his district will establish before the god that his property is not missing, and he will give his district twice whatever he had contested.

145–147 145 *šumma awīlum nadītam īḫuz-ma mārī lā ušaršīšū-ma ana šugītim aḫāzim pānīšu ištakan, awīlum šū šugītam iḫḫaz; ana bītīšu ušerrebši; šugītum šī itti nadītim ul uštamaḫḫar.* 146 *šumma awīlum nadītam īḫuz-ma amtam ana mutīša iddim-ma mārī ittalad, warkānum amtum šī itti bēltīša uštatamḫir, aššum mārī uldu bēlessa ana kaspim ul inaddišši; abbuttam išakkaššī-ma itti amātim imannūši* 147 *šumma mārī lā ulid, bēlessa ana kaspim inaddišši.* 145 If a man married a *nadītum* but she did not help him acquire children and he has decided to marry a *šugītum*, said man may marry a *šugītum*; he may bring her into his house; said *šugītum* will not compare herself with the *nadītum*. 146 If a man married a *nadītum* and she gave her husband a slave and she has born children, (and) later on said slave has compared herself with her mistress, her mistress will not sell her, since she bore children; she will give her a slave's hairstyle and include her with (the rest of) the slaves. 147 If she has not born children, her mistress may sell her.

206 *šumma awīlum awīlam ina risbātim imtaḫaṣ-ma simmam ištakaššu, awīlum šū "ina īdû lā amḫaṣu" itamma; u asâm ippal.* If a man has struck a man during a quarrel and inflicted a wound on him, said man will swear "I did not knowingly strike"; he will also pay the physician.

227 *šumma awīlum gallābam idâṣ-ma abbutti wardim lā šêm ugdallib, awīlam šuāti idukkūšū-ma ina bābīšu iḫallalūšu; gallābum "ina īdû lā ugallibu" itammā-ma ūtaššar.* If a man deceived a barber and he has shaved the hair-style of a slave that is not his, that man will be killed and hung on his gate; the barber will swear "I did not knowingly shave" and be released.

233 *šumma itinnum bītam ana awīlim īpuš-ma šipiršu lā uštesbī-ma igārum iqtūp, itinnum šū ina kasap ramānīšu igāram šuāti udannan.* If a house builder built a house for a man but did not do his work properly so that the wall buckled, said house-builder will reinforce that wall with his own silver.

124 *šum-ma a-wi-lum a-na a-wi-lim* KUG.BABBAR KUG.SIG$_{17}$ *ù mi-im-ma šum-šu ma-ḫar ši-bi a-na ma-ṣa-ru-tim id-di-in-ma it-ta-ki-ir-šu a-wi-lam šu-a-ti ú-ka-an-nu-šu-ma mi-im-ma ša ik-ki-ru uš-ta-ša-na-ma i-na-ad-di-in.*

šumma awīlum ana awīlim kaspam ḫurāṣam ū mimma šumšu maḫar šībī ana maṣṣarūtim iddim-ma ittakiršu, awīlam šuāti ukannūšū-ma mimma ša ikkiru uštašannā-ma inaddin. If a man gave a man silver, gold, or anything for safekeeping before witnesses but then he has denied it, that man will be convicted and will give twice whatever he denied.

160–161 160 *šum-ma a-wi-lum a-na* É *e-mi-im bi-ib-lam ú-ša-bi-il ter-ḫa-tam id-di-in-ma a-bi* DUMU.MUNUS DUMU.MUNUS-*i ú-ul a-na-ad-di-ik-kum iq-ta-bi mi-im-ma ma-la ib-ba-ab-lu-šum uš-ta-ša-an-na-ma ú-ta-ar.* 161 *šum-ma a-wi-lum a-na* É *e-mi-šu bi-ib-lam ú-ša-bíl ter-ḫa-tam id-di-in-ma i-bi-ir-šu uk-tar-ri-sú e-mu-šu a-na be-el aš-ša-tim* DUMU.MUNUS-*i ú-ul ta-aḫ-ḫa-az iq-ta-bi mi-im-ma ma-la ib-ba-ab-lu-šum uš-ta-ša-an-na-ma ú-ta-ar ù aš-ša-sú i-bi-ir-šu ú-ul i-iḫ-ḫa-az.*

160 *šumma awīlum ana bīt emim biblam ušābil, terḫatam iddim-ma, abi mārtim "mārtī ul anaddikkum" iqtabi, mimma mala ibbablūšum uštašannā-ma utār.* 161 *šumma awīlum ana bīt emīšu biblam ušābil, terḫatam iddim-ma, ibiršu uktarrissu, emūšu ana bēl*

aššatim "mārtī ul taḫḫaz" iqtabi, mimma mala ibbablūšum uštašannā-ma utār; u aššassu ibiršu ul iḫḫaz. 160 If a man sent a marriage-gift to his father-in-law's house, gave a bride-price, but the father of the daughter has said "I will not give you my daughter," he will return twice what was brought to him. 161 If a man sent a marriage-gift to his father-in-law's house, gave a bride-price, and then his colleague has slandered him (and) his father-in-law has said to the wife's lord "you will not marry my daughter," he will return twice what was brought to him; and his colleague will not marry his wife.

G. 1. *[šumma ina bāb] ekallim qûm ubānam iṭṭul, wāšib maḫrīka pirištaka uštenesse.* If in the palace gate a thread faced the finger, one who lives with you will keep revealing your secret(s).

2. *[šumma ina] ṣēr birītim kakkum šinā [itt]aṭlū-ma warki išdīšu [ ]û nadû, šarrān [ina pu]ḫrim ul uštaddanū.* If above the border area two weapons faced each other and behind its base [ ]s were lying, two kings will not engage in discussion in the assembly.

3. *šumma maskiltum ša ubān ḫašîm ḫurḫudam iṭṭul, sinništum awât puḫrim uštenesse.* If the *maskiltum* of the finger of the lung faced the throat, a woman will keep revealing matters of the assembly.

4. *šumma immerum pīšu iptenette, rigmū; šumma immerum lišāššu uštenesseam, niprū; šumma immerum lišāššu ištanaddad, ana šarrim awātum damiqtum imaqqut.* If the sheep keeps opening its mouth, noises; if the sheep keeps sticking out its tongue, progeny; if the sheep keeps pulling in its tongue, something good will happen to the king.

5. *šumma ina kišād iṣṣūrim kīma nīrim sūmam parik, ili awīlim šuteqrubam irriš.* If in the neck of the "bird" it is lying crosswise before the red spot like a yoke, the man's god is asking for constant petitioning.

H. 1. *Amat-Šamaš nadīt Šamaš ana Umm[ī-A]raḫtum ana aplūtim irgum-ma dayyānū dīnamušāḫizūšinātī-ma šībīšina ana Šamaš u Adad ana tumāmītum*[!] *iddinū-ma maḫar Šamaš u Adad kiam umma šunū-[ma]: "Ša Šamaš-gamil u Ummī-[Araḫtum] ana Amat-Šamaš nadānam lā nīdû." U dayyānū šībī ul imgurū; umma dayyānū: "Kīma šībū itmû, u atti ana Eštar tatammî." Ummī-araḫtum ina bāb Eštar kiam iqbi, umma šī-ma: "Anāku u Šamaš-gamil ṭuppam lā ništuru; u aplūtni lā niddinu." Nīš Šamaš Ayya Marduk u Ḫammurapi itmû.*

When Amat-Šamaš the *nadītum* of Šamaš took Ummī-Araḫtum to court over inheritance, the judges granted them a hearing and put their witnesses under oath by Šamaš and Adad; they (said) as follows before Šamaš and Adad: "We do not know what Šamaš-gamil and Ummī-Araḫtum gave to Amat-Šamaš." But the judges did not concur with the witnesses, saying, "Since the witnesses swore, you too will swear by Eštar." Ummī-Araḫtum said as follows in the gate of Eštar, "Šamaš-gamil and I did not make out a document, and we did not give our inheritance." They swore by the life of Šamaš, Ayya, Marduk, and Ḫammurapi.

I. 1. *Ana awīlim qibī-ma; umma Warad-Marduk-ma. Šamaš u Marduk dāriš ūmī liballiṭūka. [Lū š]almāta, lū balṭāta. [Ilum nāṣ]irka rēška [ana da]miqtim likīl. [Š]u[lumk]a maḫar Šamaš u Marduk lū dāri. Aššum dibbatim ša Sîn-šēmi, aḫīšu ša ina bīt abarakkim kalû, Marduk-muballiṭ mār wakil tamkārī itti našparim ša Bēlšunu aḫi Sîn-nādin-šumim ana Bābilim ittalkam. Atta u mār aḫi abīka šutātiā; maḫar awīlim Bēlšunu puṭṭerāšū-ma ana Sippar littalkam. Baluššu lā tallakam. [Ana ā]l Dūr-Šamaš ṭurdaššu. [Ina] annītim atḫûtam kullim.*

Speak to the man, thus Warad-Marduk. May Šamaš and Marduk keep you well forever. Be healthy, be well. May the god who protects you treat you well. May your health endure before Šamaš and Marduk. Concerning the agreement with Sîn-šēmi, the brother of him who is held in the steward's house, Marduk-muballiṭ the son of the chief merchant has come to Babylon with the envoy of Bēlšunu the brother of Sîn-nādin-šumim. Your cousin and you must meet; release Bēlšunu in the presence of the man that he may come away to Sippar. Do not come without him. Send him to the town of Dūr-Šamaš. Show a brotherly attitude in this.

2. *[Ad]i [ṭ]ēmka lā ašpuram-[ma] šipir nārim ša iḫḫerû lā īmurūnim, mû ana šiprim gamrim lā uštardû. U ištu šipir nārim ša inanna ṣabtāti ina ḫerêm tagdamru, Purattum ša ištu Larsa adi Ur miqtīša usuḫ; ḫāmīša šutbi, šutēšerši.*

Before I send your report and the work on the river that was dug out is seen, the water must not be conducted to the completed work. Also, after you have completed digging the river work with which you are now occupied, remove the debris of the Euphrates from Larsa to Ur; remove its litter (and) make it flow properly.

3. *Ana Sîn-iddinam, kār Sippar, u dayyānī Sippar qibī-ma; [umma A]bī-ešuḫ-ma. Bunene-nāṣir u Ṣillī-Šamaš mārū Rī[š-Šamaš] kiam ulamm[id]ūninn[i], um[m]a šunū-ma: "Ilī-iddinam aḫūni rabû[m] ḫablanniāti. Ištu šittā šanātim maḫar kār Sippar ništanakkam-[m]a ul uštešššerūniāti." Kiam ulammidūninni. Ṭuppī annia[m] ina amār[im] Ilī-iddinam šuāt[i] u šībī mūdê aw[âtīšu š]a Bunene-nāṣir u Ṣillī-Šamaš mārū Rīš-[Šam]aš ukallamūkun[ūt]i ana Bābilim ṭurdāni[m-ma] awâtūšun[u li]nnamrā.*

Speak to Sîn-iddinam, the merchants of Sippar, and the judges of Sippar; thus Abī-ešuḫ. Bunene-nāṣir and Ṣillī-Šamaš the sons of Rīš-Šamaš informed me as follows: "Our older brother Ilī-iddinam wrongs us. For two years we have been presenting (our case) before the merchants of Sippar, but they will not give us justice." Thus they informed me. On seeing this tablet of mine, send said Ilī-iddinam and the witnesses who know his affairs, whom Bunene-nāṣir and Ṣillī-Šamaš the sons of Rīš-Šamaš will point out to you, to Babylon, that their affairs may be considered.

4. *[An]a šāpirīya qibī-ma; umma Nūr-Amurrim-ma. Šamaš u Marduk dāriš ūmim liballiṭūka. Marduk-nāṣir ša ašpurakkum uḫḫiram-ma Rabût-Sîn aṭṭardakkum. Ṭuppātum ša mār bīt ṭuppim ḫamšum ittalkānim. Ana 24 iku eqlim ṣibit Mār-erṣetim ana sikkatim maḫāṣim kiam ašpuršunūšim, umma anākū-ma: "Ana šukūs rēdîm šutamlîm ištu ištēn warḫim wašbātunu. Ṭupšar ummānim šukūssû šutamlât-mâ, ina eqel ṭupšar ummānim ana rēdîm sikkatam tamaḫḫaṣā?" Ana Attâ šassukkim išpurūnim; qadum ašlim u rēdîm ana Lammayya illikam-ma nīš šarri ina pīšu aškum-ma ašlam ana tarāṣim u sikkatam ana maḫāṣi ul addiššum. Išpurūnim-ma ana qātātim ittadnūninni, ummā-mi, "Ašal šarri kubburat." Awīlû mādiš ṣurrumū. Ṭuppātūka ul irraḫānim-ma kīma alākīšunu sikkatam imaḫḫaṣū. Ana Ilī-imguranni ṭuppam ušābil-ma meḫer ṭuppi ušābilam-ma uštābilakkum. [Rē]dûm, ša ana e[q]lim ṣabātim [ir]teneddûniššu, itti Šū-ilīšu illak; ṭuppaka ana Šū-ilīšu lillikam. [I]na 29 ūmim Marduk-nāṣir aṭrudakkum; [i]na Ayyār(im) šanîm ūmim Rabût-Sîn aṭrudakkum.*

Speak to my director; thus Nūr-Amurrim. May Šamaš and Marduk keep you well forever. Since Marduk-nāṣir, whom I sent to you, was delayed, I have sent you Rabût-Sîn. Five tablets of the state scribe have come. I wrote to them as follows about driving in a peg at the 24-*iku* field held by Mār-erṣetim: "You have been in residence for one month to assign a subsistence plot of a *r dûm*. Is the subsistence plot of the military scribe to be assigned, that you drive a peg in the field of the military scribe for a *r dûm*?" They wrote to the land-registry officer Attâ; he came with a rope and a *r dûm to Lammayya* and I put him under the king's oath, but I did not allow him to stretch out the rope or drive in the peg. They gave order to hand me over for security(?), as follows: "The king's rope is thick." The men were very concerned. If your documents do not come quickly then as soon as they come they will drive in a peg. I dispatched a tablet to Ilī-imguranni and he dispatched an answer to me, so I have dispatched (it) to you. The *r dûm* whom they keep conducting here to seize the field is going with Šū-ilīšu; your tablet should come to Šū-ilīšu. On the 29th I sent you Marduk-nāṣir; on the second of Ayyār I sent you Rabût-Sîn.

5. [1] *[a-na* ^{f}*]ši-ib-tu* [2] *[qí-b]í-ma* [3] *[um-m]a be-el-ki-i-ma* [4] *eš-me-e-ma* ^{f}*na-an-na-mì* [5] *sí-im-ma-am mar-ṣa-at* [6] *ù it-ti* É.GAL-*lim* [7] *ma-ga-al wa-aš-ba-at-ma* [8] MUNUS.MEŠ *ma-da-tim it-ti-ša-ma* [9] *i-sa-ab-bi-ik* [10] *i-na-an-na dan-na-tim šu-uk-ni-ma* [11] *i-na ka-ás i-ša-at-tu-ú* [12] *ma-am-ma-an la i-ša-at-ti* [13] *i-na* ^{giš}GU.ZA *ša úš-ša-bu* [14] *ma-am-ma-an la úš-ša-ab* [15] *ù i-na* ^{giš}NÁ *ša it-ti-il-lu* [16] *ma-am-ma-an la it-te-e-el-ma* [17] MUNUS.MEŠ *ma-da-tim* [18] *it-ti-ša-ma* [19] *[la] i-sa-ab-bi-ik* [20] *[sí-im-m]u-um šu-ú mu-uš-ta-aḫ-ḫi-iz.*

[Ana] Šibtu [qib]ī-ma; [umm]a bēlkī-ma. Ešmē-ma Nanna-mi simmam marṣat; u itti ekallim magal wašbat-ma sinnišātim mādātim ittīšā-ma isabbik. Inanna dannātim šuknī-ma ina kās išattû mamman lā išatti; ina kussîm ša uššabu mamman lā uššab; u ina eršim ša ittillu mamman lā ittêl-ma, sinnišātim mādātim ittīšā-ma [lā] isabbik. [Simm]um šū muštaḫḫiz.

Speak to Šibtu; thus your lord. I heard that Nanna is sick with a disease;

also that she dwells at the palace a lot and brings many women into contact with her. Now then, give strict orders that no one may drink from the cup from which she drinks; no one may sit in the chair in which she sits; and no one may lie in the bed in which she lies, lest she bring many women into contact with her. That disease is contagious.

J. *Nanna šar šamê (u) erṣetim atta; atkalkum-ma Elali mār Girni-isa iḫtablanni. Dīnī dīn. Kaspam ula īšū-ma iṭheam; ina kaspīya ḫubullīšu uppil. Ana bīt emim iššī; māram u mārtam irši. Libbī ula uṭīb. Kaspī šalmam ula uterram; u nāš ṭuppātīšu iḫtablanni.*

Ana Nanna atkal-ma ina kirâtim meḫret Ekišnugal "lā aḫabbalūkā-ma" itma. Ina Kamaḫ šapal kakkim ša tarammu itma. Libbu kisalmaḫḫim meḫret Ekišnugal meḫret Ningal ša Egadi maḫar Nin-Šubur maṣraḫ? kisalmaḫḫim maḫar Alammuš maḫar Nanna-igidu u Nanna-adaḫ itmâm. "Kâti u mārū'ka lā aḫabbalūkā-ma" itma; "ilānū annûtum lū šībūyā-mi" iqbi. Appūnā-ma ina kirâtim meḫret Ekišnugal maḫar Nanna maḫar Šamaš "Elali Kuzzulam lā aḫabbalū-ma" maḫar Nanna maḫar Šamaš "Apil Elali ayy-ibši" — kiam itma.

Tāmi Nanna u Šamaš epqam imalla, ilappin, u aplam ula eraššī. Nanna u Šamaš Elali itmā-ma iḫtablanni. Nin-Šubur šar makkūrim lizziz-ma Nanna u Šamaš dīnī lidīnū. Rabût Nanna u Šamaš lūmur-ma.

Nanna, you are king of heaven (and) earth; I trusted you, yet Elali son of Girni-isa has wronged me. Judge my case. He had no silver and approached me; I/he paid his debts with my silver. He had a wedding; he acquired a son and daughter. He did not satisfy me. He did not return all my silver to me; and he has wronged his creditor, me.

I trusted Nanna, but, in the orchards facing Ekišnugal, "I will not wrong you" he swore. In Kamaḫ beneath the weapon you love he swore. Within the courtyard facing Ekišnugal, facing Ningal of Egadi, before Nin-Šubur the *emblem* of the courtyard, before Alammuš, before Nanna-igidu and Nanna-adaḫ he swore to me. "I, will not wrong your sons and you" he swore; "May these gods be my witnesses" he said. Moreover, in the orchards facing Ekišnugal before Nanna, before Šamaš "I, Elali will not wrong Kuzzulum," before Nanna, before Šamaš "May Elali have no heir" thus he swore.

He who has sworn (falsely) by Nanna and Šamaš becomes covered with leprosy, becomes poor, and acquires no heir. Elali swore by Nanna and Šamaš and has wronged me. May Nin-Šubur, king of property, stand forth that Nanna and Šamaš may judge my case. Let me see the greatness of Nanna and Šamaš.

LESSON THIRTY-SEVEN

C. 1. ŠUKU ERIN$_2$ ZIMBIR^{ki}
2. É.GAR$_8$ É GÌR.NITA(Ḫ)$_2$
3. KU$_6$.ḪI.A *i-na* ^{íd}BURANUN *i-mi-du*
4. SIG$_4$ É AN*(-nim)*
5. *i-na* NÁ-*ia a/at-til/ti-il*
6. UZU MUŠEN

D. 1. *nittanmar/nittammar*
2. *itaplas!*
3. *ittenenmidū/ittenemmidū*
4. *išātum ittananpaḫ*
5. *ana itaplusim*
6. *littasḫurūnim*
7. *izzazzā*
8. *nittazizzam*
9. *izizzā!*
10. *šuzissunūti!*
11. *azziz*
12. *ušzissi*

E. 185–187 185*šumma awīlum ṣeḫram ina mêšu ana mārūtim ilqē-ma urtabbīšu, tarbītum šī ul ibbaqqar.* 186 *šumma awīlum ṣeḫram ana mārūtim ilqe, inūma ilqûšu abāšu u ummašu iḫīaṭ, tarbītum šī ana bīt abīšu itâr.* 187 *mār gerseqqêm muzzaz ekallim ū mār sekretim ul ibbaqqar.* 185 If a man adopted a baby at birth and has raised it, that offspring will not be (re-)claimed. 186 If a man adopted a baby but after he has adopted it it looks for its (biological) father and mother, that offspring may return to its (biological) family. 187 The child of a domestic, a palace attendant, or the child of a *sekretum* will not be (re-)claimed.

253 *šumma awīlum awīlam ana pānī eqlīšu uzuzzim īgur-ma aldâm [i]qīpšu [l]iātim ipqissum [ana] eqlim erēšim urakkissu, [šu]mma awīlum šū zēram ū lū ukullâm išriq-ma ina qātīšu ittaṣbat, rittašu inakkisū.* If a man hired a man to oversee his field and entrusted him with a store of barley (or) provided him with cattle (or) contracted with him to cultivate the field, if that man stole seed or fodder and it has been caught in his possession, his hand will be cut off.

F. 1. *šumma ina amūtim erbe naplasātum ištēniš izzazzā, nakrum ana libbi ālīka itebbeam-ma ālānīka ikkim-ma itabbal.* If in the liver four lobes stand together, the enemy will invade your town, deprive you of your towns and take them for himself.

2. *[šumma ... it]taṭlū ilū zenûtum ana māt[im i]turrūnim.* If ... faced each other, angry gods will return to the land.

3. *šumma naplaštum ana* ŠU.BAR *iqtereb, ilum zenûm ana awīlim iturra.*If the lobe has approached the ..., an angry god will return to the man.

4. *šumma martum būdāša damam bullâm paššā, dipār nikurtim; išātum ina mātim ittananpaḫ.* If the "shoulders" of the gall bladder are smeared with ... blood, the torch of war; fire will constantly break out in the land.

5. *šumma warkat ḫašîm ittenmid, salīmu[m] iššakkan.* If the back of the lung has come together, peace will be established.

6. *šumma ina rēš iṣṣūrim ina imittim sūmū ištu šalāšat adi šeššet ittaškanū, erišti niqîm ša bīt ṣābi.* If from three to six red spots have been placed at the top of the "bird," desire for an offering of the troop quarters.

7. *šumma izbum pānī iṣṣūrim lemu[ttim] šakin, mātum šī sunqam immar; nakerša elīša ittazzaz.* If the anomaly has the face of an evil bird, that land will experience famine; its enemy will stand against it.

8. *an-ni-tum a-mu-tum ša šar-ri-im* ᵈEN.ZU-*i-din-am ša i-na* É ᵈUTU *i-na e-lu-ni-im* I.DÍB.BA *im-qú-ta-šum be-el im-me-ri-im na-ak-ra-am i-da-ri-is-ma e-li la ša-tim i-ta-za-az.*

   annītum amūtum ša šarrim Sîn-iddinam ša ina bīt Šamaš ina Elūnim askupp(at)am imqutaššum; bēl immerim nakram idarris-ma eli lā šattim ittazzaz. This is the liver omen of King Sîn-iddinam, upon whom a doorsill fell in the temple of Šamaš in Elūnum; the owner of the sheep will trample the enemy and preside over what is not his.

9. *šum-ma mar-tum it-bé-e-ma iz-zi-iz ru-bu-um i-na da-an-na-tim ú-ṣí-am.*

   šumma martum itbē-ma izziz, rubûm ina dannatim uṣṣiam. If the gall bladder rose up and stood, the prince will emerge from difficulty/the fortress.

G. 1. *..., napḫarum: 36 ṣēnū ša Ibni-Uraš ana Aḫa-nirši rēʾîm paqdā. Ana pissātim u ḫaliqtim izzaz.*

   ..., total: 36 sheep and goats of Ibni-Uraš are entrusted to Aḫa-nirši the shepherd. He is responsible for (any) *lame* or missing one(s).

H. 1. *Ištu (waraḫ) Simānim aššum ṣeḫḫerūtīya itaplusim unaʾʾidka. Erbet ūmī adi inanna ṭēm šiprātim mala ippušū u eqel šamaššammī ša ippušū ul tašpuram. Nabi-Sîn ana Bābilim īliam-ma ṭēmka rīqam ul tašpuram. Inanna Nabi-Sîn ana maḫrīka aṭṭardam; ittīšu ana eqlim rid-ma, eqel šiprātim mala ippušū u eqel šamaššammī ša ippušū itaplas-ma, ina ṭuppīka pānam šuršiam-ma šupram. Lušpurakkum-ma ûm ana kurummat ṣeḫḫerūtim u tuḫḫu raṭbum ana ukkulê alpī linnadin. Taklāku-ana-Marduk itti Nabi-Sîn ana Bābilim ṭurdam.*

   Since Simānum I (have) instructed you about keeping an eye on my boys. For four days, until now (i.e., for the last four days), you have not sent me a report of whatever preparations they are making and the sesame field they are working. Nabi-Sîn came up to Babylon and (yet) you did not send me (even) an empty report of yours. I have now sent Nabi-Sîn to you; go down to the field with him and look over whatever field preparations they are making, and the sesame field they are working, and address the issue in your tablet when you send it. I would command you that grain be given as food for the boys and moist bran as fodder for the oxen. Send Taklāku-ana-Marduk here to Babylon with Nabi-Sîn.

2. *Ana Awīl-Ištar qibī-ma; umma Ninsianna-mansum-ma. Šamaš u Marduk dāriš ūmī liballiṭūka. Aššum ṣuḫārīya ša qāti Betâ Betâ igre. Aššum amtim Aššumīya-libluṭ dibbatum māttum īliam-ma Betâ idi mārīša idabbum-ma pānīya udannim-ma pānīša ul ubil. Kīma niṭlīya ittīša adbub; kiam aqbīšim, umma anāku-ma: "Aḫūni ṣeḫrum aššatam ul aḫiz-ma, Saggīya abūni aššatam ušāḫissu. Inanna mārūšu ibtaqrūniāti. Šumma dabābum annûm lā ṭābakkim-ma mārūki ina taʾištīki lā idabbubū, attī-ma lā tadabbubī-ma ana pānīki lā tušzazzīni[āt]i. Nīnu u mārūki ana dayyānī i nisniq; awâtīni līmurū-ma šumma ša Saggīya iqīšanniāšim mārūšu leqûm kašid, dayyānū iqabbûniāšim-ma amtam nutār." Ina awâtim ussiršī-ma ana lā dabābim annam uštassīši. Mimma lā tanazziq; kīma lā nazāqīki eppuš.*

U Marduk-mušallim issanqam. Ṭēmam anniam maḫrīšu ašakkan. U atta arḫiš atlakam-ma, lāma Marduk-mušallim ayyīšam-ma ištapr[u], i nigmuršināti. Kīma tīdû, napištam ul īšu; ina ṭūbīya uštamarraṣ-ma erbet iku ušallam ša ana idīka ippeš. Kīma tīdû, eqlum epēšī u ana kaprim Gabiba qerēbī ana Ilī-šullimanni ul ṭāb-ma ušēpišannī-ma ištēn iku eqlam ana Ipqu-Šala addin. Ina ṭūbātim-ma eqlam šuāti lā epēšam Ipqu-Šala šudki. Ripqātīšu šudud-ma ša mānaḫātīšu anāku appalšu. Kīma anāku eppešu qibīšum. Šumma niṭilšu, qaqqadam ša šēpīt ušallim ša teppušu līpuš. Erbet iku eqlam šuāti ul tušadda, ul tušeppešannī-ma ittīka ezenne. Šumma ina kīnātim tarammanni la tuštaʾʾā-ma libbī lā imarraṣakkum. Eqlam šuāti ina qātim killaššū-ma lā anazziq. Ṭēmka šupram.

Speak to Awīl-Ištar; thus Ninsianna-mansum. May Šamaš and Marduk keep you well forever. Concerning my servant who is in the charge of Betâ, Betâ sued. Concerning the slave Aššumīya-libluṭ considerable dispute arose, and Betâ will plead on the side of her children; so I have *fortified myself* and not favored her. I spoke with her about my opinion, (and) said to her as follows: "Our young brother was not married, so our father Saggīya acquired a wife for him. Now his children have laid claim against us. If this complaint is not pleasing to you and your children will not plead in your loss, you yourself must not plead, lest you make us stand *before* you. Your children and we should go to the judges; let them look into our affairs, and if it is fitting for his sons to take what Saggīya gave us, the judges will say so to us, and we will return the slave." I pressed her about the matters and have made her consent not to plead. Do not worry at all; I am acting so that you need not worry.

Further, Marduk-mušallim has come here. I will inform him of this. But you must come here quickly so that, before Marduk-mušallim has written somewhere else, we can settle matters (lit., them). As you know, I have no livelihood; I would voluntarily wear myself out working the four-*iku* meadow next to you. As you know Ilī-šullimanni is not pleased with my working a field or going near the village of Gabiba, and he directed me to give the one-*iku* field to Ipqu-Šala. Persuade Ipqu-Šala not to work that field voluntarily. Measure his *dug-up land,* and I myself will pay him for his labors. Tell him that I will work (it). If it is his judgment, let him work the top of the lower meadow that you are working. You will not leave that four-*iku* field fallow; if you do not let me work it, I will become angry with you. If in truth you do love me, do not be negligent, lest I become annoyed with you. Hang onto that field for me lest I become upset. Send me a report.

3. *Ana awīlim qibī-ma; umma Zinû-ma. Šamaš u Nin-Šubur aššumīya ana dāriātim liballiṭūka. Aššum eqel šamaššammim ša Ašdubba mamman ul taškum-ma šamaššammum immašša*ʾ. *Šulpae-nāṣir ṭurdam-ma šamaššammam liṣṣur-ma lā* [*i*]*ḫalliq. Bītum šalim. Šulumka šupram. Libbī lā itteneḫ*[*p*]*e.*

Speak to the man; thus Zinû. May Šamaš and Nin-Šubur keep you well for my sake forever. Since you have not appointed anyone concerning the sesame field of Ašdubba, the sesame could be plundered. Send Šulpae-nāṣir to watch over the sesame, lest it disappear. The house is in order. Send me (news of) your health. Let my heart not be constantly broken.

4. ^{1} *a-na* ^{d}NANNA-*tum* ^{2} *qí-bí-ma* ^{3} *um-ma* ZIMBIR^{ki}-*lu-mur* ^{4} *a-ḫu-ka-ma* ^{5} ^{d}UT[U *l*]*i-ba-al-li-iṭ-ka* ^{6} *a-*[*nu-um*]*-ma* [*x*]*-hu-lu-um* ^{7} 1 SAG.ÌR ^{l}[^{ú}TÚG] ^{8} *uš-ta-bi-la-ku* ^{9} *i-zi-iz-ma* ^{10} KUG.BABBAR *šu-te-ṣí-ma* ^{11} KUG. BABBAR *mu-ḫu-ur* ^{12} *i-na ge-er-ri* ^{13} *ma-aḫ-ri-im* ^{14} KUG.BABBAR *ma-ri ši-ip-ri* ^{15} ^{I}*ip-qú-*^{d}*ša-la* ^{16} *šu-bi-lam* ^{17} ^{Id}EN.ZU-*re-me-ni* ^{18} *la-aš-šu-ma* ^{19} *ú-ul aṭ-ru-da-ku-šu.*

Ana Nannatum qibī-ma; umma Sippar-lūmur aḫūkā-ma. Šam[*aš l*]*iballiṭka. A*[*num*]*ma* [..]*ḫulum ištēn wardam ašlākam uštābilakku; iziz-ma kaspam šuteṣṣī-ma kaspam muḫur. Ina gerri maḫrîm kaspam mārī šipri Ipqu-Šala šūbilam. Sîn-rēmēnī laššū-ma ul aṭrudakkuššu.*

Speak to Nannatum; thus Sippar-lūmur your brother. May Šamaš keep you well. I have herewith dispatched to you the slave [..]ḫulum, a fuller. Be ready to produce silver frequently and to receive silver. In the first trip dispatch the silver to me with the messenger Ipqu-Šala. Sîn-rēmēnī is not here and so I have not sent him to you.

I. *Ḫammurapi šarrum dannum šar Bābilim šarrum muštešmi kibrātim arbaʾim kāšid irnitti Marduk rēʾûm muṭīb libbīšu anāku inu Anum u Enlil māt Šumerîm u Akkadîm ana bêlim iddinūnim ṣerrassina ana qātīya umallû, nāram "Ḫammurapi-nuḫuš-nišī" bābilat mê ḫegallim ana māt Šumerîm u Akkadîm lū eḫre. Kišādīša kilallēn ana mērešim lū utēr. Karê ašnan lū aštappak. Mê dārûtim ana māt Šumerîm u Akkadîm lū aškun. Māt Šumerîm u Akkadîm nišīšunu sapḫātim lū upaḫḫer, merītam u mašqītam lū aškuššināšim. In nuḫšim u ḫegallim lū erēšināti, šubat nēḫtim lū ušēšibšināti.*

Inūmīšu Ḫammurapi šarrum dannum migir ilī rabûtim anāku, in emūqēn gašrātim ša Marduk iddinam, dūram ṣīram in eperī rabûtim, ša rēšāšunu kīma šadîm eliā, in pī nārim "Ḫammurapi-nuḫuš-nišī" lū ēpuš. Dūram šuāti "Dūr-Sîn-muballiṭ-abim-wālidīya" ana šumim lū abbi. Zikir Sîn-muballiṭ abim wālidīya in kibrātim lū ušēpi.

I, Ḫammurapi, the mighty king, the king of Babylon, the king who makes the four quarters obedient, who achieves the victory of Marduk, the shepherd who pleases him, when Anum and Enlil gave me the land of Sumer and Akkad to rule, handed their halter over to me, I verily dug the canal "Ḫammurapi-is-the-abundance-of-the-people," which brings abundant water to the land of Sumer and Akkad. I verily turned both its banks into cultivated land. I verily stored up piles of grain constantly. I verily provided a continual (supply of) water for the land of Sumer and Akkad. I verily gathered the scattered people of the land of Sumer and Akkad, (and) provided pasture land and irrigation for them. I verily pastured them in abundance and plently, (and) let them live in security.

At that time I, Ḫammurapi, the mighty king, the favorite of the great gods, with the powerful strength that Marduk gave me, verily made an august wall with great (mounds of) earth, the tops of which are as high as a mountain, at the mouth of the canal "Ḫammurapi-is-the-abundance-of-the-people." I verily gave that wall the name "Wall-of-Sîn-muballiṭ-the-father-who-begot-me." I verily proclaimed the name of Sîn-Muballiṭ, the father who begot me, throughout the regions.

LESSON THIRTY-EIGHT

B.

1. *ibbalakkatā*
2. *iggarrarrū*
3. *inʾarir / iʾʾarir*
4. *nipparki*
5. *uškennū*
6. *uštepēlā*
7. *ušbalkissināti*
8. *iḫḫelesṣe*
9. *išqalil*
10. *inʾarrarrū / iʾʾarrarrū*

C.

1. *šumma šarrum šanûm awâtīya nasqātim uštepēl, uṣurātīya uttakker, šumī šaṭram ipšiṭ, šumšu ištaṭar, Šamaš dayyānum rabium ša šamê u erṣetim muštēšer šaknāt napištim bēlum tukultī šarrūssu liskip, dīššu ayy-idīn, išid ummānīšu lišḫelṣi, ina bīrīšu šīram lemnam ša nasāḫ išid šarrūtīšu u ḫalāq mātīšu liškuššum.* If another king has changed my well-chosen words, has altered my plans, effaced my inscribed name, has inscribed his name, may Šamaš the great judge of heaven and earth, the one who guides those endowed with life, the lord whom I trust, overturn his kingship, not judge his case, cause the organization of his army to slip, (and) in his divinations produce for him an evil omen of the uprooting of the foundation of his kingship and the destruction of his land.
2. PN *wardam itti* PN$_2$ *bēlīšu īgur; wardum šū iḫalliq innabbit ipparakkū-ma* PN$_2$ *wardam irīab.* PN hired a slave from PN$_2$, his master; should said slave escape, flee, (or) stop working, PN$_2$ will replace the slave.

D. 240 *šumma [elep] ša māḫirtim elep ša muqqelpītim imḫaṣ-ma uṭṭebbi, bēl eleppim ša eleppašu ṭebiat mimma ša ina eleppīšu ḫalqu ina maḫar ilim ubār-ma ša māḫirtim ša elep ša muqqelpītim uṭebbû eleppašu u mimmâšu ḫalqam irīabšum.* If the boat of an upstream skipper struck and has sunk the boat of a downstream skipper, the owner of the boat whose boat is sunk will establish before god whatever was lost in his boat and the upstream skipper who sank the boat of the downstream skipper will repay him his boat and his lost property.

E.

1. *šumma naplaštim eliš išqu, ilū ša mātim išaqqû.* If the lobe has become tall on top, the gods of the land will become elevated.
2. *šumma ina išid māt ubānim kakkum šakim-ma eliš iṭṭul, ṣibittum ibbalakkat.* If a weapon was situated in the base of the finger region and looked up, the prison will revolt.
3. *[šumma padā]nu imittam uḫtallal u ina libbi šumēlim šullum nadi, ina muḫḫelṣītim šēp awīlim iḫḫelesṣe.* If the path was suspended on the right side and a wart was lying in the middle of the left side, the man's foot will slip on slippery ground.
4. *šumma bāb ekallim nepelku, ḫušāḫum ibbašši.* If the palace gate is wide open, there will be hunger.

5. [*šumma q*]*ûm išqallal-ma u libbum kubbut-ma ina appīšu šakin, nišū bišāšina ana maḫīrim ušeṣṣeā.* If a filament is suspended and the heart is also fattened and situated in its tip, the people will bring their possessions to the market place.
6. [*šumma ḫašûm*] *naparkud*[*a*]*t, māssu ibbalakkassu.* If the lung is lying flat, his land will rebel against him.
7. *šumma šēpum īliam-ma ana rēš martim ana warkat amūtim* [*nadi*], *āl pāṭīka ša ibbalkitūka qātka ikaššad.* If the foot emerged and is lying at the top of the gall bladder at the back of the liver, you will personally conquer your border town that rebelled against you.
8. *šum-ma ú-ba-an ḫa-ši-im qá-ab-li-tum ib-ba-al-ki-it-ma ḫu-ur-ḫu-da-am iṭ-ṭù-ul na-ru-um i-sé-ke-er-ma mu-ša i-ba-lu-ú er-ṣé-tam i-lu-ša i-zi-bu-ši ma-tum ḫa-ar-bu-tam i-la-ak ú-lu-ú pa-lu-um i-na-ke-er.*

   šumma ubān ḫašîm qablītum ibbalkit-ma ḫurḫudam iṭṭul, nārum issekker-ma mûša ibbalū; erṣetam ilūša izzibūši; mātum ḫarbūtam illak ū lū palûm inakker. If the middle finger of the lung slipped out of place and faced the windpipe, the river will become blocked and water will dry up; its gods will abandon the land; the land will experience devastation, or the reign will change.

F. 1. *Eqlum ša Ḫaramatum itā eqel Lamassī mārat Šērum-ilī kirbānam ana Ḫaramatum issuk, kirbānam ana Purattim issuk. Ša Rīš-Šamaš Kīma-aḫīya u Zarriqum mārū Šamaš-abum itti Amat-Šamaš mārat Būr-Sîn u Lamassī mārat Šērum-ilī ušpēlū-ma itūrū-ma Rīš-Šamaš Kīma-aḫīya u Zarriqum ibqurū-ma ḫamšat šiqil kaspam niplāt eqlim Amat-Šamaš u Lamassī aššum* [*wa*]*tartim išqulā-ma baqrīšunu u rugummānīšunu ša Rīš-Šamaš Kīma-aḫīya u Zarriqum issuḫā. Ul iturrū-ma Rīš-Šamaš Kīma-aḫīya u Zarriqum mārū Šamaš-abum ana Amat-Šamaš mārat Būr-Sîn u Lamassī mārat Šērum-ilī ul iraggamū. Nīš Šamaš Ayya nīš Marduk u Sîn-muballiṭ itmû.*

   The field of Ḫaramatum beside the field of Lamassī daughter of Šērum-ilī became eroded toward Ḫaramatum (and) became eroded toward the Euphrates. It is the one that Rīš-Šamaš, Kīma-aḫīya, and Zarriqum the sons of Šamaš-abum exchanged with Amat-Šamaš daughter of Būr-Sîn and Lamassī daughter of Šērum-ilī, and that Rīš-Šamaš, Kīma-aḫīya, and Zarriqum came back and contested, and for which Amat-Šamaš and Lamassī had weighed out five shekels of silver as compensation for the field because of the excess (size), so that they rejected the claims and suits of Rīš-Šamaš, Kīma-aḫīya, and Zarriqum. Rīš-Šamaš, Kīma-aḫīya, and Zarriqum the sons of Šamaš-abum will not again lay claim against Amat-Šamaš daughter of Būr-Sîn and Lamassī daughter of Šērum-ilī. They swore by the life of Šamaš, Ayya, the life of Marduk and Sîn-muballiṭ.

G. 1. *Ana Mann*[*atum*?] *qib*[*ī-ma*] *umma* NI[*-m*]*a. Aššum ṭēmīki i*[*nanna*?] *ana Zamirī a*[*na ṭ*]*ēm awīltim šukbutim all*[*ik*]. *Ana Bābilim allak u abbalakkatam. Ana ūm tašapparīm ana awīltim šuprīm-ma, eleppam ana rakāb ṣuḫārtim liskipam. Ištū-ma ana šubalkutim lā tamgurī ebūrum lā ikaššadam. Ṣuḫārtam arḫiš idnīm.*

Speak to Mann[atum$^?$]; thus NI[ ]. Because of your (fs) instructions I have now gone to Zamirū in order to lend weight to the report of the lady. I will go to Babylon and then cross (back) over here. On the day you write me, write to the lady to send a boat for the servant to board. If indeed you do not agree to send (*her*) across, the harvest must not arrive. Give me the servant quickly.

2. *Ana Nabium-mušallim qibī-ma; umma Sîn-nādin-šumī-ma. Šamaš u Marduk liballiṭūka. [L]ū šalmāta. Šulumka maḫar Šamaš u Marduk lū dāri. Aššum ana pišertim nagarruri adi ešrīšu aštaprakkum-ma diʾtam ul tašāl-ma ul tāliam. Kīdam-ma šū iḫtaliq. I[n]a[nn]a ṣe[ʾ]pī uštābilakkum. Šumma talliam, arḫiš [u]ddidam-ma aliam. Šumma lā talliam, arḫiš ṭēmam gamram šupram-ma ša pānīya luppalis-[m]a anākū-ma luggarir. Ana Ḫunnatum qibī-ma, šumma illiam, līliam. [K]īma pānīka šinā šūši pišannātim leqeam. U [...]tim elīšu ṣeʾ[pī] uštābilam.*

Speak to Nabium-mušallim; thus Sîn-nādin-šumī. May Šamaš and Marduk keep you well. May you be healthy. May your good health endure before Šamaš and Marduk. I have written to you some ten times about moving on the surplus harvest$^?$, but you have neither asked for information nor come up. It has disappeared outside. I have now dispatched my letter to you. If you are coming up, hurry and come up quickly. If you are not coming up, quickly send me a complete report so that I can look to what is before me and move myself. Speak to Ḫunnatum, and if she is coming up, let come up. Get me a hundred twenty (two shocks of) boxes immediately. Also, I have dispatched my letter ... *against* it.

3. *Ana ummīy[a qibī-ma]; umma Awī[l-...] mārūkī-ma. Šamaš u [Marduk dāriš ūm]im liba[lliṭūki]. Ištu te[...] kīma šinn[i]m [nadīt]im ana pānī Šamaš tad[dî]nni. Ilkum esrannī-ma naparkâm ul eleʾʾi. U atti matī-ma kīma ummātim ul tašpurīm. Libbī ul tuballiṭī. Anumma Mannaši aštaprakkim; šinā qa šamnam šūbilīm. Murṣum iṣbatannī-ma ina napištim annadi.*

Speak to my mother; thus Awīl-..., your son. May Šamaš and Marduk keep you well forever. Since ... you have thrown me before Šamaš like a knocked-out tooth. The *ilkum*-service has me under pressure and I am unable to stop. Yet you have never written me like (other) mothers. You have not revived my spirits. I have herewith sent you Mannaši; dispatch two *qûm* of oil to me. Illness seized me and I have been *neglected in (regaining my) health.*

4. (No salutation.) ^{1} ^{I}*tam-la-tum* DAM.GÀR DUMU *qi-iš-*^{d}*nu-nu* ^{2} MÁ *ša ib-ba-tum* MÁ.LAH$_5$ *i-gu-ur-ma* ^{3} *a-na* KÁ.DINGIR.RA^{ki} *uš-qé-el-pí* ^{4} *ki-ma* MÁ *šu-a-ti ša um-mi-du-ši-i-ma* ^{5} *a-di i-na-an-na* SIG$_4$.ḪI.A *iz-bi-lu* ^{6} *ù i-na-an-na a-na* GIŠ.ÙR GIŠIMMAR *na-še-e-em* ^{7} *a-na ma-aṣ-ṣa-ar-tim ta-ap-qí-du-ši* ^{8} *iq-bi-a-am* ^{9} *a-di i-na-an-na-a* SIG$_4$. ḪI.A *iz-za-ab-la* ^{10} *ù i-na-an-na «a-na»* GIŠ.ÙR GIŠIMMAR.ḪI.A ^{11} *ta-ṭar-ra-ad-ma* ^{12} MÁ *ši-i i-ša-al-li-ma-am-ma* ^{13} *i-tu-ur-ra-am* ^{14} ^{I}*ib-ba-tum šu-a-ti* ^{15} *a-na ma-aḫ-ri-ka aṭ-ṭar-dam* ^{16} *ki-ma ra-bu-ti-ka* ^{17} MÁ *šu-a-ti pu-uṭ-ṭe*$_4$*-er* ^{18} *pí-qí-is-sú-um-ma* ^{19} *a-na* ZIMBIR^{ki} *li-ša-aq-qí-a-aš-ši.*

Tamlatum tamkārum mār Qīš-Nūnu eleppam ša Ibbatum malāḫim īgur-ma ana Bābilim ušqelpi. Kīma eleppam šuāti ša ummidūšī-ma adi inanna libnātim izbilu u inanna ana gušūr gišimmārim našêm ana maṣṣartim tapqidūši iqbiam. Adi inanna libnātum izzablā u inanna «ana» gušūrī gišimmarim taṭarrad-ma eleppum šī išallimam-ma iturram? Ibattum šuāti ana maḫrīka aṭṭardam. Kīma rabûtīka eleppam šuāti puṭṭer; piqissum-ma ana Sippar lišaqqīašši.

Tamlatum the merchant, the son of Qīš-Nūnu rented the boat of Ibbatum the sailor and sailed it down to Babylon. He told me that that boat, which he had moored and until now had transported bricks, you however have now assigned to carry palm logs for safekeeping. Until now bricks were transported, but now you are sending palm logs, so will that boat return in safety? I have sent said Ibbatum to you. In accord with your high office, release that boat; assign him to bring it upstream to Sippar.

H.

Pullusū rubû;	Princes are diverted;
Wašrū sikkūrū, šērētum šaknā.	Door-bolts are set, rings in place.
Ḫabrātum nišū šaqummā.	The noisesome people are silent.
Petûtum uddulū bābū.	Doors that were open are locked.
Ilī[!] mātim ištarāt mātim	The gods and goddesses of the land,
Šamaš, Sîn, Adad, Eštar,	Šamaš, Sîn, Adad, Eštar,
Īterbū ana utūl šamê.	Have entered heaven to sleep.
Ul idinnū dīnam,	They render no verdict(s),
ul iparrasū awâtim.	they decide no suits.
Pussumat mušītim[!];	Night is veiled;
Ekallum šaḫur, šaqummū ṣērū.	The palace is still, the countryside silent.
Ālik urḫim ilam išassi, u ša dīnim ušteberre šittam.	A traveler calls a god, and a litigant remains asleep.
[Da]yyān kīnātim, abi ekiātim,	The judge of just causes, father of the homeless,
Šamaš, īterub ana kummīšu.	Šamaš, has entered his cella.
Rabûtum ilī[!] mušītim,	May the great gods of the night,
Nawirum Gibil,	Bright Gibil,
Qurādum Erra,	Warrior Erra,
Qaštum, Nīrum,	Bow, Yoke,
Šitaddarum, Mušḫuššum,	Orion, Dragon,
Ereqqum, Inzum,	Wagon, Lyra,
Kusarikkum, Bašmum,	Bison, Hydra,
Lizzi‹z›ū-ma.	Stand ready.
Ina têrti eppušu,	In the divination I perform,
Ina puḫād akarrabu,	In the lamb I dedicate,
Kīttam šuknān.	Place the truth.
24 šumātūšu, ikrib mušītim.	24 (are) its lines, prayer of the night.